HALAL MATTERS

In today's globalized world, halal (meaning 'permissible' or 'lawful') is about more than food. Politics, power and ethics all play a role in the halal industry in setting new standards for production, trade, consumption and regulation. The question of how modern halal markets are constituted is increasingly important and complex. Written from a unique interdisciplinary global perspective, this book demonstrates that as the market for halal products and services is expanding and standardizing, it is also fraught with political, social and economic contestation and difference. The discussion is illustrated by rich ethnographic case studies from a range of contexts, and consideration is given to both Muslim majority and minority societies. *Halal Matters* will be of interest to students and scholars working across the humanities and social sciences, including anthropology, sociology and religious studies.

Florence Bergeaud-Blackler is an anthropologist and Research Fellow at the Institut de recherches et d'étude sur le monde arabe et musulman (IREMAM) in the Centre national de la recherche scientifique (CNRS), France.

Johan Fischer is an Associate Professor in the Department of Society and Globalization at Roskilde University, Denmark.

John Lever is a Senior Lecturer in the University of Huddersfield Business School, UK.

HALAL MATTERS

Islam, politics and markets in global perspective

Edited by
Florence Bergeaud-Blackler, Johan Fischer
and John Lever

LONDON AND NEW YORK

First published 2016
by Routledge
2 Park Square, Milton Park, Abingdon, Oxon OX14 4RN

and by Routledge
711 Third Avenue, New York, NY 10017

Routledge is an imprint of the Taylor & Francis Group, an informa business

© 2016 Florence Bergeaud-Blackler, John Lever and Johan Fischer

The right of Florence Bergeaud-Blackler, John Lever and Johan Fischer to be identified as authors of this work has been asserted in accordance with sections 77 and 78 of the Copyright, Designs and Patents Act 1988.

All rights reserved. No part of this book may be reprinted or reproduced or utilised in any form or by any electronic, mechanical, or other means, now known or hereafter invented, including photocopying and recording, or in any information storage or retrieval system, without permission in writing from the publishers.

Trademark notice: Product or corporate names may be trademarks or registered trademarks, and are used only for identification and explanation without intent to infringe.

British Library Cataloguing-in-Publication Data
A catalogue record for this book is available from the British Library

Library of Congress Cataloging in Publication Data
Halal matters: Islam, politics and markets in global perspective / edited by Florence Bergeaud-Blackler, John Lever and Johan Fischer. – First Edition.
pages cm
Includes index.
1. Halal food industry. 2. Muslims--Dietary laws. 3. Food--Religious aspects--Islam. 4. Globalization--Religious aspects. I. Bergeaud-Blackler, Florence, editor. II. Lever, John, editor. III. Fischer, Johan, editor.
HD9000.5.H3424 2015
381'.41091767--dc23
2014047404

ISBN: 978-1-138-81275-8 (hbk)
ISBN: 978-1-138-81276-5 (pbk)
ISBN: 978-1-315-74612-8 (ebk)

Typeset in Bembo
by Taylor & Francis Books

CONTENTS

List of figures vii
List of contributors viii
Acknowledgements x

1 Introduction: Studying the politics of global
   halal markets 1
   Florence Bergeaud-Blackler, Johan Fischer and John Lever

2 Re-imagining Malaysia: a postliberal halal strategy? 19
   John Lever

3 From an implicit to an explicit understanding: new
   definitions of halal in Turkey 38
   John Lever and Haluk Anil

4 Remembering the spirit of halal: an Iranian perspective 55
   Maryam Attar, Khalil Lohi and John Lever

5 Beldi matters: negotiating proper food in urban Moroccan
   food consumption and preparation 72
   Katharina Graf

6 Islamizing food: the encounter of market and
   diasporic dynamics 91
   Florence Bergeaud-Blackler

7	The halal certification market in Europe and the world: a first panorama *Florence Bergeaud-Blackler*	105
8	Green halal: how does halal production face animal suffering? *Manon Istasse*	127
9	Halal, diaspora and the secular in London *Johan Fischer*	143
10	Muslim food consumption in China: between qingzhen and halal *Yukari Sai and Johan Fischer*	160
11	Halal training in Singapore *Johan Fischer*	175
12	Who owns halal? Five international initiatives of halal food regulations *Florence Bergeaud-Blackler*	192

Index   198

LIST OF FIGURES

2.1	Islamic schools of jurisprudence (or Madh'hab)	28
2.2	Micrograph of a heterogeneous stem cell colony isolated from human corneal cells at different stages of differentiation	33
3.1	Traditional slaughter during Kurban Bayrami	47
5.1	Vegetable and fruit shop display in Marrakech's medina	79
5.2	White meat shop in Marrakech's medina	80
5.3	Sorting beldi lentils in a Marrakchi home	83
10.1	A qingzhen sign with "traditional" motifs at a Muslim shop in Beijing in the 1990s	161
12.1	International standards: the quest for a unique halal standard	193

LIST OF CONTRIBUTORS

Haluk Anil, former Senior Research Fellow of the Veterinary School, University of Bristol, UK, is a consultant scientist. His research interests include farm animal physiology, animal welfare with particular reference to stunning and slaughter and food safety.

Maryam Attar started her PhD degree in poultry halal supply chain management after completing a Masters degree in Food Science at the University of Huddersfield. Maryam has years of experience in poultry production both as an entrepreneur and as a commercial director.

Florence Bergeaud-Blackler is Research Fellow at the French National Centre for Scientific Research (CNRS). She has specialized in the study of Islamic normativity in secularized societies. She has published several book and papers on the production of religious trading norms and standards, and on the social and cultural determinants of halal commodities consumption.

Johan Fischer is an Associate Professor in the Department of Society and Globalization, Roskilde University, Denmark. His work focuses on modern Islam and consumer culture in Southeast Asia and Europe. More specifically, Johan explores the interfaces between class, consumption, market relations, religion and the state in a globalized world.

Katharina Graf is currently a research student in the Anthropology and Sociology Department at SOAS, University of London. Since 2008 she has been conducting ethnographic research on both natural resource management and food preparation in Morocco.

Manon Istasse works as a researcher in cultural anthropology at the Université libre de Bruxelles, Belgium. Her two main topics of interest are cultural heritage and food culture.

John Lever is a Senior Lecturer in sustainability at the University of Huddersfield Business School. He has conducted research and published on many aspects of the food industry and is particularly interested in farm animal welfare, local food production and halal and kosher meat markets.

Khalil Lohi completed his PhD at the University of Westminster in Wireless Communication Systems. Khalil has held research and academic positions and has published extensively on various topics related to telecommunications technology and has worked on major integrated EC-funded projects.

Yukari Sai is an Adjunct Researcher in the Organization for Islamic Area Studies, Waseda University, Japan, and specializes in cultural anthropology of food and eating. She is the author of several books, articles and chapters in edited volumes.

ACKNOWLEDGEMENTS

Some of the papers edited in this book were initially presented by the authors at a conference organized by Florence Bergeaud-Blackler on 7–8 November 2013. The conference – 'Did you mean *halal*? Islamic Normativities, Globalization and Secularization' – was supported by the CNRS, the IISMM and the Collège de France.

1
INTRODUCTION
Studying the politics of global halal markets

Florence Bergeaud-Blackler, Johan Fischer and John Lever

This book argues that answering the question *how are modern halal markets constituted?* is increasingly important and complex in a globalized world. In Arabic halal literally means "permissible" or "lawful". Traditionally it has several significations such as "pure" or "wholesome" with regard to meat in particular in proper Islamic practice, for example ritual slaughter and pork avoidance. Yet in the modern and globalized industry, halal is not only about food; it is also about biotechnology, tourism and care products. A number of Muslim requirements have already been met in the international arena, including an injunction to avoid any substances that may be contaminated with porcine residues or alcohol, gelatine, glycerine, emulsifiers, enzymes, flavours and flavourings. In a globalized market these requirements are setting new standards for halal production, preparation, handling, storage and certification. Optimistically, market players have estimated the value of the halal food market to be around $632 billion annually (Agriculture and Agri-Food Canada, 2011).

Drawing on studies from around the world, this book explores how global halal production, trade, consumption and regulation are taking place. In spite of these global transformations in halal, this topic has only attracted sporadic academic attention. The research question answered is: *How and by whom, for whom, and for what reasons are objects, discourses and practices actually called "halal" or "haram"* (literally, "unlawful" or "prohibited")? Hence, in this book readers will learn that even if the global market for halal products and services such as certification is expanding and standardizing, this market is still fraught with contestation in terms of politics and power/knowledge.

There exists no edited book from an interdisciplinary perspective that explores how modern forms of halal production, consumption, trade and regulation take place in diverse contexts. This research moves beyond previous works on halal consumption in the everyday lives of Muslims in a globalized market (Bergeaud-Blackler, 2004,

2005, 2007; Bergeaud-Blackler and Bernard, 2010; Fischer 2008, 2011; Lever, 2013; Lever and Miele, 2012).

Existing studies of halal and Islamic consumption in general explore microsocial aspects. For example, from an interdisciplinary perspective the edited volume *Muslim Societies in the Age of Mass Consumption* (Pink, 2009) argues that in spite of the intensifying globalization of markets and consumption, these processes have received modest scholarly attention. More specifically, this volume explores issues such as the changing spaces of consumption, branding and the marketing of religious music as well as the consumption patterns of Muslim minority groups. Another important study looks at urban Muslims in China, where the Hui's halal food and eating habits stood out as the most important identity marker in contradistinction to the surrounding Han majority. Besides nutritional and economic functions, food and eating practices expressed values and traits that they regarded as fundamentally Hui (Gillette, 2000). Lastly, in Turkey the politics of identity among Islamists and secularists has been deeply influenced by an expanding consumer market, a "market for identities", in the context of the globalization of the 1980s and 1990s (Navaro-Yashin, 2002). Many of the chapters in the present book explore halal from microsocial or everyday perspectives, but they do so by taking into consideration the "bigger institutional picture" that frames the everyday consumption of halal products.

We are inspired by practice theory that is used as a general framework for the project's analyses. A "practice" can be defined as "a routinized way in which bodies are moved, objects handled, subjects are treated, things are described" (Reckwitz, 2002, 250). Such a practice-theoretical perspective involves assumptions about "performativity of social practices" as in Bourdieu's classic study *The Logic of Practice* (1990). Reflexive and strategic practices also evoke the question of ideas/ intentionality versus practice in public/private domains (Goffman, 1971). Hence, a central issue in the chapters that follow is the extent to which ideas, ideals, policies, discourses and intentions about what halal is or ought to be are translated into actual practices at different levels of the social scale in everyday life and by halal certifying bodies. Theoretically, we also draw on recent scholarship on the interfaces between markets and regulation such as Ong and Collier's *Global Assemblages: Technology, Politics, and Ethics as Anthropological Problems* (2005).

What is modern halal understanding and practice?

Industrial players, merchants and some Muslim scholars involved in halal trade and standardization have based their halal food rulings on statements from selected verses from the Qur'an such as: "Allah makes good things lawful to them and bad things unlawful" (7: 157) and:

> You who believe, eat the good things We have provided for you and be grateful to God, if it is Him that you worship. He has only forbidden you carrion, blood, pig's meat, and animals over which any name other than God's has been invoked. But if anyone is forced to eat such things

> by hunger, rather than desire or excess, he commits no sin: God is Most Merciful and Forgiving.
>
> *(Abdel Haleem, 2008, 2: 172–73)*

It is repeated that

> You are forbidden to eat carrion; blood; pig's meat; any animal over which any name other than God's has been invoked; any animal strangled, or victim of a violent blow or fall, or gored or savaged by a beast of prey, unless you still slaughter it [in the correct manner]; or anything sacrificed on idolatrous altars.
>
> *(Abdel Haleem 2008, 5: 3)*

Halal is that which is beneficial and not detrimental to Muslims. A number of conditions and prohibitions must be observed. Muslims are expressly forbidden from consuming carrion, spurting blood, pork and foods that have been consecrated to any being other than God himself: these substances are called haram ("unlawful" or "forbidden"). The lawfulness of meat depends on how it is obtained. During ritual slaughter, *dhabh*, animals should be killed in God's name by making a fatal incision across the throat, with the blood being drained as fully as possible. Among Muslim groups and individuals, the question of the stunning of animals prior to slaughter is highly contested. While some Muslims only consider meat from unstunned animals halal, others accept that stunning is part of modern and ethical food production.

Sea creatures and locusts are considered halal by most Sunni groups. Because the sea is seen to be pure in essence, all marine animals, even if they have died spontaneously, are halal. Despite the fact that they are not mentioned in the Qur'an, land creatures such as predators, dogs, and, in the eyes of some jurists, donkeys are haram. What is more, crocodiles, weasels, pelicans, otters, foxes, elephants, ravens and insects have been condemned by the *ulama* (literally, 'those who know the law' or 'religious scholars'). Another significant Islamic prohibition relates to wine and any other alcoholic drink or substance, all of which are haram whatever the quantity or substance (Denny, 2006, 279). As we shall see, alcohol has become a highly controversial issue.

With the advent of Islam, ancient negative attitudes towards pigs and pork were reinforced (Benkheira, 1996). Inspired by Jewish law, the Prophet Mohammad banned the flesh of pigs and in the Qur'an the prohibition is repeated several times (Simoons, 1994, 32). In effect, Muslims were distinguished from their Christian adversaries (Simoons, 1994, 33). Some Muslim groups came to abhor pigs and pork to such an extent that everything touched by them was regarded as contaminated and worthless (Simoons, 1994). Under Western colonialism, pig abhorrence declined in many parts of the world, only to increase again at the end of European colonial rule and the advent of Islamic revivalism (Simoons, 1994).

The reasons for the ban on pork within Islam follow the five main types of explanation advanced to analyse the origin of the Hebrew food laws. One is that these are arbitrary and make no sense to humans and can only be understood by God. Another is that injunctions were based on sanitary concerns (Simoons, 1994). A symbolic explanation proposed by Mary Douglas (2004) argues that acceptable animals represented proper human behaviour versus the sinful behaviour of banned animals. Yet another explanation is that Hebrew food laws originated in their rejections of cultic practices of alien peoples and the worship of deities other than Jehovah. Involved in both the third and fourth hypotheses is the notion that the Hebrews wanted to set themselves apart from other peoples. Some anthropologists, most famously Marvin Harris, have argued for a fifth and recent explanation, according to which the prohibitions are grounded in economic, environmental, and/or ecological reasons (Simoons, 1994, 64–65). According to Harris (1977, 1998), the Israelite taboo on pigs was reconceptualized with the rise of Islam as a new set of sanctioned dietary laws "ecological" in essence, that is, religious ideas traced to the cost–benefit analysis of ecological processes.

The proliferation of halal can be seen as distinct sets of invocations of haram or taboo. Taboo can protect distinctive categories of the universe, consensus and certainty about the organization of the cosmos, thus reducing intellectual and social disorder (Douglas, 2004, xi). However, certainty and order can easily mirror feelings of uncertainty and disorder. These doubts mostly surface in everyday strategies about how to practise the ever-intensifying demands of proper Islamic consumption. Elsewhere, Douglas (1975, 275) argues that when people become aware of encroachment and danger, dietary rules that control what goes into the body function as an analogy of the corpus of their cultural categories at risk.

The debate over the origins of the ban on pork in Judaism and Islam is far from resolved. One central reason for this is that there is not sufficient historical evidence in existence. The prohibition of pork is one of the rare food taboos that lives on in Islam, but the true reason for its prohibition is unknown. Our brief discussion of the arguments of Douglas and Harris provides the reader with key arguments in a debate that has spanned decades, and which still seems to inform scholarly and popular controversy over the prohibition of pork and the nature of taboo itself. Taboos distinguish between groups and individuals within their own society. Moreover, they operate in terms of the production, preparation and distribution of food (Manderson, 1986).

The understanding and practice of halal requirements vary among import countries and companies producing halal food. This is the point made in the book *Halal Food Production* (Riaz and Chaudry, 2004, vii). This book by two US scholars is a popularized guide to producing and marketing halal (foods) for professionals in an expanding global food market. Chaudry is President of the Islamic Food and Nutrition Council of America (IFANCA), a leading halal certifier based in the US, and Riaz is a Senior Auditor in the same organization. Riaz is also Texas A&M University's Director of Food and Protein R&D Center; the Islamic Food Council of Europe is a kind of subsidiary of IFANCA. To our knowledge, this is the only book of its kind and it is widely used by companies worldwide to understand and comply with the current transformation of halal and it is a unique piece of empirical material. It is the guide to modern and global halal.

In classical *fiqh* (Islamic jurisprudence), there are five qualifications: obligatory, recommended, indifferent, reprehensible and forbidden. Therefore, in addition to halal and haram, doubtful things may be avoided; that is, there is a grey area between the clearly lawful and the unlawful. The doubtful or questionable is expressed in the word *mashbooh*, which can be evoked by divergences in religious scholars' opinions or the suspicion of undetermined or prohibited ingredients in a commodity (Schacht, 2014). Hence, individual and fuzzy aspects of context and handling are involved in determining the halalness of a product. The problem in certifying food and other products with regard to these substances is that they are extremely difficult to discover. The interpretation of these *mashbooh* areas is left open depending on the nature of the food product and how/where it is obtained/processed.

Knowledge of the above requirements is, of course, essential to innovative companies seeking to establish themselves in an expanding global halal market. The increased demand for halal products by conscious and educated Muslim consumers has encouraged developed countries to export halal products. Moreover, the proliferation of Western franchised food has changed the international food market and subjected it to new standards of halal certification (Riaz and Chaudry, 2004, 29–30).

In countries such as Malaysia, Singapore and Indonesia even paper/plastic labels and printing on food are seen as problematic. Glue used for labels as well as edible printing and dyes used directly on food may contain non-permissible ingredients. Some halal certifying bodies in importing countries feel that such seepage or cross-contamination may violate the halal status of food (Riaz and Chaudry, 2004, 134). What is more, packaging food in a halal environment is essential (Riaz and Chaudry, 2004, 134–35).

Divergences between jurists of the different schools of Islamic jurisprudence (Hanafi, Maliki, Hanbali and Shafi'i) exist on halal understanding and practice (see Chapter 2). This point is of particular relevance in relation to Ong and Collier's (2005) notion of a global assemblage (see p. 10) in which theology, politics and regulation diverge and overlap across different countries and contexts. The book *Issues on Halal Products* (2007) is a fatwa (opinion concerning Islamic law issued by an Islamic scholar) published by the State Mufti's Office in the Prime Minister's Office, Brunei Darussalam. In Brunei and other Southeast Asian countries such as Malaysia and Singapore (as we shall see in subsequent chapters) the Shafi'i school of jurisprudence within the Sunni division of Islam is dominant. For a number of reasons halal has taken on a special meaning in these Southeast Asian countries in the interfaces between revivalist Islam, state and market. The State Mufti's fatwa, for example, goes to great lengths to define and "standardize" halal understanding and practice among consumers and companies involved in the market for halal products and services. The book offers its opinions on issues such as monosodium glutamate in prawn crackers and emulsifiers and sausages wrapped in pigs' intestines (food);

soft drinks in beer bottles (drinks); displaying signs that particular locations are not suitable for Muslims at companies, restaurants and other eating places where the majority of employees or customers are not Muslims (restaurants); tranquillizers for slaughtered chickens (slaughter); medicines mixed with gelatine or alcohol (treatment); involvement of conventional banks in halal projects and the buying and selling of pork in supermarkets (trading); hair dye and praying using perfume that contains alcohol (cosmetics); the word "Carlsberg" on clothes (adornment); utilizing a building that was once a pig market (premises); and transport of pork (transportation). The limited space here does not permit us to go into detail with all these rulings, but it suffices to say that halal is subjected to strict and highly regulated understandings and practices in this fatwa originating in the heartland of Southeast Asian Sunni Islam.

Another example is *The Lawful and the Prohibited in Islam* (1995), published in Arabic by the Egyptian Islamic scholar Yusuf al-Qaradawi, a leading figure in the Muslim Brotherhood, and translated into several languages for global distribution. The book explains that the Islamic view of halal and haram is simple and clear: it is a divine order and part of the total legal system of Islam (Sharia) whose primary objective is the good of mankind (al-Qaradawi, 1995, 6). The book covers a wide range of topics including the Islamic principles of halal and haram in relation to food and drink; clothing and adornment; working and earning a livelihood; physical appetites; marriage; the relationship between husband and wife; contraception; divorce; parents and children; beliefs and customs; business transactions; recreation and play; social relations; and the relations of Muslims and non-Muslims. The last example of a guide to proper halal understanding and practice is *The Islamic Laws of Animal Slaughter* (2006) by the Pakistani Mufti Muhammad Taqi Usmani of the Islamic Fiqh Academy of the Muslim World League.

This book is a guide to Islamic slaughter with regard to slaughtering methods, the religious status of the slaughterer and automated methods of slaughtering. The book accepts the stunning of animals prior to slaughter (Usmani, 2006, 81), which as we shall see is a highly controversial issue. While an increasing number of Muslims advocate slaughter without stunning – a practice that animal rights activists in some countries want to be banned – many Muslims consider meat from pre-stunned animals to be halal (Lever and Miele, 2012).

These rulings or guides raise some bigger questions that we develop to explain the relationship between knowledge and power in the assemblage of global halal. Many of the book's chapters explore how the (anthropological) knowledge of halal emerges in terms of politics of scientific authority and representation; the phenomenology of expertise; historicized and contextualized (halal) skills as abilities/capacities; and epistemic devices of anthropological analysis and representation. Running through many of these discussions are how ethnographic encounters generate particular types of knowledges (Boyer, 2005) of halal across diverse settings. From diverse perspectives authors explore the production of knowledge about halal in national/nationalist settings or complexes, that is, what Lomnitz (2001) has described as the role of intellectual production in shaping the national idea. We draw on Foucauldian conceptualizations of power/knowledge as new sets of operations/procedures that Foucault calls technologies. Such technologies come together around the objectification of the body and are disciplinary technologies in institutional forms that aim at subjecting, transforming and improving bodies (Rabinow, 1984, 17). Fatwas and powerful discourses about proper halal understanding and practice are all examples of how the power/knowledge complex plays into the global assemblage of halal.

Muslim dietary rules assumed new significance in the twentieth century, as some Muslims began striving to demonstrate how such rules conform to modern reason and the findings of scientific research. Another common theme in the revival and renewal of these dietary rules seems to be the search for alternatives to what are seen to be Western values, ideologies and lifestyles and this is reflected in globalized halal.

Halal Matters between Islam, politics, markets

The title of this book signifies a point that runs through all chapters: that halal materiality matters on a global scale. We consider halal commodities to be things with a particular type of social potential (Appadurai, 1999, 6). Thus, in the following we examine how this social potential is translated into ambiguous halal conceptualizations and practices.

These discussions also evoke the relationship between Islam and politics in diverse settings. Soares and Osella (2010) critically reflect on the study of Islam based on a broad understanding of politics involving various actors and organizations, everyday politics and micropolitics. Our analysis of global halal is situated at the intersection of these different levels where the field of politics is constituted in practice (Soares and Osella, 2010, 1). Halal is an example of the way in which Islam and modernity are compatible. Arguably, it is publicly engaged Islam that generates "enchanted modernity" that at its core has a dual emphasis on both material and spiritual progress. Similar to Deeb's (2006) analysis of gender and public piety in Lebanon, our take on halal is focused on how everyday public piety is performed in the interfaces between Islam and politics. The pious modern is an ethos or a way of being in the world and a self-representation (Deeb, 2006, 227).

Contrary to the commonly held notion that "Islamists" in general endeavour to transform the state/nation itself, the book's chapters demonstrate that this idea is a simplification. As in Egypt, with regard to the cultural politics of a women's grassroots piety movement, Islamic revivalism is much more focused on personal forms of piety, freedom and agency – and escaping nationalist politics altogether (Mahmood, 2004). This contention is supported by the argument that in Egypt the concerns, loyalties, sentiments and practices of Islamic revivalism has given rise to a form of community for which the nation is a contingent but not an essential component (Hirschkind, 2001, 26). Thus, the book's contributors explore the everyday effects of politicized and commercialized halal.

Our understanding of the global market for halal products and services is inspired by studies that question what global markets in the wake of neoliberalism actually mean in practice (Caliskan, 2010). We take seriously the argument that following a commodity's growth and circulation is a way of mapping the multisited fields of a global market (Caliskan, 2010, 13). In this kind of understanding the market is characterized by calculative dynamics of power and it is made of multiple fields that produce its commodities and prices (Caliskan, 2010). Most importantly perhaps, the market can be studied as fields of power made and maintained by various human and nonhuman agents that confront each other on asymmetrical platforms (Caliskan, 2010, 188). This requires researchers to locate how different market participants engage in and understand the sustenance, production and market fields of power (Caliskan, 2010, 191).

Current studies on the entanglements of capitalism, Islam and the state in Southeast Asia explore, for example, how moderate Islamic "spiritual reform" movements in Indonesia combine business management principles and techniques from popular life-coaching seminars with Muslim practice. This form of "market Islam" and "spiritual economies" merge Muslim religious practice and capitalist ethics and effective self-management by attempting to make people "better from the inside" (Rudnyckyj, 2009, 2010). In the global and expanding market for halal capitalism, Islam and states fuse in a similar way and we situate our analysis of halal in the intersections of Islam, politics and markets in the making.

Emerging standards

Over the past three decades, Southeast Asian countries such as Malaysia and Singapore have become world leaders in the global expansion of halal markets. This has come about in large part because the state governments of Malaysia and Singapore have taken on the role of halal-certifying authorities within those countries. In effect, they have certified, standardized and bureaucratized halal production, trade and consumption in a way that made it possible to extend these standards abroad. Attempts to regulate halal production, trade and consumption also characterize the global market for halal outside Southeast Asia and this is a question that runs through many of the book's chapters. Consequently, the global market for halal is currently characterized by a marked tension between emerging forms of regulation on the one hand and attempts at challenging these on the other.

We take halal standards and standardization to mean several things. First, they can refer to the design and qualities of products as well as proper conduct of companies, for example with regard to the production, preparation, handling and storage of halal, states, organizations and individuals. Standards and standardization can be seen as instruments of control and forms of regulation attempting to generate elements of global order (Brunsson and Jacobsson, 2000). Unlike non-state certifying bodies around the world, the Malaysian and Singaporean states can impose legal sanctions on companies that do not live up to the expectations standards impose.

What is more, standards can also refer to persons with certain qualifications, knowledge or skills. Hence, standards can generate and reinvigorate social norms and directives. At the same time, the meanings of standards may evoke ideas of similarity and uniformity – the standardized is that which supposedly is similar and follows rules. Such rules also specify what is proper behaviour, and ideas of appropriateness thus become associated with standardization; the standard way of doing things is often understood not only as the most usual, but also the generally accepted, normal and best way (Brunsson and Jacobsson, 2000, 15). Even powerful organizations like states and large corporations go by rules that others have provided about how to organize, what policies to pursue, what kind of services to offer, or how to design their products (Brunsson and Jacobsson, 2000, 1).

This process of standardization is apparent in halal certification, but standardization is also market driven. Halal extends between Islam, state certification and markets, and standards and standardization are important, but also highly contested, issues, as we shall see. An important theme that runs through this book is the emergence, consolidation and expansion of an audit culture around halal practice. Not only the state in Malaysia and Singapore, but also independent certifiers such as the Islamic Food Council of Europe (IFCE) regulate halal by performing "on site" audits and inspections in shops, restaurants and factories. There is a large body of literature on the rise of an "audit society" but there is need for further scholarship on the ways in which audits and inspections are understood and practised in locally specific contexts. The pervasiveness of an audit culture within and around halal practices is not well understood, but, as we will show, it links Islam, state and markets in novel ways.

Audit and inspection systems are a feature of modern societies. They exist to generate comfort and reassurance in a wide range of policy contexts (Power, 1999, xvii). To a large extent auditing is about cultural and economic authority granted to auditors (Power, 1999, xvii), based of course on the assumption that those auditors are competent and their practices effective. There are some basic conceptual ingredients of any audit practice. These include "independence from the matter being audited; technical work in the form of evidence gathering and the examination of documentation; the expression of a view based on this evidence: a clearly defined object of the audit process" (Power, 1999, 5). A central aspect of audit culture that is also highly relevant to the market for halal is the pushing of control and self-control further into organizations to satisfy the need to connect internal organizational arrangements to public ideals (Power, 1999, 10). The governments in Malaysia and Singapore have become increasingly and explicitly committed to an indirect supervisory role in halal and audit is both a solution to a technical problem as well as a way of redesigning the practice of government. Staff policies such as setting up a Halal Committee/Team to handle halal properly, as well as establishing sections in companies that specialize in halal compliance, are examples of the increasingly prominent role of internal control systems that can be audited.

Audit culture has been explored from an anthropological perspective focusing on consensus endorsing government through economic efficiency and good practice.

In this form of modern accountability the financial and the moral converge to form a culture of what are deemed acceptable forms (Strathern, 2000, 1). Audits and audit practices are discussed as descriptors "applicable to all kinds of reckonings, evaluations and measurements" and as "distinct cultural artefacts" in the market that works as a platform for both individual interest and national politics (Strathern, 2000, 2). A key question we explore is to what extent audit culture is compatible with the point made above that the underlying principle behind halal remains a "divine order" and that the "halalness" of products is not easily verifiable: smell, texture or taste cannot fully determine whether a product is halal or not.

Global halal assemblages

We also explore halal as integral to globalized Islam. The spread of Islam around the globe has blurred the connection between religion, specific societies and territories. One-third of the world's Muslims now live as members of a minority, as is the case in Buddhist Burma. In the wake of democratic reforms and openness transnational Islam strives to establish an imaginary *ummah*, or Muslim community, that is a product and an agent of the complex forces of globalization (Roy, 2002).

Modern halal is explored as part of "global assemblages", that is, it is a product of multiple and emergent determinations that are not reducible to a single logic (Ong and Collier, 2005, 12). As a composite concept, the term "*global* assemblage" suggests inherent tensions: global implies broadly encompassing, seamless and mobile; assemblage implies heterogeneous, contingent, unstable, partial and situated (Ong and Collier, 2005, 12). In short, we analyse how Islam and regulation make up halal as a global assemblage. As we shall see, the proliferation of the halal market signifies broader global shifts in domains such as circuits of licit and illicit exchange; systems of administration of governance; and regimes of ethics or values. These phenomena are distinguished by a particular "global" quality. They are abstractable, mobile, dynamic, and move across and reconstitute "society", "culture" and "economy". Simultaneously, these phenomena are domains in which the forms and values of individual and collective existence are subject to technological (the problem of choosing the most appropriate means for achieving technoscientific, organizational or administrative ends); political (concerning the appropriate form and scope of juridico-legal institutions); and ethical reflection on questions of value and morality (Ong and Collier, 2005, 4). Hence, we shall combine several disciplines and methodologies to disassemble these multiple determinations, that is, Islamic studies, anthropology, sociology and marketing. This book moves beyond existing work on individualized halal understandings and practice as part of everyday consumption to also explore the "bigger picture" that frames modern and global halal consumption.

There is a large and growing body of literature on Islamic banking (Maurer, 2005; Kuran, 1995, 1997) and even accounting in Islamic banking and finance (Maurer, 2002), but very little on halal production, trade, consumption and regulation.

A central question in this literature on Islamic finance is regulation. However, the regulation of Islamic products, that is halal products, has not attracted the same level of attention. Halal certification in the form of logos has added a new layer of legal signification to production and marketing of these products, and at the same time two regimes of intellectual property are at play simultaneously, a commercial one and an Islamic one, making halal irreducible to one single logic or determination. Halal as a cultural or religious form has created new fields of potential economic value in new industries and has raised legal and ethical quandaries (Coombe, 1998). We explore how the law is at work in the case of halal shaping social worlds of meaning institutionally, that is, law in the everyday lives of Islamic organizations, states and companies. Both trademarks and halal logos represent legal and institutional forms that struggle to establish and legitimate authoritative meanings in public spheres. Consequently, the legal protection of halal forms creates new relations of power in contemporary cultural politics. In other words, as the law legitimizes new sources of cultural authority it also fixes social meanings.

What is more, a large number of statutes bestow upon "public authorities" such as government agencies, state-owned corporations and non-profit organizations rights to control particular signifiers such as national symbols. Unauthorized use of these can result in a fine or imprisonment (Coombe, 1998, 135). Trademarks play a central role in the visual culture of the nation and point to different politics of ownership and protest, domination and resistance. To sum up, we explore how halal is subjected to novel forms of intellectual property law with its specialized traditions, codes and practices.

This focus also entails broader questions such as the spectacle of attempts at directed control and planning, and publicly rationalized imperative decision-making (Moore, 1978, 8) as well as emphasis on legal transactions, disputes and rules seen in the dimension of time (Moore, 1978, 256). Hence, there is a clear aspect of economic anthropology in these analyses of halal production, trade, consumption and regulation as forms of economic life or activities. We situate halal in larger social and cultural frames in order to see how markets affect and are affected by the thoughts and beliefs of people and institutions.

Methodologically, this study endeavours to follow "the people" (consumers, bureaucrats, representatives from halal certifying bodies, activists and company representatives); "the thing" (the circulation of halal commodities as manifestly material objects of study) (Marcus, 1995, 106) as well as "the metaphor" (halal embedded in particular realms of discourse, modes of thought and practices) (Marcus, 1995, 108). Thus, the contributions in this book all follow people, halal things and metaphors between Islam, states, certifiers and markets on the one hand and inside and across divergent settings on the other. Despite the emergence of halal trade on a global scale, there have been no attempts to systematically disassemble halal as a global assemblage. To sum up, the chapters of this book are based on the following types of material: participant observation, in-depth interviews among Muslim producers, entrepreneurs, traders, non-governmental organizations (NGOs), Islamic organizations, food authorities, restaurant owners, *imams* (Muslim men who lead the prayers in a mosque) and Muslim consumers as well as the proliferation of halal in media such as magazines, newspapers, e-mails, websites, advertisements and pamphlets.

This book is to a large extent based on the interdisciplinary conference 'Did you say *halal*? Islamic normativities, globalization and secularization' organized by Florence Bergeaud-Blackler at Collège de France in Paris on 7–8 November 2013. This conference was the first of its kind to explore global halal production, trade, consumption and regulation. The study of Islamic normative dynamics and halal qualification/disqualification processes was at the heart of the conference: how and by whom, for whom, for what reasons objects, discourses, practices can or are actually called "halal" or "haram"? What methods, institutions, arguments of Islamic legitimation/de-legitimation are used? What are the procedures for monitoring compliance with standards and how and by whom are they developed or institutionalized? The seven sessions of the conference covered different fields in the social sciences, humanities, history, law and philosophy based on wide spectrum of case studies.

Chapter overviews

The book's 12 chapters are not organized into neat thematic sections. Instead, they are organized so that they move from discussions of Muslim-majority to Muslim-minority societies. Chapter 2 *Re-imagining Malaysia: a postliberal halal strategy?* by John Lever examines the emergence of Malaysia as a leading player in the global halal industry. Drawing on documentary research undertaken to augment findings from the EU-funded Dialrel project (www.dialrel.eu), it examines the ongoing attempt to position Malaysia as a leading player in the international halal market by building new economic and social alliances that cut across transnational space on the vertical plane. Moving beyond a concern with nation building through halal consumption and regulation to a position targeting halal consumers in selected global locations, the chapter argues that Malaysia is pursuing a "postliberal" halal strategy by inserting new hegemonic claims into transnational space – the overall aim being to reimagine Malaysia's place in the world.

Chapter 3 by John Lever and Haluk Anil is entitled *From an implicit to an explicit understanding: new definitions of halal in Turkey*. For the majority of the Turkish population all meat is taken prima facie to be halal. The major concern in the market revolves around illegal slaughter, yet most production companies only need a letter from the local Mufti to operate. Although some meat arrives at supermarkets with a label saying "this is halal", it is only recently that debates about halal standards and certification have emerged. These debates are reflected in tensions between reformist groups linked to the modernizing Turkish state and the ruling Justice and Development Party (AKP) backed by the electoral support of political Islam. However, Lever and Anil argue that the growth of greater halal awareness in Turkey is as much about agricultural modernization and the spread of neoliberal technologies as it is about global halal discourses and internal political tensions. The chapter discusses these issues and the move from an implicit to an explicit understanding of halal through a case study of the Turkish meat industry.

Chapter 4 *Remembering the spirit of halal: an Iranian perspective* is by Maryam Attar, Khalil Lohi and John Lever. Research on halal supply and consumption is mainly focused on the physical rather than the spiritual realm. This chapter reverses this trend and explores the halal concept through the definition presented by Ali ibn Abi Taleb in his sermons based on verses from the Qur'an. The chapter explores an approach to the adoption of technological innovations in poultry farming through a case study of an award-winning egg producer in northeast Iran. It highlights a method of poultry production that challenges emergent notions of Iranian halal at the global level through a production process aligned with alternative food ethics within a spiritual economy. If the Iranian poultry industry is to become a producer of poultry products for external as well as for internal markets – a reoccurring theme in state policy – the chapter calls for greater leadership and innovation and better support for Iranian poultry producers.

In Chapter 5 Katharina Graf looks at *Domestic cooking in Marrakech's medina*. She examines how for most domestic cooks in the medina the halalness of food products is taken for granted and embodied in daily practice rather than questioned and explicit. For these cooks, who are predominantly women preparing daily meals for their families, religion frames their everyday practices of food preparation, and as such demands respect for all edible produce. However, in light of ongoing changes of cooking practices related to shifting aspirations of younger generations, halal/haram distinctions are interpreted flexibly. The chapter explores the complex linkages and changes between embodiment, consumption and the religious dimensions of food production and preparation in the medina as embedded in a larger economy of food. Graf aims to show how, apart from a rather taken-for-granted yet changing halal/haram distinction, the local concept of a *beldi* or *rumi* provenance of commodities is equally important to a cook's negotiation of food properties and determines to a large extent their tactics of consumption.

In Chapter 6 Florence Bergeaud-Blackler considers *Islamizing foods*. The conversion to mass distribution of halal meat has revealed the existence of an already well-structured market. By considering the "halal" concept as a "quality" in the conventional sense, this chapter moves beyond the pitfalls of a theological approach by illustrating how the concomitant normative dynamics of "a diasporic, religious market" interfere and combine to produce religious products. It describes the impact of production on the redefinition of religious norms and the relational modalities of those who produce and consume halal products. The more general aim of the chapter is to shed new light on the relationship between politics, religion and economics and examine theories of secularization through these dynamics.

In Chapter 7 *The halal certification market in Europe and the world: a first panorama* Florence Bergeaud-Blackler shows that halal standardization has developed differently in Muslim and non-Muslim countries. Halal markets are instruments for economic development in Muslim countries in Southeast Asia, while they are not yet developed in Muslim majority countries where everything is deemed to be halal. The plurality of halal guarantees in the US and in the different European countries is more complex and cannot be explained only by economics. It is related to the structural characteristics of markets, as well as to the different status accorded by each country to religion and religious practices, the acceptability of religious visibility in general and Islam in particular, the level of Islamic organized activism and the population's sensitivity to animal welfare issues. The chapter proposes a first classification of halal certification, concluding that the distinction between certification agencies does not lie in ritual or cultural differences between Islamic schools of jurisprudence, but rather in the local economic and politico-religious issues at stake.

Chapter 8 *Green halal: how does halal production face animal suffering?* Manon Istasse explores an alternative ethical approach to halal in Belgium. In Brussels, members of the association Green Halal define themselves as "eco-Muslims". To them, Islam invites Muslims to love and to take care of Creation. From this ethical stance, halal is "a Divine order and not simply about consumption". Green Halal members demand a reduction in the consumption of meat, a healthy way of life, good eating practices and respect in animal farming and slaughtering. On the basis of ongoing research with Green Halal members, this chapter questions the qualification of food (and food practices) as halal and ethical, and explores how Green Halal consumers appropriate this qualification. Green Halal relies on a charter about ethical halal and on the confidence of consumers in Green Halal's products and activities. More generally, the chapter investigates the identifications and the investments of humans around "good food" in Belgium.

Chapter 9 *Halal, diaspora and the secular in London* by Johan Fischer examines how halal markets are expanding on a global scale in the wake of Islamic revivalism. London has emerged as a centre for halal production, trade and consumption at a time when the meaning and practices of halal are being transformed and contested. In this chapter, Fischer argues that in the eyes of many Muslims in Britain, this proliferation of halal calls attention to a form of impotent state secularism: the more the culture of Islamic consumption asserts itself, the more the state's incapacity to define what is legitimate in the community's life is felt. Discussing ethnographic material from fieldwork among Malay Muslim migrants living in London, the chapter illustrates how halal evokes a range of sensibilities, attitudes, assumptions and behaviours that may support or undermine secularism as a political doctrine and "the secular" as an epistemic category in everyday life.

Chapter 10 *Muslim food consumption in China: between qingzhen and halal* by Yukari Sai and Johan Fischer explores discourses and practices of halal consumption among Chinese Muslims in China. Based on ethnographic fieldwork, the chapter argues that halal availability and consumption are premised on the state's halal food policies and the sentiments of the surrounding Han majority. While the state and local governments have regulated "ethnic" foods since the 1950s it was not until

2009 that a general guideline for halal food certification was issued. Halal food has been redefined culturally and economically, particularly through the standardization of production. Besides nutritional and economic functions, food and eating practices express values and traits that Chinese Muslims regard as fundamental to ethnic and religious distinctions. "Halal" and the term *qingzhen* (the Mandarin translation for Islam) have been negotiated through the institutionalization of halal food regulation, but policies are also shaped by international connections and cooperation to ensure the reliability and authority of halal marks. The culinary image of *qingzhen*, constructed by religious, ethnic and local factors, influences the marketing of and access to halal food. Even if personal attitudes to halal understanding and practice vary, regulation and trust in the honesty of producers play essential roles in the everyday lives of Chinese Muslims.

Chapter 11 *Halal training in Singapore* by Johan Fischer investigates why and how halal production, trade and certification have become essential to state-regulated Islam and companies in contemporary Singapore. In the rapidly expanding global market for halal products Singapore holds a special position; it is one of the few countries in the world where a state body certifies halal products. Building on ethnographic material from Singapore, this chapter explores the workings of Islamic bureaucracies with particular focus on halal training arranged by Majlis Ugama Islam Singapura (MUIS) – the Islamic Religious Council of Singapore. The everyday political economy of halal commodities and services such as certification and training by MUIS raises some broader questions about how the state and Islamic authorities in Singapore attempt to create and regulate new markets around halal products in a local context.

Chapter 12 by Florence Bergeaud-Blackler is entitled *Who owns halal? Five international initiatives of halal food regulations*. The chapter looks at the many different halal food certifications, standards and logos operating in the international arena. It argues that this plurality of definitions is problematic for economic operators and regulators, and that it is unclear how trade can flow smoothly and fairly in this market. Some international regulatory initiatives have recently emerged. This chapter describes these initiatives, their context and what is at stake for each. How were they born and at what level? In what and how are they different from other supranational regulations? What competitive advantages do they expect or confer? Who decides what standards international bodies use? In conclusion, the chapter suggests that the trend towards the convergence of halal norms may never reach its ultimate goal of creating a universal halal standard.

Bibliography

Abdel Haleem, M. A. S. (translator) (2008). *The Qur'an*. Oxford: University Press.
Agriculture and Agri-Food Canada (2011). *Global Halal Food Market*. Ottawa, ON: Agriculture and Agri-Food Canada.
Appadurai, Arjun (1999). "Introduction. Commodities and the Politics of Value." In *The Social Life of Things: Commodities in Cultural Perspective*, ed. Arjun Appadurai, 3–63. Cambridge: Cambridge University Press.

Benkheira, Mohamed H. (1996). "Chairs Illicites en Islam: Essai d'Interprétation Anthropologique de la Notion de Mayta." *Studia Islamica* 84: 5–33.

Bergeaud-Blackler, Florence (2004). "Social Definitions of Halal Quality: The Case of Maghrebi Muslims in France." In *The Qualities of Food: Alternative Theories and Empirical Approaches*, eds. Mark Harvey, Andrew McMeekin and Alan Warde, 94–107. Manchester: Manchester University Press.

——(2005). "De la Viande Halal à l'Halal." *Food Revue Européenne des Migrations Internationales* 21(3): 125–47.

——(2006). "Halal: d'une norme communautaire à une norme institutionnelle, des normes à boire et à manger. Production, transformation et consommation des normes alimentaires." *Le Journal des Anthropologues* 106–7: 77–103.

——(2007). "Religious Slaughter: A European Perspective." *Journal of Ethnic and Migration Studies* 33(6): 965–80.

Bergeaud-Blackler, Florence and Bernard, Bruno (2010). *Comprendre le Halal*. Liège: Edipro.

Bonne, Karijn, Vermeir, Iris, Bergeaud-Blackler, Florence and Verbeke, Wim (2007). "Determinants of Halal Meat Consumption in France." *British Food Journal* 109(5): 367–86.

Bourdieu, Pierre (1990). *The Logic of Practice*. Cambridge: Polity.

Bowen, John R. (2007). *Why the French Don't Like Headscarves: Islam, the State, and Public Space*. Princeton and Oxford: Princeton University Press.

Boyer, Dominique (2005). "Visiting Knowledge in Anthropology: An Introduction." *Ethnos* 70(2): 141–8.

Brunsson, Nils and Jacobsson, Bengt (2000). "The Contemporary Expansion of Standardization." In *A World of Standards*, eds. Nils Brunsson and Bengt Jacobsson, 1–20. Oxford and New York: Oxford University Press.

Caliskan, Koray (2010). *Market Threads: How Cotton Farmers and Traders Create a Global Economy*. Princeton and Oxford: Princeton University Press.

Coombe, Rosemary J. (1998). *The Cultural Life of Intellectual Properties: Authorship, Appropriation, and the Law*. Durham and London: Duke University Press.

Deeb, Lara (2006). *An Enchanted Modern: Gender and Public Piety in Shi'i Lebanon*. Princeton and Oxford: Princeton University Press.

Denny, Frederick M. (2006). *An Introduction to Islam*. Upper Saddle River: Pearson Prentice Hall.

Douglas, Mary (1975). *Implicit Meanings*. New York and London: Routledge.

——(2004). *Purity and Danger*. London: Routledge.

Fischer, Johan (2008). *Proper Islamic Consumption: Shopping among the Malays in Modern Malaysia*. Copenhagen: NIAS Press.

——(2011). *The Halal Frontier: Muslim Consumers in A Globalized Market*. New York: Palgrave Macmillan.

Gillette, Maris B. (2000). *Between Mecca and Beijing. Modernization and Consumption among Urban Chinese Muslims*. Palo Alto: Stanford University Press.

Goffman, Erving (1971). *The Presentation of Self in Everyday Life*. London: Penguin Books.

Harris, Marvin (1977). *Cannibals and Kings: The Origins of Cultures*. New York: Random House.

——(1998). *Good to Eat: Riddles of Food and Culture*. Illinois: Waveland Press.

Hirschkind, Charles (2001). "Civic Virtue and Religious Reason." *Cultural Anthropology* 16(1): 3–34.

Kuran, Timor (1995). "Islamic Economics and the Islamic Subeconomy." *The Journal of Economic Perspectives* 9(4): 155–73.

——(1997). "The Genesis of Islamic Economics: A Chapter in the Politics of Muslim Identity." *Social Research* 64(2): 301–38.

Lever, John (2013). "The Postliberal Politics of Halal: New Trajectories in the Civilizing Process?" Special Issue of *Human Figurations* 2(3).

Lever, John and Miele, Mara (2012). "The Growth of Halal Meat Markets in Europe: An Exploration of the Supply Side Theory of Religion." *Journal of Rural Studies* 28(4): 528–37.

Lomnitz, Claudio (2001). *Deep Mexico: An Anthropology of Nationalism*. Minneapolis: University of Minnesota Press.

Mahmood, Saba (2004). *Politics of Piety: The Islamic Revival and the Feminist Subject*. Princeton: Princeton University Press.

Manderson, Lenore (1986). "Introduction: The Anthropology of Food in Oceania and Southeast Asia." In *Shared Wealth and Symbols: Food, Culture and Society in Oceania and Southeast Asia*, ed. Lenore Manderson, 1–25. Cambridge and Melbourne: Cambridge University Press.

Marcus, George E. (1995). "Ethnography in/of the World System: The Emergence of Multi-Sited Ethnography." *Annual Review of Anthropology* 24: 95–117.

Maurer, Bill (2002). "Anthropological and Accounting Knowledge in Islamic Banking and Finance: Rethinking Critical Accounts." *Journal of the Royal Anthropological Institute* 8(4): 645–67.

——(2005). *Mutual Life, Limited: Islamic Banking, Alternative Currencies, Lateral Reason*. Princeton: Princeton University Press.

Moore, Sally F. (1978). *Law as Process: An Anthropological Approach*. London, Henley, Boston: Routledge.

Navaro-Yashin, Yael (2002). *Faces of the State: Secularism and Public Life in Turkey*. Princeton: Princeton University Press.

Ong, Aihwa and Collier, Stephen J. (2005). "Global Assemblages, Anthropological Problems." In *Global Assemblages: Technology, Politics, and Ethics as Anthropological Problems*, eds. Stephen J. Collier and Aihwa Ong, 3–21. Oxford: Wiley-Blackwell.

Pink, Johanna (2009). *Muslim Societies in the Age of Mass Consumption: Politics, Religion and Identity between the Local and the Global*. Newcastle upon Tyne: Cambridge Scholars Publishing.

Power, Michael (1999). *The Audit Society: Rituals of Verification*. Oxford: Oxford University Press.

Al-Qaradawi, Yusuf (1995). *The Lawful and the Prohibited in Islam*. Kuala Lumpur: Islamic Book Trust.

Rabinow, Paul (1984). "Introduction." In *The Foucault Reader*, ed. Paul Rabinow, 3–32. New York: Pantheon Books.

Reckwitz, Allan (2002). "Toward a Theory of Social Practices: A Development in Culturalist Theorizing." *European Journal of Social Theory* 5: 243–63.

Riaz, Mian N. and Chaudry, Muhammad M. (2004). *Halal Food Production*. Boca Raton: CRC Press.

Roy, Olivier (2002). *Globalised Islam: The Search for a New Ummah*. London: Hurst & Company.

Rudnyckyj, Daromir (2009). "Market Islam in Indonesia." *Journal of the Royal Anthropological Institute* (N. S.): S183–S201.

——(2010). *Spiritual Economies: Islam, Globalization, and the Afterlife of Development*. Ithaca: Cornell University Press.

Salvatore, Armando (2007). *The Public Sphere: Liberal Modernity, Catholicism, Islam*. New York: Palgrave Macmillan.

Schacht, Joseph. 2014. "Aḥkām." In *Encyclopaedia of Islam*, Second Edition, eds. Peter J. Bearman et al.: http://referenceworks.brillonline.com/entries/encyclopaedia-of-islam-2/ahkam-SIM_0376.

Simoons, Frederick J. (1994). *Eat Not This Flesh: Food Avoidances from Prehistory to the Present*. Madison and London: The University of Wisconsin Press.

Soares, Benjamin and Osella, Filippo (2010). "Islam, Politics, Anthropology." In *Islam, Politics, Anthropology*, eds. Benjamin Soares and Filippo Osella, 1–22. Oxford: Wiley Blackwell.

State Mufti's Office, Prime Minister's Office (2007). *Issues On Halal Products*. Brunei Darussalam: Prime Minister's Office.
Strathern, M. (2000). "Introduction: New Accountabilities." In *Audit Cultures. Anthropological Studies in Accountability, Ethics, and the Academy*, ed. Marilyn Strathern, 1–18. London and New York: Routledge.
Tarlo, Emma (1995). "Hijab in London." *Journal of Material Culture* 12(2): 131–56.
Usmani, Muhammad Taqi (2006). *The Islamic Laws of Animal Slaughter*. Santa Barbara: White Thread.
Werbner, Pnina (2007). "Veiled Interventions in Pure Space: Honour, Shame and Embodied Struggles among Muslims in Britain and France." *Theory, Culture and Society* 24(2): 161–86.

2

RE-IMAGINING MALAYSIA: A POSTLIBERAL HALAL STRATEGY?

John Lever

Introduction

This chapter draws on documentary research conducted to build on insights that emerged through the European Union (EU) funded Dialrel project (www.dialrel.eu). One aspect of the Dialrel project was to examine and gather information on the functioning of the supply chains for halal and kosher meat markets in five countries (Lever and Miele 2012).[1] This chapter examines the ongoing attempt to position Malaysia as a major player in the global halal market by inserting hegemonic claims into the transnational spaces where these markets operate (Lever 2013). Moving beyond a concern with halal as a feature of internal state policy to a position from which Malaysia now targets diverse groups of halal consumers in selected global locations, I argue that Malaysia is pursuing a 'postliberal' halal strategy that cuts across transnational, horizontal space on the vertical plane (Lever 2013). Malaysia is doing this, I argue, through the development of public–private partnerships that foster new economic and social alliances in the international arena.

The social and economic antecedents of postliberalism can be traced back to the second half of the twentieth century. As the modern nation state failed to deal with claims made of it by rising outsider groups, so it turned towards transnational forms of governance and neoliberal forms of regulation and control (Papadopoulos et al. 2008; Lever 2013). The forces that had bound competing social groups together within the confines of the nation state over many centuries (Elias 2012) thus began to unravel, as the processes of subjectification described so intimately by Foucauldians came to the fore (Barry et al. 1996; Burchell et al. 1991; Rose 1996). Papadopoulos et al. (2008) argue that a similar process is under way today. Much as transnational regimes of control emerged as a response to a crisis at the heart of the nation state, so postliberalism, they argue, is *now* emerging as a response to the crisis of multiculturalism at the heart of transnationalism.

This chapter draws on and develops this argument. Just as the modern nation state mobilized the most intimate aspects of subjectivity escaping regulation from the 1960s onwards through transnationalism, I argue here that Malaysia is perusing a postliberal halal strategy to target Muslims excluded under transnational conditions (Lever 2013). It is important to note, however, at this juncture, that the modern nation state does not become irrelevant under postliberal conditions. Nor do transnational institutions take complete control. As Papadopoulos et al. (2008) note, the difference is that the state chooses when to represent itself; it splits itself and pursues change through vertical aggregates of power where its strategic outcomes can be achieved. To a greater or lesser extent this process involves targeting and articulating the interests of competing social and economic actors through the 'strategic rearrangement' of transnational, horizontal space (Papadopoulos et al. 2008, 28).

As politics has combined with demographics to manufacture demand of global magnitude (*New Straits Times* 2006; Fischer 2011; Lever 2013), Malaysia has attempted to position itself centrally within the rapidly expanding global halal market. With the Muslim population expected to increase from 1.6 billion to 2.2 billion by 2030 (Miller 2009) the potential benefits to be accrued are vast. During this period, the Muslim population is expected to increase by 180 per cent in Canada, 140 per cent in the US and by more than 100 per cent in a number of European countries (Miller 2009) – thus providing significant opportunities to target new segments of economy and society in these locations. It is my argument that Malaysia is attempting to position itself in these lucrative future markets by inserting new hegemonic claims into transnational space. This strategy is directly linked, I argue, to *Vision 2020*, a national vision for the future set in motion at the height of the Asian economic boom in the early 1990s. Launched with the intention of making Malaysia a fully industrialized nation by the year 2020, the initiative is based on state-led demands for economic liberalization and cultural reinvention. Arguably it was this discursive process that created the heightened sense of '*national reimagining*' (Goh 2012) on which Malaysia's postliberal halal strategy now stands.

In the first part of the chapter, I trace the origins of this strategy through the development of a hegemonic ethnocratic state regime that emerged after Malaya gained independence from Britain in 1957 (Yiftachel 2006; Wade 2009). From this point onwards, I show how the standardization of halal – in what was to soon become Malaysia – was wrapped up in a state-led process of secular Islamic nationalism that transformed the country into a regional centre for halal trade, commerce and industry (Fischer 2011). As the global conditions for expanding the state's national halal vision began to intensify during the early twenty-first century, I argue that Malaysia began to expand the reach of its halal standardization and regulatory agenda in the international arena by laying the foundations for a postliberal halal strategy. In the second half of the chapter, I explore the process through which Malaysia is operationalizing this strategy by inserting new hegemonic claims into transnational space. This involves an examination of the dual halal strategy employed to extend the reach of Malaysian branded halal and position Malaysia as a central player in the global halal market.

The chapter draws on the notion of postliberalism from the work of Papadopoulos et al. (2008) alongside Ong and Collier's (2005) work on global assemblages. The paper is based on work conducted during the Dialrel project and recent documentary analysis of online media and marketing sources. Malaysia has been perusing a discursive media and marketing strategy to enhance the state's internal halal agenda for decades. More recently, the Internet has become significant as a way of mediating the management of meaning in a process of online nation building (Uimonen 2003) at the global level. Malaysia now promotes its halal ambitions in the international arena through a discursive media and marketing campaign involving state agencies such as Bernama and Matrade, online media such as *Malay Mail Online* (www.themalaymailonline.com) and the *New Straits Times* (www.nst.com.my), and state-supported private sector agencies such as Halal Media (http://halalmedia.net; http://halalsme.com). Arguably all such developments play a central role positioning Malaysia internationally. The chapter draws on these sources throughout to gain a greater understanding of the wider discursive context within which Malaysia's postliberal halal strategy is emerging.

The foundations of ethnocracy in Malaysia

Ethnic diversity has always been a central feature of the geographical territories that make up Malaysia (Hilley 2001; Spaan et al. 2002; Bunnell 2002; Hing 2007; Wade 2009). In the early stages of the state formation process, slaves from the surrounding regions were traded in towns such as Malacca and Singapore, while merchants from China, India and the Middle East mixed openly with soldiers and administrators from European colonial powers jostling for supremacy. Before the rise of the colonial state, indigenous peoples were tied to the land and Malay chiefs were heavily dependent on Chinese coolie and migrant labour to work the large plantations and tin mines set up by the British. The first task of the colonial administration, which emerged after the Anglo-Dutch Treaty of 1824, was to set up a state apparatus that could rationalize the underlying economic and political processes. While this allowed the British to categorize and regulate the population, it also laid the foundations for the exclusionary form of nationalism that privileged Malays and other indigenous peoples over and above the needs of Chinese and Indian migrants (Hilley 2001; Hing 2007).

The territories that make up peninsular Malaysia were united as the Malayan Union in 1946. They were restructured as the Federation of Malaya in 1948, which achieved independence from Britain in August 1957. In September 1963, Malaya was united with Sabah, Sarawak and Singapore as Malaysia. However, Singapore's large Chinese majority presented significant problems for the priorities of the Malay majority, and amid much controversy and social unease Singapore was ousted in August 1965 through a process that gave Malays and other indigenous groups special rights (Bunnell, 2002). This firmly fixed 'multiple fragmented nationalisms into the Malayan political consciousness' (Hing 2007, 224) and laid the foundations on which Malaysia's distinctive brand of *ethnocracy* was to stand (Yiftachel 2006; Wade 2009; Khoo 2013).

Although religious symbols were used to bridge tribal, sectarian and ethnic differences and mobilize support for independence in Muslim countries ruled by European colonial powers during the twentieth century, secular nationalist ideologies also had a profound impact (Sutton and Vertigans 2005). The consequences of these developments are clearly evident in Malaysia, where the constitutional arrangements that emerged at the time of independence provided the foundations for a distinctive brand of ethno nationalism (Yiftachel 2006; Wade 2009). While Islam is the official religion of Malaysia, practised by over 60 per cent of the population, the United Malays National Organisation (UMNO) was heavily involved in the development of the constitution and Malaysia was thus founded as a secular state. As Yiftachel (2006) confirms, under conditions of ethnocracy the national question is intimately linked to a politicized religion – in this case Islam – and Malays are only classed as Malay if they are also Muslim, speak the Malay language and follow Malay cultural traditions.

After independence in 1957 Malaya was governed by an alliance made up of the UMNO and organizations representing Chinese and Indian minorities. The alliance had emerged in the run up to independence, but the new institutional arrangements increased fears between these constituent groups considerably. While ethnic Malays were anxious about the economic power of the Chinese, ethnic Indian and Chinese Malays were concerned about the erosion of their cultural traditions. In the following decades, the UMNO's project of nationalizing Islam had far-reaching social and political consequences, with Chinese and Indian minorities increasingly viewed as questionable and problematic citizens (Nonini 1997). In the period up until 1970, the greatest socioeconomic inequalities were *intra* rather then *inter* racial (Hilley 2001). However, it was disparities between the average incomes of Malays and Malaysia's Chinese and Indian population (Spaan et al. 2002) that heightened sensitivities about the constitution, thus bringing inter-ethnic rivalries to the fore (Hilley 2001).

It was in this discursive context that the New Economic Policy (NEP) was introduced by the UMNO to address the concerns of the Malay majority. Throughout the 1970s and 1980s the number of Malays employed in the state bureaucracy increased significantly, with ethnic Malays receiving favourable quotas in many areas of state policy (Bunnell 2002). In education, for example, over 95 per cent of scholarships were reserved for Malay students (Courbage and Todd 2007). The overall ideological aim was to produce an educated, entrepreneurial and consuming Malay middle class in line with the emergence of a dominant, Western economic model (Fischer 2011; Hilley 2001).

Building on reformist ideas that reached Malaysia from the Middle East during the late nineteenth century, throughout this period UMNO consistently idealized Islam as rational, *of-this-world* and compatible with modern capitalist society (Fischer 2011). While most political activity was banned, some degree of Islamic political activity was tolerated, thus allowing the rise of radical Islam and *dakwah* (revival) groups focused on making Malays better Muslims. As economic development intensified from the 1980s onwards, and the Islamic resurgence intensified transnationally (Sutton and Vertigans 2005), the underlying political controversies became more pronounced. Throughout this period, *dakwah* groups and the Islamic opposition Parti Islam Se-Malaysia (PAS) criticized the UMNO-led government for its un-Islamic separation of the political and religious spheres. This continued to further the ethnicized tensions on which ethnocracy stood, as UMNO and PAS consistently tried to out Islamize each other (Kessler 2008). From this point onwards, as the state selectively mobilized nationalist sentiment to position ethnic Malays *vis-à-vis* the non-Malay *other*, halal became increasingly visible in Malaysian politics.

Regulating halal practices

In the 1970s the Trade Description Act 1975 made it illegal to falsely label food as halal (Sadek 2006). On coming to power in 1981 Prime Minster Mahathir Mohamad furthered this process by initiating the regulation of halal within the state bureaucracy. As consumption practices and shopping/eating spaces were institutionalized in line with the expansion of the dominant Western economic model, centralized state incentives strengthened halal production, trade and consumption (Fischer 2008, 2011). As the state was criticized throughout the 1980s for secular practices and colonial traditions that were seen to undermine the role of religion in everyday life (Jomo and Cheek 1992), halal became increasingly important as a means of maintaining hegemony and advancing a strong Islamic identity (Khoo 2009; Fischer 2011).

With the consequences of neoliberalism and the free market agenda becoming more visible and opposition growing, Malaysian state and federal organizations attempted to maintain authority by regulating the groups they regarded as representative of '*deviant Islam*'. Established in 1971, Darul Arqam promoted a vision of Malay nationalism and independence based on communal development and self-sufficiency. This included the production of a wide range of halal food products that were marketed and traded openly across peninsular Malaysia. However, by the early 1990s the state's halal vision was in full swing and in 1994 Darul Arqam was accused of 'deviationism' and banned on the grounds that they represented the Islamic 'other' that threatened the state's nationalized version of Islam. Fischer (2011, 2015) argues that the state brand of Islamic nationalism is thus intimately linked to the challenges posed by *dakwah* groups and by the concurrent attempt to fuse Malay ethnicity with notions of a fit and proper Islamic way of life in the modern world. Referring to what he calls '*shopping for the state*', he argues that Islamic ritual and practice have been transformed through the production, trade and consumption of halal products to illustrate the compatibility of state-led nationalism with '*proper Islamic consumption*' (Fischer 2008).

By emphasizing Yiftachel's (2006) claim about the significance of settlement for expanding the control of dominant ethnic groups into new regions, Fischer (2011) illustrates how debate over what Islam *is or ought to be* is played out in the modern and affluent suburbs of the capital city Kuala Lumpur. He argues that state engineering through NEP moulded new moral and aesthetic halal communities through a range of spatial practices at the interfaces where policy, Islamic revivalism and the market meet. Fischer's work illustrates how these new suburbs have been squeezed into the spaces between mosques and shopping malls, where the invocation of Islam as a worldview and consumer practices meet and are negotiated within middle-class families *vis-à-vis* other ethnic groups, particularly Chinese and Indian minorities.

Re-imagining Malaysia

From the early 1990s UMNO was compelled by emerging global pressures to think about developing a less exclusive form of nationalism than had been propagated through NEP during the 1980s. In a national context driven by economic globalization, Malaysia started to peruse a multicultural strategy to redefine nationalism in line with the objectives of *Vision 2020* (Bunnell 2002). Introduced by the influential Prime Minister Mahathir Mohamad in 1991, *Vision 2020* outlines plans for Malaysia to become a self-sufficient industrialized nation by 2020 through interlinked initiatives in business, finance and education. The media – which played a significant role resisting the counter hegemonic forces revolving around PAS during the economic crisis (Hilley 2001) – now became a means of promoting *Vision 2020* in line with the work of state and federal organizations.

Halal became increasingly central to these endeavours. The overall objective of the Ministry of Trade and Industry (MITI) (www.miti.gov.my), for example, which articulates strategies and incentives to encourage trade and investment in halal products and services across Malaysia, is to plan, legislate and implement policies to achieve *Vision 2020*. It was during this period, at the height of the economic boom during the early 1990s, that a heightened sense of '*national reimagining*' came to the fore through state-led demands for economic liberalization and cultural envisioning (Goh 2012). It was this inclusionary *imagining* at the official level, Goh (2012) argues, that intensified debate at the everyday level, where the valorization of Islam by the state strengthened Islam's role in Malay identity in ways that challenged existing cultural boundaries between Malay Muslims, non-Malays and non-Muslims.

We can see this process at work in the development of eating practices over an extended period of time. While eating was once an aspect of sociality that brought ethnic Malays, Indians and Chinese closer together, over recent decades eating has been used to indicate the essential difference between halal consuming Malays and the '*bad Malay other*' (Fischer 2011). However, the rise of halal awareness and consumption does not simply preclude forms of sociality. As Khoo (2009) notes, eating spaces are often defined along ethnic lines through the work of state-supported halal entrepreneurs who challenge the dominance of ethnic Chinese in other areas of the domestic economy. This situation, which positions Malays as permanent 'hosts' vis-à-vis non-Malay 'guests', means the food of Chinese and Indian minorities can never be trusted by their Malay 'hosts' (Khoo 2009). This process clearly illustrates the working of the halal–haram dichotomy in Malaysia, with Malay Muslims often rejecting the social invitations of non-Malay Muslims because of the perceived threat to their piety (McKinley 2003). As we observe in the next section, this process also provides insights into Malaysia's attempt to insert a new hegemonic claim into transnational space under postliberal conditions.

Extending hegemony

As a former colony, Malaysia has strong ties with Britain and London is the centre of the Malaysian diaspora (Fischer 2011). As debate about religious slaughter began to influence Muslim identity in Britain during the 1990s, halal presented significant market opportunities (Lever and Miele 2012). During the 1970s a new class of Malay entrepreneurs had emerged through NEP to push the state's halal vision, and throughout the 1980s and 1990s state agencies encouraged and funded ethnic Malays to set up restaurants in London. This process advanced the development of a national halal cuisine (Bunnell 2007) and encouraged the development and visibility of a Malaysian halal brand (Fischer 2015).

Much as they are in Malaysia, Fischer (2011) argues that individuals in the diaspora were subjected to the state's dominant halal discourses. He argues further that the consumption of Malaysian state-certified halal products in the *diaspora* can thus be seen as '*a form of state sovereignty in the diaspora*' that attempts to control Islamic expression (Fischer 2011, 87). This argument is significant when we consider the global expansion of halal and Malaysia's ongoing attempt to develop a postliberal strategy targeting diverse groups of halal consumers in selected locations (Lever 2013). Indeed as Fischer (2011, 120) notes, the 'Malaysian vision to become a world leader in halal is intimately linked to a particular dimension of modern diasporas in urban spaces'.

By positioning halal at the centre of internal trade, commerce and industry throughout the 1970s and 1980s, Malaysia initiated a process through which it became a major halal hub in Southeast Asia through collaboration with countries such as Brunei, Indonesia and Australia. This was part of a long-term strategy – evident in consecutive Industrial Master Plans – to position Malaysia as a global halal hub by improving global competitiveness and transforming the domestic manufacturing and service sectors (Badawi 2006; Muhammad et al. 2009; Noordin et al. 2009; *Marketeer* 2011). As the global conditions for perusing these objectives started to intensify at the start of the new millennium, a Malaysian state standard for halal food (MS 1500:2004) (Department of Standards Malaysia 2004) was launched at the first Malaysian International Halal Showcase (MIHAS) in Kuala Lumpur. The Swiss food giant Nestlé played a significant role in the development of the standard in partnership with the Malaysian Department of Islamic Development (JAKIM) (Bergaud-Blackler 2012). The standard is wide ranging and covers, among other things, slaughter practice, processing, distribution, storage, hygiene, sanitation, packaging and labelling (Tieman and Ghazali 2014).

From this point onwards, Malaysia also began a process of more widespread international engagement. In 2005, the first global halal food exhibition was held in London, which Malaysia's national trade agency Matrade (www.matrade.gov.my) attended in 2006. At the same time, to strengthen its international position and push forward the notion of a global halal hub, Malaysia established the Halal Industry Development Corporation (HDC) (www.hdcglobal.com) to oversee market expansion. They also launched a Halal Knowledge Centre (www.knowledge.hdcglobal.com) as a reference point for all things halal, while promoting the halal food industry at the local level in Malaysia through an online portal (www.Halal.gov.my) that encourages small and medium enterprises (SMEs) to enter the halal market (Seong 2011).

The number of halal hubs and halal parks across Malaysia, comprising various SMEs and associated infrastructure support services in one place, also began to increase in this period (Saifuddeen et al. 2006; Khalid 2009). As stated on one of the HDC's linked websites: '*One of the initiatives undertaken by the government in making Malaysia a Global Halal Hub is providing the necessary infrastructure to facilitate investments in the Malaysian halal industry*'. There are currently around 20 regional halal parks across Malaysia developing new halal knowledge and expertise claims through collaborations between state and private sector agencies (Khalid 2009). Bunnell's (2002) stress on the positioning of Malaysia as a transnational hub for 'high-tech' research and development is clearly evident in this context, where there has been a strong commitment by state and federal agencies to support and promote the development of appropriate internal halal infrastructure and expertise (Khalid 2009).

A global halal standard?

To advance the Malaysian halal brand in the international arena the state has pursued a dual halal strategy. While Malaysia has pursued plans to become a global halal hub over the last decade by expanding their standards and certification regime internationally, they have also been involved in a project to develop a global halal standard by aligning MS 1500:2004 with the diverse concerns and practices of all 57 member states of the Organization of the Islamic Cooperation (OIC) (Lever and Miele 2012). Arguably it is the prioritization of the former over the latter that underpins Malaysia's postliberal ambitions.

A number of standard-setting organizations – including the International Organization for Standardization (ISO), the Codex Alimentarius Commission and the OIC Standing Committee for Economic and Commercial Cooperation (COMCEC) (Hashim 2010, 2012) – have been implicated in plans to develop a common halal standard at the global level. From 2008 until 2010, Malaysia worked in partnership with the OIC to develop a global standard through the International Halal Integrity Alliance (IHIA). Launched at the 5th World Halal Forum in Kuala Lumpur in 2010 to uphold the integrity of halal in global trade, one of the major issues facing this self-styled non-government organization (NGO) was the issue of stunning animals before slaughter, as it is the entailed animal welfare concerns that dominate debate about halal in European markets (Lever and Miele 2012).

Until the end of the last century, most Muslim communities in Europe considered the meat sold in supermarkets and restaurants, and provided in public institutions, to be acceptable if it was slaughtered by people of 'the Book' – i.e. by Muslims, Jews and Christians; in practice this meant that all halal meat came from animals stunned before slaughter. More recently, as the legitimacy of Islam has been questioned in line with changing political discourses at the global level (Marranci 2009), some European Muslims have questioned the status of meat from these sources and there have been calls for 'authentic' halal meat in a number of European countries (Lever and Miele 2012). It is a requirement of European legislation for the protection of animals at the time of killing (EU 1993, 2013) that all animals are stunned *prior* to slaughter in line with the science underpinning mainstream animal welfare claims (FAWC 2009). However, EU member states are allowed to grant an exception to this requirement on religious grounds in line with freedoms granted by Article 9 of the European Convention on Human Rights (Ferrari and Bottoni 2010). This legislation is subject to interpretation by EU member states, but in general it provides legitimacy for the expansion of markets for halal meat from non-stunned animals. This has created the space for the rise of a plethora of new third-party certification regimes overseen by religious and commercial organizations that define non-stunned halal meat as being of 'authentic' halal quality (Lever and Miele 2012).

As a result of these developments, there are now established markets for halal meat from both pre-stunned and non-stunned animals in a number of European countries (Lever and Miele 2012; Lever 2013). The pre-stun position, which is aligned with the Qur'an, is based on an understanding that all people of 'the Book' share common slaughter practices and, as noted, that Muslims can consume meat from animals reared and slaughtered by Jews and Christians as well as by Muslims. The non-stun position, common among Sunni Muslims, is linked more directly to Islam and to traditional halal practices in line with the principles established in the Qur'an through the lived experiences of the prophet Mohammed, as recorded in the *Hadith* (a saying of Muhammad or a report about something the prophet did). Attitudes towards stunning also differ across the four schools of jurisprudence (or *Madh'hab*) within Sunni Islam – the Hanafi, Hanbali, Maliki and Shafi'i schools – where regional differences facilitate divergent and often contradictory halal practices (Oorjitham 2009; Lever and Miele 2012); there are also differences of opinion between Sunni and Shi'ite interpretations of halal (see Chapter 4).

As Malaysia has attempted to position itself centrally within the global halal market, it has tried to accommodate both the pre-stun and non-stun positions into its state halal standard. When it was launched in 2004 the

FIGURE 2.1 Islamic schools of jurisprudence (or Madh'hab) (Adapted from Hashim 2010)

Malaysian standard (MS 1500:2004) came with the qualification that stunning was 'not recommended' (Department of Standards Malaysia 2004). However, in 2009 the standard was revisited (MS 1500:2009) with a commitment to accommodate pre-slaughter stunning under certain conditions, most notably for poultry (Department of Standards Malaysia 2009).

The OIC's Standing Committee for Economic and Commercial Cooperation (COMCEC) has also been working to develop halal standards for over three decades (Dağ and Erbasi-Gonc 2013) and for most of this period it was also against stunning. However, in 2010 scholars from the OIC's Islamic Fiqh Academy in Jeddah also announced that stunning could be used in the slaughter of poultry (Nazar 2010). This would seem to signal a coming together of the positions of the two major players in the global halal standards project at this time, but tensions over the economic aspects of standardization undermined collaboration. Research conducted during the Dialrel project drew attention to the controversial nature of these issues (Lever and Miele 2012). An interviewee at a specialist meat production company in the UK stressed the centrality of economics in all decision making in the Malaysian approach, arguing that the state standard will continue to evolve as international halal markets expand and debate intensifies. A Muslim scholar from a UK-based certification agency argued that the acceptance of stunning by Malaysia was an attempt to target the demands of *all* Muslim consumers over and above religious and scholarly opinion.

Since the launch of MS 1500 in 2004, Malaysia has emerged as a major player in the halal standards debate and there is no doubt that the standard is valued at the global level. Its significance is evident in its citation by the Codex Alimentarius Commission (CAC)[2] '*as the best example in the world in terms of justification of Halal food*' (Noordin et al. 2009, 1). However, the justification provided by CAC aligns itself directly with World Trade Organization (WTO) guidelines, which state that WTO members must give the same priority to imported products as to domestic products in order to protect commercial interests (Lonconto and Busch 2010). This means that the non-Muslim countries that currently dominate global production can export to OIC countries unhindered by claims for unanimity. This is a major source of concern within the OIC. Indeed, much as different standards and certification practices *within* the OIC erect indirect barriers to trade, there are worries that the emergence of a common halal standard from outside the OIC will further prevent economic growth and development *within* it (Muhammad et al. 2009; Dağ and Erbasi-Gonc 2013).

The underlying tensions came to the fore at the 5th World Halal Forum in Kuala Lumpur in 2010. The forum was widely promoted as the launch event of a global halal standard that would provide accreditation for different halal practices through the simultaneously launched IHIA (Oorjitham 2009; IHI Alliance 2010; Lever and Miele 2012). The Malaysian state played a big role in the development of this NGO alongside Islamic finance and private equity fund companies, committing RM15 million over three years to ostensibly improve access to the halal market for all 57 OIC countries. However, there were clear tensions over the power wielded by the Malaysians. As noted, this was particularly evident in negotiations in Kuala Lumpur over the economic aspects of standardization, where Malaysia's role as a global centre for halal certification meant that they were in a position to resist many of the demands made of them by influential members of the OIC from the Gulf Cooperation Council (GCC) (Saudi Arabia, the United Arab Emirates, Kuwait, Oman, Bahrain and Qatar) (Observations made at the World Halal Forum 2010).

It is important to note at this juncture that the boundary between government and non-government organizations is not always clear. Very often, NGOs such as the IHIA, ostensibly set up by the state to further cross-sector collaboration, have strong links *with* the state and the distinction between the public and private sector can become blurred in this context. Throughout their collaboration with the OIC, Malaysia continued to prioritize its standards and certification regime in its own terms over and above GCC demands and working in partnership with the OIC became increasingly problematic (observations made at the World Halal Forum 2010). Consequently, in 2011 the CEO of the IHIA announced that a global halal standard was no longer feasible or necessary. Arguably Malaysia became involved in the global standards project with the OIC as part of a strategy of *selective openness* (Yiftachel 2006) to bypass the collective influence of the OIC and position itself centrally within the international halal market (Lever 2013).

A postliberal halal strategy

It is the argument of this chapter that Malaysia has put a postliberal halal strategy into practice by collaborating with religious and commercial actors in selected locations in order to insert new hegemonic claims into transnational space. Malaysia is already one of the largest global exporters of halal products, with exports reaching $10 billion in 2013 (Hamsawi 2014). With the Muslim population expected to increase by

180 per cent in Canada, 140 per cent in the US and by more than 100 per cent in Italy, Norway, Finland and Sweden over the next 20 years (Miller 2009) the opportunities on the horizon are vast. Collaborations to develop new social and economic alliances is a key aspect of Malaysia's strategy to target and develop these potentially burgeoning markets.

Over the last decade, Malaysia's national trade promotion agency Matrade (www.matrade.gov.my) has been actively building relationships and influencing debate with retailers and certification bodies in selected locations. In the UK, Matrade has worked closely with the UK's major supermarket chain Tesco and the National Halal Food Group (www.nationalhalal.com) (NHFG) for a number of years (Fischer 2011). In 2006 Tesco announced a deal to source RM 1 billion – around US$ 285 million – of certified halal products into the UK (Fischer 2011) and the NHFG was subsequently presented with an award by the Malaysian Chamber of Commerce in Kuala Lumpur for introducing halal products to the UK. Tesco has sold halal meat from pre-stunned animals certified by the Halal Food Authority since 2000. From 2010 they also began selling halal meat from non-stunned animals certified by the NHFG in a number of hypermarkets and selected stores in locations with large Muslim populations (Fischer 2011; Lever and Miele 2012).

Compared with the UK, where the vast majority of halal meat originates from animals that are stunned before slaughter, most halal meat in France comes from non-stunned animals (Lever and Miele 2012). Although Matrade (2005) has drawn attention to the potential the French market offers Malaysian producers for almost a decade, the complexities of the French market have made it more difficult to penetrate than the UK market (Lever and Miele 2012). In 2007 Bernama reported that Malaysian SMEs had received orders worth US$3.5 million during a *Taste of Malaysia* event at a large Carrefour hypermarket in the shadow of the Évry Mosque in Paris – one of the major certification bodies in France. From this point onwards, Malaysian certified halal products have been widely marketed by Carrefour in an increasing number of stores. It has since been argued that many young French Muslims are slowly being seduced by the culture of halal consumption emerging around Malaysian branded halal (Haenni 2010; Bergeaud-Blackler 2012).

In Germany, the expansion of the halal market has been perceptibly slower than in the UK and France (Lever and Miele 2012). German consumers appear less aware of the underlying debates and concerns about animal welfare, and there has not been a direct impact on the availability of different types of halal products in the Aldi and Lidl supermarket chains (Schröder 2009). Links are nonetheless emerging and the German halal market is starting to expand. The Federal Association of German Food Retailers has highlighted the significance of the market, while the German Federation of Turkish Wholesalers and Retailers has advised German companies to embrace it. The Malaysian National News Agency Bernama has also drawn attention to the potential the German halal market offers Malaysian producers (Mehta 2009). Over recent years, the demand for a broader range of halal products has also started to increase (Bouckley 2012) and in 2014 the first international halal trade fair in the German-speaking world was held in Stuttgart.

As Malaysian certified halal products have penetrated European markets the need for support services to facilitate the penetration of the Malaysian halal brand has also been recognized (Muhammad et al. 2009; Othman et al. 2009). With halal evolving downstream and upstream through the supply chain to establish a halal value chain, the food industry is starting to recognize the need for more effective infrastructure and logistical support (Tieman 2014). As far back as 2005, the Port of Rotterdam (2005, 2007) developed a logistics handbook for halal with 'guidelines for suppliers, inspection, storage, packaging and transport' (Tieman and Ghazali 2014, 46). Plans to develop links between the halal designated Port Klang in Malaysia and the Port of Rotterdam in the Netherlands have also been promoted by Malaysia for over a decade (*Marketeer* 2011; Khalid 2009; Fischer 2011). The Netherlands is a potential gateway for halal products entering Europe, and Malaysia now exports more halal products to the Netherlands than any other European country. The emergence of the European Halal Food Park in Norfolk in the UK, close to ports with connections to Rotterdam, is another significant factor in these emerging international chains. Discussions have also taken place between the Malaysian state and the Port of Marseilles in France (Mehta 2010).

Despite problems with the collective voice of the OIC, Malaysia is building relationships with a number of GCC countries to further access to European and North American markets where the Muslim population is expanding. Emerging links with countries such as Turkey (see Chapter 3) and the UAE (Chibber 2014) present significant opportunities for Malaysia to develop solutions for countries wishing to export to GCC countries (Othman et al. 2009) whilst simultaneously helping to further their postliberal ambitions. The IHIA now provides members with support and expertise in a number of interlinked areas, including research and development, accreditation and certification (Azmi 2012; Khalid 2009; Hashim 2010, 2012). In 2012 the IHIA had over 100 members, including 39 countries and 53 certification bodies worldwide, all of which benefit from the continued support and expertise Malaysia provides (IHI Alliance 2010).

Discussion

Throughout the 1980s and 1990s the Malaysian state maintained hegemony through a distinctive brand of Islamic nationalism. The development of halal standards was a significant feature of a process that allowed the state to mobilize nationalism and notions of *other* selectively as and when the opportunity arose. This process was clearly evident in relation to food practices, where state incentives and entrepreneurial activities elevated Malay Muslims over and above non-Malays and non-Muslims in very particular ways.

Over the last 15 years, a similar process has been activated in the international arena. Much as Malaysia inserted hegemonic claims into national space in order to maintain the dominance of the ethnocratic state, so they are now inserting hegemonic claims into transnational space to position the country centrally within the global halal market. By allowing the stunning of poultry, for example, when the need and opportunity arose, Malaysia was able to collaborate more widely with social and economic actors to achieve greater penetration in European markets. Over recent years, this process has taken on a new trajectory as a number of Malaysian agencies have attempted to foster debate about halal and a range of ethically produced foods. The IHIA, for example, has made great efforts to highlight connections between halal, organic, fair-trade and free-range food over recent years (Hashim 2010, 2012). Links between halal and alternative food ethics are thus starting to emerge in some urban spaces (Haenni 2010; Fischer 2011; Lever 2013; Miele and Rucinska 2015) accross Europe in line with the emergence of what Haenni (2010, 335) refers to as a 'more mobile, global philosophy'. To some extent, these developments align halal more closely with the global assemblage of alternative food networks (Goodman and Sage 2013).

Arguably it is the new *subjectivities* that emerge in this context that underpin the *postliberal politics of halal* in European societies (Lever 2013). Attempts are currently being made to further this process in Malaysia through the development of a 'quality' Islamic standard that will align halal with global sustainability discourses (Porter 2014). Ong and Collier's (2005) notion of *global assemblage* is a particularly useful way of examining how theology, politics and regulation diverge and overlap in this context. It highlights how technology, politics and ethics 'are reflected upon and valued, constituted and reconstituted, through reflective practices' (2005, 7). The work of Papadopoulos et al. (2008, 32) also provides significant insights into Malaysia's attempt to position itself centrally in the global halal market to further these aims. As stated in the introduction to this chapter, under postliberal conditions the nation state does not become irrelevant nor do transnational institutions take control. The difference is that the state splits itself into competing social aggregates as and when the opportunity arises in order to achieve its wider strategic objectives.

Much as it was impossible to achieve an effective compromise including all social groups under conditions of national sovereignty, Papadopoulos et al. (2008) argue that it is impossible *now* under transnational conditions to reach a compromise that includes all social groups. Right now, at this very moment, they assert that a new phase of control is being articulated through attempts to capture the subjectivities escaping transnational governance. They argue that the postmodern identities and sensibilities that emerged under transnationalism are *now* being drawn into vertical aggregates of postliberal power through the strategic rearrangement of transnational horizontal space. Postliberalism feeds on transnationalism. It inserts new hegemonic claims into transnational space in order to facilitate new solutions to existing problems – in this case, the exclusion and ongoing vilification of European Muslims (Vertigans 2010). Under postliberal conditions, neither the centralized state apparatus of government nor the relational networks of neoliberal governance are effective ways of organizing economy and society. Postliberalism knows this and it sets out to develop new solutions to existing problems as and when the opportunity arises (Papadopoulos et al. 2008).

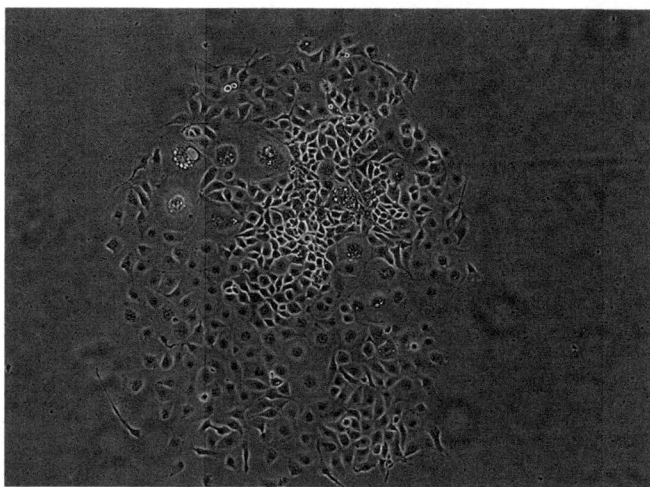

FIGURE 2.2 Micrograph of a heterogeneous stem cell colony isolated from human corneal cells at different stages of differentiation. The cell is likely to be at the centre of the colony where new cells reside. Further from the centre, the cells are older and larger and will eventually die as something new comes into being. (Image reproduced with the permission of Dr Nick Di Girolamo, School of Medical Sciences, University of New South Wales, Sydney.)

If the unbounded network is paradigmatic for the understanding of transnational governance, Papadopoulos et al. (2008, 33) argue that 'cultures or assemblages of stem cells serve as a paradigmatic figure of how artificial postliberal aggregates arise to be able to respond to the ad hoc needs of a certain situation'. The 'promise of the vertical aggregate', they argue, 'lies in its becoming and holding together a series of different actors, akin to the pluripotence of stem cells which might develop into a valued body part or into a cancerous growth' (2008, 32). However, these developments should not simply be seen as an example of the state acting in its own best interests in response to wider global pressures (Stephenson 2011). As Sassen (2008, 70–71) notes, they should be seen as an example of the nation state acting as 'one of the strategic institutional domains where critical work for developing […] foundational transformations in the relation between the private and the public domains' take place. Although the boundaries between the public and private sectors are becoming increasingly blurred, in this context this is very much the approach taken by Malaysia in the international arena.

Conclusion

As Islam has been subjected to increasing cultural and political criticism at the global level, halal has emerged as a central feature of the identity of many young Muslims in European countries with large immigrant populations. Arguably the underlying tensions between the local and the global are the foundations on which the Malaysian state is attempting to maintain internal legitimacy and further the process of *national reimagining* by inserting new hegemonic claims into transnational space. Fischer's argument about engendering state sovereignty in the Malay diaspora through new consumption practices is particularly significant in this context. Considered alongside the increasing number of commercial and religious bodies offering halal certification in Europe, it alerts us to the ways in which these organizations target diverse groups of Muslim consumers looking to reinforce their identity in the face of wider global pressures.

Malaysian branded halal, as a result, has risen from national policy objective to become an internationally recognized benchmark that fuses Islamic traditions with the demands of international markets. Just as Malaysia attempted to maintain adherence to *proper Islamic consumption*, both internally and within the diaspora by drawing on nationalism, arguably it is now drawing on state nationalist discourses to further their postliberal ambitions. Postliberalism uses nationalism arbitrarily, not because it refers to a nationalist ideology, but because it helps to maintain the coherence of the aggregate in question. Moving beyond the idea of horizontally aligned networks of transnational power as the dominant framework for understanding economic and social change, postliberalism allows us to examine how diverse elements of economy and civil society are being drawn together in new ways on the vertical plane in order to capture the subjectivities escaping transnational governance. The notion of a global halal standard is still being pursued by the OIC – latterly with Turkey leading the way (see Chapter 3) – but it remains to be seen whether external *haram* threats to the 'authenticity' of the Malaysian halal brand force a reconsideration of the benefits of a common halal standard at the global level.

Notes

1 The UK; France; Germany; Norway; and Turkey.
2 Established in 1963 to develop international food standards, CAC guidelines and codes of practice were set up to ensure fair practice in the food trade and protect the health of the consumers.

Bibliography

Agriculture and Agri-Food Canada (2011) *Global Halal Food Market*, Ottawa: Agriculture and Agri-Food Canada.
Azmi, H. J. (2012) *Challenges and Opportunities in the Halal Industry*, presented at the International Food, Agricultural and Gastronomy Congress Antalya, Turkey, 17 February.
Badawi, A. A. (2006) *Islam Hadhari: A Model Approach for Development and Progress*, Petaling Jari: MPH Publishing Sdn Bhd.
Barry, A., Osborne, T. and Rose, N. (1996) (eds.) *Foucault and Political Reason: Liberalism, Neo-liberalism and Rationalities of Government*, London: University College London Press, pp. 19–36.
Bergaud-Blackler, F. (2012) Islamising food: halal markets and dynamic norms, *Genesis*, 2013/4, 89: 69–87.
Bernama (2007) *SMEs Clinch Orders Worth RM12 Million in Paris Business*, 27 June, www.bernama.com/bernama/v3/printable.php?id=269836.
——(2013) *Malaysia's Halal Export Growth on Uptrend, says Mustapa*, Malay Mail Online, October.
Bouckley, B. (2012) *Kosher Dairy Demand on the Rise, claims German Ingredients Supplier*, 5 March, www.dairyreporter.com.

Bunnell, T. (2002) (Re)positioning Malaysia: high-tech networks and the multicultural rescripting of national identity, *Political Geography*, 21: 105–24.

——(2007) Post-maritime transnationalization: Malay seafarers in Liverpool, *Global Networks*, 7 (4): 412–29.

Burchell, G., Gordon, C. and Miller, P. (1991) *The Foucault Effect: Studies in Governmentality*, Chicago: University of Chicago Press.

Chibber, A. (2014) *Malaysia to use UAE as Gateway to Halal Markets in Africa, Europe*, www.foodnavigator.com/Regions/Middle-East/Malaysia-to-use-UAE-as-gateway-to-halal-markets-in-Africa-Europe.

Courbage, Y. and Todd, E. (2007) *A Convergence of Civilizations: The Transformation of Muslim Societies around the World*, Columbia University Press.

Dağ, H. and Erbasi-Gonc, E. (2013) SMIIC and halal food standards, *Journal of Chemical Metrology*, 7 (1): 1–6.

Department of Standards Malaysia (2004) *MS 1500:2004: Halal Food – Production, Preparation, Handling And Storage – General Guidelines* (first revision), Malaysia.

——(2009) *MS 1500:2009: Halal Food – Production, Preparation, Handling and Storage – General Guidelines* (second revision), Malaysia.

Elias, N. (2012) *On the Process of Civilisation*, The Collected Works of Norbert Elias, University College Dublin Press.

EU (1993) COUNCIL DIRECTIVE 93/119/EC of 22 December 1993 on the Protection of Animals at the Time of Slaughter or Killing.

——(2013) COUNCIL REGULATION (EC) 1099/2009 on the Protection of Animals at the Time of Killing.

FAWC (2009) *Report on the Welfare of Farmed Animals at Slaughter or Killing, Part 2: White Meat Animals*, www.fawc.org.uk/pdf/report-090528.pdf.

Ferrari, S. and Bottoni, R. (2010) *Legislation Regarding Religious Slaughter in the EU, Candidate and Associated Countries*, Dialrel Research Report, www.dialrel.eu.

Fischer, J. (2008) *Proper Islamic Consumption: Shopping Among the Malays in Modern Malaysia*, Copenhagen: Nias Press.

——(2011) *The Halal Frontier: Muslim Consumers in a Globalized Market*, Contemporary Anthropology of Religion Series, New York: Palgrave Macmillan.

——(2015) Malaysian diaspora strategies in a globalized Muslim market, *Geoforum*, 59: 169–77.

Goh, B. L. (2012) Spirits, cults and construction sites; trans-ethnic popular religion and Keramet symbolism in contemporary Malaysia, in Endres, K. W. and Lauser, A. (eds.), *Engaging the Spirit World: Popular Beliefs and Practices in Modern Southeast Asia*, New York and Oxford: Berghahn Books.

——(2013) The rise of constitutional patriotism in Malaysian civil society, *Asian Studies Review*, DOI:10.1080/10357823.2013.767309.

Goodman, M. and Sage, C. (2013) *Food Transgressions: Making Sense of Contemporary Food Politics*, Aldershot: Ashgate.

Haenni, P. (2010) The economic politics of Muslim consumption, in Pink, J. (2011) (ed.), *Politics, Culture and Identity between the Local and the Global*, Cambridge Scholars Publishing.

Hamsawi, R. (2014) Malaysia exports US$10b worth of halal products, *Business Times*, 10 April, www.nst.com.my.

Hashim, D. (2010) *The Quest for a Global Halal Standard*, presented at the Meat Industry Association of New Zealand Annual Conference, Christchurch, 19–20 September.

——(2012) *Reaching the Muslim Consumer*, presented at University of Auckland Business School, New Zealand Asian Foundation, 12 September.

HDC (2012) *Welcome to Halal Park*, Halal Industry Development Corporation: Halal Park, www.halalpark.com.my, first accessed September 2012.

Hilley, J. (2001) *Malaysia: Mahathirism, Hegemony and the New Opposition*, London: Zed Books.

Hing Y. I. (2007) Migration and the reconfiguration of Malaysia, *Journal of Contemporary Asia*, 30 (2): 221–45.

IHI Alliance (2010) *ICCI-IHI Alliance Halal Standard: Logistics – IHIAS 0100:2010* (first edition), Kuala Lumpur, Malaysia.
Jomo, K. S. and Cheek, A. C. (1992) Malaysia's Islamic movements, in Kahn, J. S. and Francis, L. K. W (eds.), *Fragmented Vision: Culture and Politics in Contemporary Malaysia*, Sydney: Allen and Unwin.
Kessler, C. S. (2008) Islam, the state and desecularization in Malaysia: the Islamist trajectory during the Badawi years, in Othman, N., Puthucheary, M. C. and Kessler, C. S. (eds.), *Sharing the Nation: Faith, Difference, Power and the State 50 Years after Merdeka*, pp. 59–76.
Khalid, N. (2009) *Malaysia: A Global Halal Hub in the Making*, www.maritimegateway.com.
Khoo, G. C. (2009) Kopitiam: discursive cosmopolitan spaces and national identity in Malaysian culture and media, in Wise, A. and Velayutham, S. (eds.), *Everyday Multiculturalism*, Basingstoke and New York: Palgrave Macmillan, pp. 87–104.
——(2013) The rise of constitutional patriotism in Malaysian civil society, *Asian Studies Review: Malaysia, Singapore, Thailand*, Special Issue: *Focus On Southeast Asia*, 38 (3).
Lever, J. (2013) The postliberal politics of halal: new trajectories in the civilizing process?, Special Issue: *Human Figurations*, 2 (3): November.
Lever, J. and Miele, M. (2012) The growth of halal meat markets in Europe: an exploration of the supply side theory of religion, *Journal of Rural Studies*, 28 (4): 528–37.
Loconto, A., Busch, L., (2010). Standards, techo-economic networks, and playing fields: performing the global market economy. *Review of International Political Economy*, 17 (3): 507–536.
McKinley, R. (2003) *DiTanggung Halal (Guaranteed Islamic): The Importance of Serving Halal Food in Religiously Plural Malaysia. Who is Host and who is Guest?*, presented at the Eat, Drink Halal, Haram: Food, Islam and Society in Asia Workshop, Asia Research Institute, Singapore, 3–5 December.
Marketeer (2011) Halal Market – Branding Malaysia as a global halal hub: call to action, *Institute of Marketing Malaysia*, 1/2006, http://imm.org.my/2011/02/marketeer-issue-12006-3.
Marranci, Gabrielle. (2009) *Understanding Muslim Identity: Rethinking Fundamentalism*, London: Palgrave Macmillan.
Matrade (2005) *Product Market Study: Halal Market in France*, July.
Mehta, M. (2009) *Germany's Halal Market Unleashes Opportunities for Malaysian Suppliers*, 19 September, www.bernama.com.
——(2010) *Port Klang & Port Of Marseilles Ink MoU To Bolster Malaysia's Halal Exports To North Africa*, Bernama, http://maritime.bernama.com/news.php?id=530068&lang=en.
Miele, M. and Karolina Rucinska (2015) Producing halal meat: the case of halal slaughter practices in Wales, UK, in Emel, J. and Neo, H. (eds.) *Political Ecologies of Meat*, London and New York: Routledge.
Miller, T. (2009) *Mapping the Global Muslim Population*, Pew Research Centre.
Muhammad, N., Isa, F. M. and Kifli, B. C. (2009) Positioning Malaysia as halal hub: integration role of supply chain strategy and halal assurance scheme, *Asian Social Science*, 5 (7).
Nazar, S. (2010) *Stunning Is Halal, Says OIC's Islamic Fiqh Academy*, http://halalmedia.net/stunning-is-halal-says-oic-islamic-fiqh-academy.
New Straits Times (2006) *The Halal Way to Free Trade*, 11 May.
Nonini, D. M. (1997) Shifting identities, positioned imaginaries: transnational traversals and reversals by Malaysian Chinese, in Ong, A. and Nonini, D. M. *Ungrounded Empires: The Cultural Politics of Modern Chinese Transnationalism*, London and New York: Routledge.
Noordin, N., Noor, N. L. M., Hashim, M. and Sanicho, Z. (2009) *Value Chain of Halal Certification System: a Case of the Malaysia Halal Industry*, presented at the European and Mediterranean Conference on Information Systems, Izmir, Turkey, 13–14 July.
Ong, A. and Collier, S. J. (2005) *Global Assemblages: Technology, Politics, and Ethics as Anthropological Problems*, Oxford: Wiley-Blackwell.
Oorjitham, S. (2009) Draw halal standard from all 4 Sunni schools, *New Straits Times*, 20 April.

Othman, S., Sungkar, I. and Wan Hussin, W. S. (2009) Malaysia as an international halal food hub: competitiveness and potential of meat-based industries, *ASEAN Economic Bulletin*, 26 (3): 306–20.
Papadopoulos, D., Stephenson, N. and Tsianos, V. (2008) *Escape Routes: Control and Subversion in the 21st Century*, London: Pluto Press.
Porter, L. (2014) Halal guide to consumer faith, *Delivering Impact: Monash University Magazine*, February.
Port of Rotterdam (2005, 2007) *Halal Logistics Handbook*, Rotterdam, the Netherlands: Port of Rotterdam.
Rose, N. (1996) *Inventing our Selves: Psychology, Power and Personhood*, Cambridge: Cambridge University Press.
Sadek, Mohamed (2006) Marketing Niche for Halal Food Supply: A Framework for the Establishment of an International Halal Food Market, in Saifuddeen, S., H., Salleh, S., M. and Sobian, A. (eds.), *Food and technological progress: an Islamic perspective*, MPH Group.
Saifuddeen, S. H., Salleh, S. M. and Sobian, A. (eds.) (2006) *Food and Technological Progress: An Islamic Perspective*, Petaling Jari: MPH Group Publishing.
Sassen, S. (2008) Neither global nor national: novel assemblages of territory, authority and rights, *Ethics & Global Politics*, 1: 61–79.
Schröder, D. (2009) Halal is big business: Germany waking up to growing market for Muslim food, *Spiegel Online International*, www.spiegel.de/international/germany/halal-is-big-business-germany-waking-up-to-growing-market-for-muslim-food-a-653585.html.
Seong, L. K. (2011) Halal certification as a spring board for SMEs to access the global market, *The Star*, 27 May, www.thestar.com.my/story.aspx?sec=b&file=%2f2011%2f5%2f28%2fbusiness%2f8633743.
Spaan, E., Naerssen, T. van and Kohl, G. (2002) Re-imagining borders: Malay identity and Indonesian migrants in Malaysia, *Tijdschrift voor Economische en Sociale Geografie*, 93 (2): 160–72.
Stephenson, N. (2011) Emerging infectious disease/emerging forms of biological sovereignty, *Science, Technology & Human Values*, first published 22 November 2010.
Sutton, W. P. and Vertigans, S. (2005) *Resurgent Islam: A Sociological Approach*, Cambridge: Polity Press.
Tieman, M. (2014) Synergy in halal supply chains, *Islam and Civilizational Renewal*, 5 (3): 538–42.
Tieman, M. and Ghazali, M. C. (2014) Halal control activities and assurance activities in halal food logistics, *Procedia – Social and Behavioral Sciences*, 121: 44–57.
Uimonen, P. (2003) Mediated management of meaning: on-line nation building in Malaysia, *Global Networks*, 3 (3): 299–314.
Vertigans, S. (2010) British Muslims and the UK Government's 'war on terror' within: evidence of a clash of civilizations or emergent de-civilizing processes, *The British Journal of Sociology*, 61 (1): 24–44.
Wade, G. (2009) The origins and evolution of ethnocracy in Malaysia, *The Asia-Pacific Journal: Japan Focus*, http://japanfocus.org/-geoff-wade/3259.
Yiftachel, O. (2006) *Ethnocracy: Land and Identity Politics in Israel/Palestine*, University of Pennsylvania Press.

3

FROM AN IMPLICIT TO AN EXPLICIT UNDERSTANDING: NEW DEFINITIONS OF HALAL IN TURKEY

John Lever and Haluk Anil

Introduction

The controversies associated with the expansion of the global halal market are as evident in Turkey as they are in any other global location, particularly in Istanbul and regional urban centres. Located at the crossroads of Europe and Asia, bordering the Middle East, at the heart of the once mighty Ottoman Empire (Sutton and Vertigans 2005), Turkey has significant trading interests with the Organisation of the Islamic Cooperation (OIC) *and* with the European Union (EU). When it comes to halal this situation creates many tensions. For the majority of the Turkish population all meat marketed within the country is taken prima facie to be halal and most production companies only need a letter from the local mufti (or cleric) to operate. Some meat arrives at supermarkets with a label saying *this is halal*, but it is only recently that concerns over halal standards and certification have emerged. While debates about new forms of Islamic consumption in Turkey are commonplace (Navaro-Yashin 2002; Yavuz 2003; Gokariksel and Secor 2009; Tunç 2009; Sandıkcı and Ger 2010), halal has only recently been recognized as part of the underlying *market for identities* (Izberk-Bilgin 2012).

This chapter explores the rise of greater halal awareness in Turkey by examining agricultural modernization alongside the simultaneous rise of competing halal discourses at the national and global level. The underlying tensions revolving around halal are evident in relations between reformist groups linked to the modernizing Turkish state and the ruling Justice and Development Party (AKP) backed by the electoral support of political Islam. Although the AKP has re-legitimized Islam in the public sphere (Turner and Arslan 2013) and pushed for a national halal standard along the lines of the Malaysian model (Cagatay and Yegenoglu 2006), Turkey's secular foundations also bring them into direct conflict with a state bureaucracy pursuing modernization in line with the EU's animal welfare (Miele and Lever 2013) and halal agendas (Lever and Miele 2012). Turkish consumers can therefore choose between different understandings of halal aligned with these competing political priorities. However, in this chapter we argue that concerns over agricultural modernization and the spread of neoliberal technologies (Ong 2007) have been just as important as the rise of global halal discourses in facilitating greater halal awareness. We argue that as the poultry (white) meat sector has expanded and modernized, concerns over the spread of new technology and more visible forms of avian disease have contributed towards an increased awareness of the value of halal certification. This is in stark contrast to the red meat sector, where long-standing concerns over illegal slaughter can be more directly aligned with a traditional Turkish way of life and taken-for-granted assumption about Islam and halal food practices in everyday life (Yesilada et al. 2010; Durmus et al. 2012; Trépanier 2014).

The chapter draws on mixed methods research conducted during the Dialrel project (www.dialrel.eu) on halal and kosher supply chains, consumer issues and slaughter regulations. It complements this – building on a well-established strand of work on animal welfare and slaughter practice (see Anil 2012) – with detailed documentary research and data from ongoing consultancy work in Turkey and Central Asia. Theoretically we draw on the work of Papadopoulos et al. (2008) alongside Ong and Collier's (2005) notion of global assemblages to examine the rise of competing understandings of halal and the underlying technological, political and ethical practices.

We begin by charting the decline of the Ottoman Empire and the subsequent rise of the Turkish state. The long-standing tensions between proponents of modernization and political Islam provide insights into the social, political and economic tensions that underpin competing definitions of halal in modern-day Turkey. We then examine how these tensions are reflected in the global assemblage of halal and through competing definitions and understandings. This is followed by an examination of the taken-for-granted assumptions about red meat, which is taken to be halal at face value by producers and consumers alike, and an emerging and more explicit recognition of the need for halal certification and labelling in the poultry sector. The Turkish red meat industry has suffered many problems over recent decades including, most notably, widespread concern over illegal slaughter. As the price of red meat has increased significantly on the back of these trends, the poultry sector has undergone a rapid process of modernization using imported Western technology. Arguably the subsequent increase in the production and consumption of poultry meat has – combined with concerns over agricultural modernization and the spread of neoliberal technologies (Ong 2007) – increased calls for halal certification (Yesilada et al. 2010; Durmus et al. 2012) in line with the rise of global halal discourses.

The birth of the Turkish state

In the Ottoman Empire Islam was the dominant force in all areas of social life. The sultan was the ruler of the empire and as caliph the leader of the Muslim world, a situation that 'symbolized the Islamic ideal of a political community based on religious legitimacy' (Toprak 1981, 1–2). Ottoman society was organized around a *millet* system of multi-ethnic and multi-religious communities, each with its own leadership. In this early system of pre-modern religious pluralism (Sachedina 2001), there were no Turkish or Arab *millets* nor any other openly recognized ethnic groups, only Ottomans, as any form of nationalism was seen as a threat to the stability of the empire (Eligür 2010). While the central administration was Islamic, the social, economic and religious rights of minorities were recognized and it has been argued that there was no direct threat towards religious and ethnic groups (Nasr 2004). However, as Turner and Arslan (2013) point out, there were also rules to maintain the division between these groups and preserve the hierarchy between Muslims and non-Muslims.

After a series of military defeats in the late eighteenth century, the Ottomans initiated a process of modernization to prevent the growing threat and influence of Europe. The pace of modernization quickened during the reformist *Tanzimat* period in the nineteenth century, when European-style laws replaced key tenets of *Sharia* law (Sutton and Vertigans 2005). While modernization led to more freedom, many of the reforms were seen to be un-Islamic and in the short term this increased autocracy (Lewis 2002). However, modernization continued to reduce the influence of the religious elite and power was gradually transferred to the state through a new bureaucratic class educated in the West (Turner and Arslan 2013). The 'Young Turks' accelerated the process of reform in the early twentieth century, initiating progressive movements in the spheres of education, law and military. Modernization eventually failed in the late Ottoman period because of the challenges presented by competing nationalist ideologies and the rise of new institutions, all of which left the majority of the population outside the reform process (Sutton and Vertigans 2005).

When the Ottoman Empire was finally dissolved at the end of World War I the notion of 'Turkey' emerged as a clear marker of identity for the first time. The Treaty of Sèvres in 1920 was a defining moment in this process. Initiated by the Allies as a peace treaty with the Ottomans, the treaty was never ratified, yet it had far-reaching social, economic and political consequences. As large parts of modern-day Turkey were divided between Britain (Istanbul administration), France, Italy and Greece, and the Kurds and Armenians were promised independence (Sutton and Vertigans 2005), radical opposition emerged amongst Turkish nationalists. The Turkish War of Independence (1919–1922) thus culminated in the rise of an independent Turkish Republic in 1923.

The process through which 'Turkey' emerged a symbol of what was to be typical of the new polity was complex (Navaro-Yashin 2002). While those at the forefront of building the new republic were not interested in maintaining links with Ottoman culture, there was nevertheless a need for some historical continuity to give influential Western notions of national culture some credibility. As the monarchy was removed and religious influence declined, modernization intensified and strong links were thus forged with Turkic groups in Central Asia to justify an authentic nationalism along European lines (Navaro-Yashin 2002). The Atatürk revolution (1923–38) was to some extent a struggle against Western imperialism and domination (Eligür 2010). However, while it is often seen as the start of a long process of secularization, it is better off viewed as a process that consigned Islam to the private sphere (Turner and Arslan 2013) and laid the foundations for the rise of a secular Muslim state. Mustafa Kemal Atatürk's aim was profound in that he attempted 'to create a distinct Turkish culture, Muslim born, yet secular, different from Arabs and keen to adopt Western lifestyles and technologies' (Navaro-Yashin 2002, 48). Rabasa and Larrabee (2008, 32) argue that this was a *'revolution from above'*, imposed on a reluctant traditional society by a state-led *'military-bureaucratic elite'*.

Throughout the Kemalist period, everything associated with the Ottoman era was effectively cast aside in favour of modernization and a series of reforms that attempted to sever Turkey's links with its Islamic past. The notion of 'Turkey' was associated with all citizens regardless of ethnicity or class, yet the impact of the reforms initiated by Atatürk was felt most closely in urban areas and the countryside was largely unaffected. Consequently, as Rabasa and Larrabee (2008, 33) note, from this point onwards 'two Turkeys coexisted in uneasy harmony: an urban, modern, secular "centre" and a rural, traditional, religious "periphery"'. Religion was not banned or eliminated: it was simply relegated from the public sphere and supervised as an arm of the state by the Directorate of Religious Affairs. Despite a ban on religious orders in 1925 (Turner and Arslan 2013), Islam retained strong social roots in the countryside and for the most part remained beyond state control.

The rise of political Islam

To some extent, the rise of political Islam in Turkey can be linked to a series of modernizing reforms that took place during the late Ottoman period and failed attempts to stop the growing power and influence of the West (Eligür 2010). However, the political upheavals that emerged after the rise of the Turkish republic were also significant. Atatürk's death in 1938 intensified the authoritarian tendencies of the regime significantly and one party rule enabled further social transformations. As more than 75 per cent of the population lived in rural areas at the time, many people maintained their traditional customs and beliefs because they simply did not understand what was happening (Eligür 2010). Rabasa and Larrabee (2008, 35) argue that the rise of political Islam over the last few decades is thus best seen as an expression of a marginalized periphery's attempt to *'find its political voice'* – a process that was greatly enhanced by the emergence of a multi-party system in 1946.

In 1950 the Democratic Party won the general election by appealing to those areas and groups that felt marginalized by the state. As Islam and the values of traditional society were re-legitimized, political Islam was drawn into the political arena and there was some movement away from state-led policies towards a more liberal economic model (Rabasa and Larrabee 2008; Eligür 2010). In 1960, the Turkish military intervened following civil unrest ignited by the ruling party's divisive policies, alienation of the army and allegations of corruption. After power was given back to the civilian government there were changes to the constitution in 1961. At the same time, the number of autonomous groups, both religious and non-religious, began to proliferate. This culminated in the rise of the National Order Party in 1970. However, throughout the 1970s there was an upsurge in violence by left- and right-wing groups and the military had to intervene again in 1980 to restore order and prevent civil war. In order to combat the rise of the left and rising communist sympathies, the military now turned to Islam (Rabasa and Larrabee 2008; Eligür 2010). By instituting a state-led process of '*Islamisation from above*', the military attempted to fuse Islamic symbols with nationalism to highlight the threat posed by ideological fragmentation and initiate a more homogenous political community. However, while Turkey had long been defined as a secular state in the constitution, the promotion of moral and religious education as a means of reinforcing Turkish nationalism inadvertently undermined modernization, thus strengthening political Islam still further (Rabasa and Larrabee 2008).

As well as economic and political change, Turkish society underwent some profound demographic changes during the twentieth century. The policies of successive governments – perused to encourage industrialization in the 1930s and agricultural modernization in the 1980s – undermined the agricultural basis of the economy and encouraged a massive influx of rural migrants into towns and cities. These migrants did not leave empty handed and they arrived in urban areas with their traditional beliefs and customs intact, thus presenting Islamic parties with a significant pool of potential new voters (Rabasa and Larrabee 2008; Eligür 2010). However, while the changing demography of Turkish society helped to further new forms of Islamic consumption during the 1980s, all meat was largely taken to be halal at face value in line with traditional Turkish customs and widely accepted Islamic practices (Delaney 2014; Trépanier 2014).

Neoliberalism, consumption and identity

The political and economic reforms carried out by Prime Minister Turgut Özal during the 1980s continued to strengthen the position of Islamic groups *vis-à-vis* powerful bodies in the secular state bureaucracy. Özal's administration emerged following three years of martial law and military leaders were initially sceptical of his move towards economic and political liberalization. However, public life in Turkey was transformed during this period and success quickly emerged as the greatest social value (Navaro-Yashin 2002). The number of retail chains, cafés and cinemas in Istanbul increased dramatically and the city became a hub for emerging lifestyle consumption practices. Significantly, these changes did not simply take place in the lives of secular urbanites, they also created a new class of capitalists and entrepreneurs with strong Islamic roots. These new groups were hugely in favour of economic and political liberalization, not least because it entailed a lesser role for the state and greater religious freedom (Navaro-Yashin 2002; Rabasa and Larrabee 2008). It was during this period that preparations for a formal application to

EU membership also gained pace, with Turkey eventually beginning accession talks in the 2000s.

In line with emerging forms of consumption, Islamic groups began to form strong identities of their own throughout the 1980s and 1990s (Navaro-Yashin 2002; Yavuz 2003; Mutlu 2009; Gokariksel and Secor 2009; Tunç 2009). A subject of particular controversy in the literature is the issue of women's headscarves, which has sparked intermittent controversy between conservative Muslims and modernist reform groups (Olson 1985; Gokariksel and Secor 2009). Halal is notable in this literature by its omission. While Navaro-Yashin (2002) discusses how Islamic groups changed their consumption habits considerably during this period, halal still remained a largely implicit and taken-for-granted aspect of Turkish life. Izberk-Bilgin (2012) argues that the recent rise of a market for halal products in Turkey is inseparable from the changes highlighted by Navaro-Yashin. However, the simple focus on Islamic consumption as a challenge to Western modernity to some extent overlooks the influence of the hegemonic contestation revolving around halal at the global level. It also overlooks the freedom Muslims have in contemporary Turkey to choose between competing definitions and understandings of halal.

The rise of greater halal awareness in Turkey can be traced back to 2002 when the ruling AKP came to power and re-legitimized Islam (Turner and Arslan 2013) in the public sphere through an ideology fusing conservative Islam with neoliberalism (Tugal 2009). As they attempted to reassert Islam in the public sphere, the AKP began pushing for a national halal standard along the lines of the Malaysian state model to inform consumers (Lever 2013; Fischer 2014). This was controversial and questions were raised about the government of a secular country telling people what they could and could not eat on religious grounds (Cagatay and Yegenoglu 2006). It was in this context, characterized by tensions between a modernizing Turkish state and the ruling AKP Government, that the debate about halal standardization and certification began to intensify.

The global assemblage of halal

Over recent years, the underlying tensions have been reflected in debates between the state-led Turkish Standards Institute (Turk Standartlari Enstitusu or TSE) and the third-party certification body GİMDES (the Food Auditing and Certification Research Association). On coming to power in 2002, the AKP instructed TSE (https://www.tse.org.tr) to develop an official halal standard for the consumer market (Cagatay and Yegenoglu 2006). However, tensions within the workings of the state bureaucracy held up this process significantly. Subsequently, in 2005, GİMDES (www.gimdes.org) emerged as the first third-party halal certification body in Turkey.

GİMDES started out by issuing halal certificates to Turkish companies exporting to markets in Asia and the Middle East – and it is only recently that they have started to focus on the national market. They issued their first export certificate in 2009 and during the first six months of 2010 further certificates were issued to Turkish companies 'on demand'. At the time of writing, GİMDES claimed to have checked and certified 350 firms and 5,000 products, exporting goods worth $5 billion to 67 countries. As well as overseeing certification, it appears that GİMDES has some capacity to conduct annual audits of halal manufacturers and train halal certifiers. They also promote public halal awareness through conferences, a website and a bi-monthly magazine, all of which are seen to provide consumers with the resources and information they need to live a halal lifestyle.

The chairman, Dr Hüseyin Kami Büyükzer, has positioned GİMDES in direct opposition to the social and economic problems posed by Western modernity (Izberk-Bilgin 2012), consistently questioning the practices of TSE and the Ministry for Agriculture and Food (www.tarim.gov.tr). In 2008, Büyükzer claimed that fewer than 40 per cent of all products imported into Turkey were investigated and that Turkish producers do not always disclose what ingredients are in their products; the implication here was that this situation increases public mistrust and cynicism. Büyükzer cited the example of a German drug firm that named gelatine amongst a product's list of ingredients but which was erased when the product was imported into Turkey. He claimed that consumers should pay more attention to such issues and that the Government should do more to make the public aware (Hava 2009).

When TSE started issuing halal certificates for export in collaboration with the Directorate of Religious Affairs in 2011 (TSE 2012) a debate soon emerged in the national media about who could legally issue halal certificates (Aznam 2011). It was clear that TSE was uncomfortable with private sector bodies issuing halal certificates without their consent. GİMDES responded by challenging the Government to amend the constitution and provide consumers with food produced in accordance with their religious beliefs. It was in this discursive context that Büyükzer claimed a common halal standard was needed at the global level (Hava 2009) to bring some coherence to international markets. He argued that halal certification should take place at the international level in line with the expertise of muftis and clerics, and that it should not involve governments. It was because individual members of the OIC had not agreed a common standard, he argued, that some countries had started to introduce separate halal rules and standards of their own (Aznam 2011).

TSE had been working with the OIC to develop a global halal standard through the OIC's Standards and Metrology Institute for Islamic Countries (SMIIC) for some time. Turkey has been a key player in the development of SMIIC since the OIC's Standing Committee for Economic and Commercial Cooperation (COMCEC) announced plans for such an organization at a meeting in Istanbul in 1999. SMIIC was eventually ratified in 2010 when it received the full backing of the required number of OIC members (Dağ and Erbasi-Gonc 2013). As SMIIC was located in Istanbul near COMCEC, this gave great impetus to Turkey's plans to develop a global standard for the OIC. While the proposal was rejected by a number of OIC countries, most notably Malaysia and Saudi Arabia (Boyacioglu

2010), Turkey's position has nonetheless been strengthened by Malaysia's unwillingness to work with the OIC. Since 2011, TSE has issued over 200 halal certificates, and with companies operating in Iraq, the Gulf States and the rest of the Middle East are starting to take interest (*Today's Zaman* 2014). At the same time, however, GİMDES has been working with Malaysia as the country attempts to position itself as a global halal hub and centre for halal certification. As GİMDES immersed itself in the activities of the World Halal Forum and obtained accreditation from the Malaysian State Department of Islamic Development (JAKIM), it came to play a central role developing the European Association of Halal Certifiers (AHC-EUROPE) to expand the wider reach of the Malaysian network. AHC-EUROPE is an umbrella organization for a single European halal certification scheme involving agencies from Belgium, Bosnia, France, Germany, Spain, the Netherlands and the UK (EMU 2010).

As a member of the EU trading block, Turkey is also involved in a number of initiatives to enhance the EU's farm animal welfare (FAW) agenda (Miele and Lever 2013). In a continuation of the process of modernization that started over a century ago, the Ministry for Agriculture and Food and TSE have been working to develop new market rules and standards for halal and animal welfare in Central Asian countries (*Today's Zaman* 2014). They have worked closely with the Food and Agriculture Organization of the United Nations (FAO) and the Royal Society for the Protection of Cruelty to Animals (RSPCA) in the UK to increase awareness of FAW. Initiatives have also been funded by the FAO and Turkish International Technical Cooperation Funds (TIKA) to improve poultry and red meat processing, and welfare assessment, in these countries. The Ministry for Agriculture and Food has also organized training for staff in rural regions and prepared new legislation in line with new EU regulation that aims to improve animal welfare at the time of killing. Turkey's representative from the FAO, a sub-regional coordinator for Central Asia, recently indicated that Turkey has the capacity and capability to become a major halal food exporter in the region. Indeed the particularly striking thing about all the initiatives being introduced by Turkey is that they all target the export market. Within Turkey itself, as noted, meat is generally taken to be halal at face value (Ergul 2013). At the time of our research (2006–10), most production companies only needed a letter from the local mufti (or cleric) to operate and it is only recently that debate about halal standardization and certification has emerged. While the rise of global halal discourses has no doubt played a part in this process, a range of cultural factors associated with agricultural modernization have also been significant (Yesilada et al. 2010; Durmus et al. 2012).

To explore this situation in more detail, the rest of this chapter looks at developments in the Turkish meat industry. First, we briefly look at the structure and organization of the industry. This is followed by an examination of the taken-for-granted assumptions about halal in the red meat sector and an emerging and more explicit recognition of the need for halal certification and labelling for poultry meat, particularly chicken. This situation has come about, we argue, not simply because of the rise of global halal discourses, but because of a series of complex socio-cultural and economic factors linked to the spread of neoliberal technology (Ong 2007).

The Turkish meat industry

The Ministry for Agriculture and Food (www.tarim.gov.tr) is the central regulator of the meat industry in Turkey. The ministry has relevant divisions and veterinarians with responsibility for animal health, animal welfare and hygiene control. All slaughterhouses have official veterinarians who oversee daily operations and carry out meat inspections; licences to operate are provided by Government veterinarians. Until relatively recently, most slaughterhouses were run by municipal authorities, but this is now changing. The red meat sector is mainly focused on the internal market and it is now made up largely of private sector companies. Private sector companies also dominate the poultry sector, which has undergone a significant process of modernization over recent years. As well as conducting primary processing and national marketing, companies in the poultry sector also produce products for export.

In 2011 red meat (cattle, sheep, goat) and poultry (chicken, turkey and hens) production in Turkey was reported to be 624,286 tonnes and 1,308,009 tonnes, respectively (FAO 2011). While the figure for red meat consumption is much lower than in other developed nations, the consumption of poultry meat is now much closer to such countries in some regions, particularly in the Mediterranean west of the country (Yesilada et al. 2010; Durmus et al. 2012). While there have been some imports of livestock over recent years, there have been objections to imports on the grounds that they entail economic losses for national producers. There have also been problems over animal welfare compromises during transportation from Europe and incentives for national production are thus seen by many to be preferable to imports.

There is no explicit halal regulation in Turkey and the production of meat according to Sharia law and Islamic principles is standard practice. All slaughter men must be Muslim and all commercial slaughter must be performed in recognized slaughterhouses. In the red meat sector, non-stunning is the standard method of slaughter. Slaughter must be preceded by the *tasmiyah* – 'Bismillah Allahu Akbar' (God is great) – and conducted with a single cut from an unserrated knife; it is believed that this method of slaughter allows the blood to drain with minimal pain. Animals must not be handled until the blood has drained completely and legislation is largely focused on the control of disease alongside animal and public health. There is an exception for slaughter carried out for personal consumption and during religious festivals. At such times, slaughter must be carried out quickly with as little pain as possible in line with religious rules and hygiene regulations.

The slaughter of animals during Kurban Bayrami (*Eid al Adha* in Arabic) is a long-standing tradition in Turkey commemorating Ibrahim's willingness to sacrifice his son

FIGURE 3.1 Traditional slaughter during Kurban Bayrami. (Copyright Kobby Dagan/Shutterstock.com)

to Allah (Delaney 2014). During this four-day festival, which marks the end of the annual pilgrimage to Mecca, large numbers of cattle, sheep and goats are slaughtered in celebration with friends and family, often in public spaces. Over the last decade, this practice has become more controversial as animal welfare demands have increased in line with EU accession talks and Turkey's commitments to the EU trading block. Kurban legislation has been enforced more regularly, particularly in urban areas, and municipal authorities have attempted to tighten controls by providing temporary abattoirs and imposing fines. In some places, supermarkets now slaughter animals for customers in temporary (tent-based) slaughter facilities during Kurban. Non-stunning, as this brief discussion indicates, is a culturally accepted method of slaughter in Turkey, with red meat taken to be halal at face value by the majority of the population. However, while most production companies only needed a letter from the local mufti (or cleric) to operate, there was also recognition at the time of our research that halal certification was on the horizon. We can see these trends more clearly by looking at developments in the red meat and white meat (poultry) production sectors, respectively.

An implicit understanding of halal

The problem of unrecorded or illegal slaughter makes it particularly difficult to get a definitive estimate of red meat production in Turkey. As an interviewee commented:

The FAO gave 650,000 [tonnes] for Turkey, but the red meat consumed in Turkey is 1.2 million tonnes. That's because of the unrecorded meat. For that reason, it's difficult to give an accurate figure.

(Interview September 2009)

Some interviewees claimed further that as much as 60 per cent of red meat in Turkey may be illegally produced. Production in the sector faces a number of other challenges and red meat has become increasingly expensive (Durmus et al. 2012). The sector has not modernized using new technology to the same extent as the poultry sector and pasture is scarce. Conflict in the east of the country (*Today's Zaman* 2014) – the major red meat production region – has, combined with poor state incentives, also undermined production and increased costs. Growing concerns about a range of health-related issues associated with red meat consumption have also been detrimental. However, despite the problems facing the sector, it appears that all red meat in Turkey is still taken prima facie to be halal by the vast majority of the population (Ergul 2013).

All the red meat production companies we spoke to during our research indicated that they only needed a letter from the local mufti (or cleric) to operate. The first red meat company we visited was established in January 1984 and production started in the late 1980s. At the time, there was no centralized system for red meat production or distribution in Turkey and the company set out to improve modern stockbreeding knowledge and develop new production techniques. The company slaughters sheep and cattle in line with EU standards to produce delicatessen products, frozen foods and ready-made meals for a number of supermarkets, including 50 per cent of the fresh meat for the Migros chain. The second red meat company was established as a family business in the early twentieth century and it is now in its third generation as a family business. For many years, it only produced a specialist *sucuk* sausage, but it has since expanded its range of products in line with demands of the Carrefour and Migros supermarket chains. Interviewees indicated that both companies follow strict Islamic rules governing slaughter and that both practise non-stunning. This involves having the *tasmiyah* recited during slaughter, a Muslim slaughter man making the first cut with a knife, and draining all blood from the animal post-slaughter. Interviews conducted with retailers and supermarkets indicated that meat sometimes arrives with a label saying '*this is halal*', yet it was clear that debate about halal certification was still in its infancy in the red meat production sector at this time. Even so, all interviewees recognized that the demand for certification was growing.

Towards explicit understandings of halal

The poultry production company we visited breeds, slaughters and processes birds in and around Istanbul, distributing poultry across every region in Turkey. The company avoids big supermarkets that impose strict conditions and pay low prices, and most of their customers are butchers and small supermarkets; all the products they produce also have coded labels that allow everything to be traced back to the company. At the time of our research, the company preferred to export to Iraq rather than the EU, primarily because market conditions were not as demanding. As with the red meat production companies we worked with, interviewees suggested that the company's products and processes would have to be certified halal at some point, particularly if they were to make the most of export opportunities. At the time, however, the only form of certification came in the form of a letter from the local mufti, who visited the plant when new clients from the Middle East and Africa were taken on.

To the same extent, interviewees suggested that emerging animal welfare standards would only become an issue if the company starts exporting to the EU. However, because the company received a better price from markets where this type of certification was not necessary, there was little sense of urgency on the matter at this time. As the company director stated:

> To be honest with you we are not that interested in exporting to Europe at present. We export to Iraq and get a good price and there are not so many conditions.
>
> *(Interview October 2009)*

Interviewees indicated that the company follows strict Islamic practices during production; all birds must be healthy and alive at the time of slaughter and all the blood must be completely drained from the body. However, while all slaughter in the red meat industry is conducted without stunning, the company uses the latest Western technology, including electrical stunning baths and automatic neck cutters to produce poultry in line with EU regulations. While there was recognition that some consumers would pay more for meat from manually killed birds, it was argued that this type of production often takes place under unhygienic conditions. While the poultry sector has undergone a significant process of modernization in recent years, it now also faces greater risks from avian disease than it did previously; with increasingly large numbers of birds being kept in smaller spaces, disease spreads more quickly than it once did. In 2005–7 the avian influenza epidemic had a significant impact on demand and this seriously undermined growth in the sector (Yesilada et al. 2010).

Trends in the sector are complex. While technology is now of a far higher standard than it is in the red meat sector, slow growing healthier breeds are increasing in popularity because of the perceived health benefits. There has also been an increase in demand for halal certification by consumers over recent years, most notably for fresh chicken products; Durmus et al. (2012) found that almost 70 per cent of the population thought halal labelling should be standard. Arguably these trends are illustrative of the cultural tensions and concerns that have emerged as the industry has modernized in line with the spread of neoliberal technologies (Ong 2007). These issues were evident in focus groups conducted with consumers during the Dialrel project.

In Turkey, a focus group was established in Istanbul with the help of the Veterinary Public Health and Social Activities Association (www.vetder.org). There were eight participants in total (six males and two females) aged from 26 to 65. All but one indicated that they were practising Muslims, three were observing regular religious practice, and the other four were observing occasional practice. It soon became clear during focus group discussions that trust in the 'authenticity' of halal meat is not as important in Turkey as it is in some European countries. While the halal status of meat was a non-negotiable characteristic for focus group participants from France, the UK and Germany (Lever and Miele 2012), for Turkish consumers factors such as hygiene, freshness and convenience appeared to be more important. However, there did appear to be large differences in shopping, food preparation and consumption practices between people living in urban and rural areas (see Box 3.1). One focus group participant from Istanbul stated that she was not particularly concerned about whether the meat she purchased in Istanbul was 'genuine' halal, but that this was a concern for members of her family living in rural areas. She indicated that this was because people in rural areas tend to buy live animals rather than meat products, conducting slaughter themselves in accordance with widely accepted halal rules and practices.

Box 3.1: Focus group discussion Istanbul

Participant: I married in September. I have been shopping since September. I do it from a market near my home. I have never paid attention about the meat whether it is halal or not. Before my marriage, I had been eating outside, from restaurants. My family and their neighbourhood pay attention about it strongly. They always slaughter their animals by themselves ... Maybe, it is because they are living in a village ... but I have never paid attention about that in Istanbul.
Moderator: Your consumption attitude is different from your family.
Participant: Because of their living place.
Moderator: It is a situation about the environment?
Participant: We can say in my family's village no one buys meat from market, instead they buy animals.

All the retailers we spoke with in Turkey had experienced consumer concerns over illegal slaughter at some point, which is perhaps directly related to the prevalence of traditional slaughter. Supermarket chains such as Carrefour now also trace product origin and many production companies indicated that they have started to provide information on a range of issues, including animal type, origin and additives used in production. There has also been an increase in veterinary controls in the meat industry more generally over recent years.

Arguably these developments have been initiated to alleviate concerns over illegal slaughter and modernize the red meat industry. However, during focus group discussions, the increase in veterinary controls was not simply seen as a solution to the problems brought about by traditional animal farming practices. They were seen more as a sign of the problems associated with modern agricultural production techniques and the threat posed by new and more visible types of avian disease. In this sense, contrary to many European countries – where Muslims are a minority population and halal is mainly viewed as a religious issue (Lever and Miele 2012) – in Turkey halal is often viewed in cultural terms as something traditional that stands in direct opposition to Western modernity. While Turkish focus group participants were less likely to question the status of halal food than participants from other countries, they displayed a more general mistrust of society overall.

Discussion

The increase in calls for halal certification identified in the previous section has been reflected over recent years in the growth of Turkish certification bodies targeting the internal market. The complexities and particularities underpinning the global assemblage of halal are evident in the vertical alliances or aggregates of power (Papadopoulos et al. 2008; Lever 2013) formed between these certification bodies and transnational actors. Two of the new certification bodies follow the lead of GİMDES and are linked closely with Malaysia; Helalder (www.helalder.org.tr) and Dünya Helal Birliği (www.dunyahelalbirligi.org) provide certification through the Malaysia-based International Halal Integrity Alliance (IHIA) (www.ihialliance.org) and World Halal Union, respectively. A third – HEDEM (www.helaldenetim.com) – is aligned more closely with national halal guidelines approved by TSE. To complicate matters still further, Helalder is also approved by TSE, while Dünya Helal Birliği is not. As we have already observed, Turkish production companies encounter these complexities and competing halal priorities in different export markets. Export to markets in the Middle East, for example, is often more viable because costs are lower and there is no need to meet the high animal welfare standards required for export to EU markets (it should be noted that Turkey can only export cooked poultry products into the EU). Although this is slowly starting to change, meat exported from Turkey to Muslim majority countries is, in most instances, it appears, despite the increase in calls for halal certification, still taken to be halal at face value. Much as they do in Muslim minority countries, these complexities give weight to Lever and Miele's (2012) argument that third-party certification bodies are driving demand for halal certification within national economies.

It is in this context that Turkey has been involved in a project to develop a global halal standard to ensure economic growth within the OIC (Muhammad 2009; Lever and Miele 2012) and challenge the influence of Malaysian branded halal. While Turkey is aligned with Malaysia's global ambitions through the work of GİMDES and some of the newer certification bodies that have emerged over recent years, a number of state agencies and the newer certification bodies are simultaneously aligned with the OIC's challenge to the Malaysian quest for market hegemony. It is these competing tensions and priorities that allow the global assemblage of halal to function. As Ong and Collier (2005) note, an assemblage is a product of multiple determinations irreducible to a single logic; it is partial, unstable and contingent – an emergent global form.

Mutlu's (2009) work on Cola Turka to some extent illustrates the tensions between halal products aligned with the rise of global Islam and Turkish nationalism, respectively. Launched as a direct competitor to the global American brands Coca Cola and Pepsi, Cola Turka was marketed in TV commercials in a way that emphasized the commodification of the traditional Turkish way of life rather than the commodification of Islam. Arguably similar developments are now evident in the Turkish halal market where consumers have the option to buy halal products aligned with developments in global Islam and the ruling AKP or, alternatively, products aligned more closely with a reforming Turkish state, EU technology and animal welfare legislation. It is not always clear where the boundary between these competing priorities lies. Modernization along European lines has, in this context, much as it did in earlier periods, arguably furthered the intensification of developments associated with the rise of political Islam in ways that reinforce the complexities associated with the global assemblage of halal. As we have observed throughout this chapter, the multiplicities within this global assemblage are constantly moving in new directions.

Conclusion

Until relatively recently, halal was an implicit and largely unquestioned part of Turkish culture, both for meat production companies and for the majority of the population. It is only over the last few years that greater halal awareness has emerged alongside more explicit and highly contested understandings of halal. As we have shown, this is not simply related to the rise of competing halal discourses at the national and global level. A number of complex cultural factors have contributed much to this process, including, most notably, concerns over agricultural modernization and the spread of neoliberal technologies. Concerns over illegal production – evident in Turkey for some time – have, combined with conflict in the east of the country, poor state incentives and concerns over health-related issues, also served to undermine red meat production at a time when the poultry meat sector has gone through a period of rapid modernization. While the production and consumption of poultry meat has increased significantly during this period, so too have concerns over the spread of new technology and avian disease, thus increasing concerns about modernization and fuelling the demand for halal certification and labelling. While it has been argued that halal is excessive and that the government of a secular state should not tell people what they can and cannot eat on religious grounds, these cultural differences have, we contend, combined with the rise of global halal discourses, increased halal awareness significantly.

Bibliography

Anil, H. (2012) Religious slaughter: a current controversial animal welfare issue, *Animal Frontiers* (the review magazine of animal agriculture), 2 (3): 64–67.
Aznam, K. (2011) *Turkey faces conflict of interest in halal certification dilemma*, http://halalmedia.net/turkey-faces-conflict-of-interest-in-halal-certification-dilemma.
Boyacioglu, H. (2010) *Helal Gida Kriterine Malezya Celmesi* (Barrier for Halal Food Criteria from Malaysia) *Radikal* (Turkish daily newspaper) 20 October, www.radikal.com.tr/ekonomi/helal_gidaya_malezya_celmesi-1024575.
Cagatay, S. and Yegenoglu, Y. (2006) *Halal Turkey*, Bitter Lemons International, www.bitterlemons-international.org/inside.php?id=503, 9 March.
Dağ, H. and Erbasi-Gonc, E. (2013) SMIIC and halal food standards, *Journal of Chemical Metrology*, 7 (1): 1–6.
Delaney, C. L. (2014) The hajj: its meaning for Turkish Muslims, in Marranci, G. (ed.), *Studying Islam in Practice*, New York: Routledge.
Durmus, I., Misrak, C., Kamanli, S., Demirtas, S. E., Kalebasi, S., Karademir, E. and Dogu, M. (2012) Poultry meat consumption and consumer trends in Turkey, *Journal of Science and Technology*, 2: 10–14.
Eligür, B. (2010) *The Mobilization of Political Islam in Turkey*, New York: Cambridge University Press.
EMU (2010) *Press Release of the AHC-EUROPE*, 9 March, Press Releases & Statements, Strasbourg: European Muslim Union.
Ergul, H. S. (2013) Religious industry in halal food (distribution and knowledge), *The Journal of Academic Social Science Studies*, (6) 2: 831–41.
Fischer, J. (2014) Malaysian diaspora strategies in a globalized Muslim market, *Geoforum*, published first online.
FAO (Food and Agriculture Organization of the United Nations) (2011) *Eastern Europe and Central Asia Agro-Industry Development Country Brief. Turkey*, Budapest: Regional Office for Europe and Central Asia.
Gokariksel, B. and Secor, A. (2009) New transnational geographies of Islamism, capitalism and subjectivity: the veiling fashion industry in Turkey, in Pink, J. (ed.), *Muslim Societies in the Age of Mass Consumption: Politics, Culture and Identity between the Local and the Global*, pp. 23–52, Newcastle: Cambridge Scholars Publishing.
Hava, E. (2009) *Exports constitute Turkey's first venture into halal food market*, Today's Zaman, 24 May, www.todayszaman.com/tz-web/news-176181-exports-constitute-turkeys-first-venture-into-halal-food-market.html.
Izberk-Bilgin, E. (2012) Theology meets the marketplace, in Rinallo, D., Scott, L. and Maclaran, S. (eds.), *Consumption and Spirituality*, pp. 41–53, New York: Routledge.
Kurt, E. (2013) *Dunyada ve Ulkemizde Helal Belgelendirme Calismalarinda Mevcut Durum* (Current Status of Halal Certification in the World and in our Country), *Standard* 52 (611): 27–32 (a monthly publication of the Turkish Standards Institute).
Lever, J. (2013) The postliberal politics of halal: new trajectories in the civilizing process?, special issue of *Human Figurations*, 2 (3).
Lever, J. and Miele, M. (2012) The growth of Halal meat markets in Europe: an exploration of the supply side theory of religion, *Journal of Rural Studies*, 28 (4): 528–37.
Lewis, B. (2002) *What Went Wrong? The Clash between Islam and Modernity in the Middle East*, New York: Perennial.
Miele, M. and Lever, J. (2013) Civilizing the market for welfare friendly products in Europe? The techno-ethics of the welfare quality assessment, *Geoforum*, 48: 63–72.
Muhammad, R. (2009) Standardization: a solution for achieving economic growth in the Muslim world, *The Halal Journal*, January/February.
Mutlu, D. K. (2009) The Cola Turka controversy: consuming cola as a Turkish Muslim, in Pink, J. (ed.), *Muslim Societies in the Age of Mass Consumption*, Newcastle: Cambridge Scholars Publishing.
Nasr, S. H. (2004) *The Heart of Islam: Enduring Values for Humanity*, New York: Harper One.

Navaro-Yashin, Y. (2002) *Faces of the State: Secularism and Public Life in Turkey*, Princeton and Oxford: Princeton University Press.

Olson, E. A. (1985) Muslim identity and secularism in contemporary Turkey: 'the headscarf dispute', *Anthropological Quarterly*, 58 (4): 161–71.

Ong, A. (2007) Neoliberalism as a mobile technology, *Transactions of the Institute of British Geographers*, 32: 3–8.

Ong, A. and Collier, S. J. (2005) *Global Assemblages: Technology, Politics, and Ethics as Anthropological Problems*, Chichester: Wiley-Blackwell.

Papadopoulos, D. S., Stephenson, N. and Vassilis, T. (2008) *Escape Routes: Control and Subversion in the 21st Century*, London: Pluto Press.

Pink, J. (2011) Introduction, in Pink, J. (ed.) *Muslim Societies and Mass Consumption: Politics, Culture and Identity between the Local and the Global*, Newcastle: Cambridge Scholars Publishing.

Rabasa, A. and Larrabee, F. S. (2008) *The Rise of Political Islam in Turkey*, Santa Monica, CA: RAND, National Defense Institute.

Sachedina, A. (2001) *The Islamic Roots of Democratic Pluralism*, New York: Oxford University Press.

Sandıkcı, Ö. and Ger, G. (2010) Veiling in style: how does a stigmatized practice become fashionable?, *Journal of Consumer Research*, 37 (1): 15–36.

Stephenson, N. (2011) Emerging infectious disease/emerging forms of biological sovereignty, *Science, Technology & Human Values*, first published 22 November 2010.

Sutton, W. P. and Vertigans, S. (2005) *Resurgent Islam: A Sociological Approach*, Cambridge: Polity Press.

Today's Zaman (2014) *Turkey poised to be key halal food exporter*, 19 January, www.todayszaman.com/business_fao-turkey-poised-to-be-key-halal-food-exporter_336959.html.

Toprak, B. (1981) *Islam and Political Development in Turkey*, Leiden: E. J. Brill.

Trépanier, N. (2014) *Foodways and Daily Life in Medieval Anatolia: A New Social History*, Austin: University of Texas Press.

TSE (2012) *Helal Hassasiyeti Olan Herkes icin Guvenilir Belge* (A trustworthy accreditation for anybody who is sensitive about halal), Ankara: Turkish Standards Institute.

Tugal, C. (2009) *Passive Revolution: Absorbing the Islamic Challenge to Capitalism*, Redwood City, CA: Stanford University Press.

Tunç, T. E. (2009) Between East and West: consumer culture and identity negotiation in contemporary Turkey, in Pink, J. (ed.), *Muslim Societies in the Age of Mass Consumption: Politics, Culture and Identity between the Local and the Global*, pp. 23–52, Newcastle: Cambridge Scholars Publishing.

Turner, B. S. (2013) Class, generation and Islamism: towards a global sociology of Islam, in Turner, B. S. and Nasir, K. M. (eds.) *The Sociology of Islam: Collected Essays of Bryan S. Turner*, Farnham: Ashgate.

Turner, B. S. and Arslan, B. Z. (2013) Shari'a and legal pluralism in the West, in Turner, B. S. and Nasir, K. M. (eds.) *The Sociology of Islam: Collected Essays of Bryan S. Turner*, Farnham: Ashgate.

Yavuz, H. (2003) *Islamic Political Identity in Turkey*, New York: Open University Press.

Yesilada, A., Ucer, M. and Aksoy, I. (2010) *Turkish Agriculture Sector*, Istanbul: Egeli and Co.

4

REMEMBERING THE SPIRIT OF HALAL: AN IRANIAN PERSPECTIVE

Maryam Attar, Khalil Lohi and John Lever

> Be like a bee; anything it eats is clean, anything it drops is sweet and any branch it sits upon does not break.
>
> *(Ali ibn Abi Talib, quoted in Masri 2007, 7)*

Introduction

Over the last 15 years, global markets have become familiar with the word halal and a prevailing understanding that refers to food products that are 'permissible' and 'lawful' according to Islamic jurisprudence. While the global rise and interest in halal matters in Europe can be aligned with the expansion of global halal meat markets (Lever and Miele 2012), in the Middle East and other Muslim countries the pressures generated by globalization compete with many other local factors. Research on halal supply and consumption is largely focused on the physical rather than the spiritual realm; it is also generally focused on Sunni understandings. In this chapter we explore a qualitative dimension of halal as a way of life that is represented by the inseparable nature of the physical and the spiritual realms from a Shia point of view.

To do this we draw on recent research on the Iranian poultry industry. We examine the reasons for the phenomenal expansion of poultry production in Iran before and after the Iranian revolution of 1979, and the ongoing attempt of those in power to control poultry production in order to maintain the status quo (Gyton 2014). While this is the context in which Iran has immersed itself in global halal networks, we argue that these developments are very much at odds with the true spirit of halal in Iranian society. We argue that the immersion of Iranian products in the global halal market is fine if the proceeds benefit the state and help to maintain the status quo; as the pressure generated by the West's sanctions has intensified over recent years, increases in poultry production have, we contend, helped the current regime to avoid social unrest and maintain internal stability (Gyton 2014). Poultry prices have to be kept at an affordable level, regardless of the cost of production, if the status quo is to be maintained.

To illustrate our argument we look at an award-winning farm in the Binalood Mountains in the north east of Iran. The farm lies outside the sphere of the state's direct influence and provides important insights into poultry production that challenge its emergent halal agenda. We explore a production process and innovatory management practices that reinforce an understanding of halal based on its true spirit as envisaged by Ali ibn Abi Talib (2009). Despite the continuing threat of disease facing the poultry industry, and the problems that arise from contradictory state policies, we argue that our case study farm has managed to stay disease free for a considerable period of time because of innovatory management practices that remember and remain close to the true spirit of halal. To some extent, this approach can be aligned with the notion of the 'spiritual economy' (Rudnyckyj 2013). However, it also illustrates our argument that halal food should be produced – much like organic food – in ways that are good for human, animal and environmental health (Akhtar 2012). This is our understanding of what 'authentic' halal (Lever and Miele 2012) can and should be.

The chapter draws on the organizational literature to examine the adoption of innovations in the Iranian poultry sector (Jassaawalla and Sashittal 2001; Benson and Palaskas 2006) that facilitate an understanding of halal that stands in direct opposition to emergent notions of global halal. We also draw on Ong and Collier's (2005) notion of global assemblages to explore the technological, political and ethical practices underpinning Iran's immersion into the halal market. However, we are interested in the conditions rather than the spatiality (Rudnyckyj 2013) of halal practices in line with the global assemblage of alternative food ethics (Goodman and Sage 2013). The chapter is based on research that utilized a qualitative case study methodology. Semi-structured interviews were conducted to examine management practice at a number of Iranian poultry farms producing meat and eggs. The key focus of the study was on the way an organization's diffusion structures, systems and/or processes influence the adoption of technology, our findings confirming that senior management support is pivotal to the successful diffusion of innovatory practice. In this chapter we look at one farm in particular where managerial support was essential for innovation (Jassaawalla and Sashittal 2001; Benson and Palaskas 2006) and the production of poultry products in line with the true spirit of halal as envisaged by Ali ibn Abi Talib (2009). This relates directly to the central research question posed by this chapter: *how are poultry products aligned with the true spirit of halal from a Shia perspective?*

The chapter begins by examining the origins and spirit of Shia Islam. This provides an avenue through which to examine the true spirit of halal and Islamic jurisprudence from a Shia perspective, thus offering a contrast with emergent notions of Iranian and global halal that are emerging within the global halal assemblage. To get a wider picture of these different approaches and understandings, we next turn our attention to the development of the Iranian poultry industry before and after the Iranian revolution of 1979. This involves a close examination of strategic state policy, overseen and introduced, we argue, to keep control of the poultry industry and maintain the status quo. While the poultry industry expanded rapidly throughout the second half of the twentieth century, we argue that many of the challenges now faced by the industry are linked to its strategic mismanagement over the proceeding half-century. We then present our case study of an award-winning egg-laying farm in north-eastern Iran to illustrate an alternative method of production based on innovatory management practice that, we argue, produces poultry products in a way that lies closer to the true spirit of halal as understood from a Shia perspective.

The origins and spirit of Shia Islam

After Sunnism, Shi'ism is the second largest denomination in Islam. The schism between Sunni and Shia Islam is well known. Theological as well as political, the break occurred as a result of political controversy over the succession of the Prophet Mohammad following his death in 632 (Ahmed 2002; Nasr 2004). At the time, friends and followers of Ali ibn Abi Talib believed that leadership of the Muslim community should pass directly to Ali in line with the views of the Prophet (Nasr 2010; Tabatabai 1979). However, at the very moment of the Prophet's death, a group of his companions and followers went to the mosque where the community was gathered. The aim was to select a caliph to solve the immediate problems of the community and the first caliph was therefore selected by a majority vote amongst the companions (Tabatabai 1975). Ali and *his* companions were not present at this time, but protested and presented evidence for their arguments. They were told that the welfare of the Muslim community was at stake and that the solution lay in what had been done (Yaqubi [581] 1992; Nasr 2010).

The second caliph was selected by the will and testament of the first, and the third by a six-man council whose members and rules of procedure were organized and determined by the second caliph. For Sunnis, the original caliphate and the companions of the Prophet represent the Prophet's heritage and are the channel through which the Prophet's message was passed on to later generations. It is through the companions that the sayings (Hadith) and manner of living (Sunnah) of the Prophet are transmitted to the Islamic community; in Arabic the word 'Sunni' refers to those who follow the traditions of the Prophet. Ali eventually became the fourth caliph after Abu Bakr, Umar and Uthman and was the first Shia Imam. Ali's two sons Hasan and Husayn followed him as Imam and all subsequent Shia Imams are decendents of Husayn, whose son Zayn al-Abidin was one of the only survivors of the battle of Karbala in 680. The Shia did not reject the authority of elected Muslim leaders as rulers and administrators of the Islamic community, but they did not accept their function as Imam and chose instead to follow a line of Imams appointed by the Prophet Mohammad as divinely appointed: in Arabic the word

'Shia' means follower and as a group or party supportive of Ali they are called Shiat of Ali or simply Shia. For the Shia, Ali and the household of the Prophet (*ahl-albayt*) is the sole channel through which the original message of Islam can be transmitted. Imams constitute a continuation and transmission of the sacred and religious knowledge associated with the spiritual authority of the Prophet, which is passed on through Imams to ensure the authenticity of Divine authority (Curtis 2013).

As this brief exegesis suggests, the difference between the two traditions is essentially a matter of governance. While Sunni Muslims considered the successor of the Prophet to be the guardian and administrator of Islamic law, Shia Muslims saw in the successor a spiritual function connected with the inner mysteries interpretation of the revelation as well as with the inherited knowledge and interpretation of Divine Law (Nasr 2010). Shi'ite Muslims believe that the leader of Islam must be a descendant of the Prophet, a 'trustee' of his esoteric knowledge and an interpreter of the religious sciences (Nasr 2010). It is this distinction that has a profound and temporal influence on 'the spiritual' in Shi'ite society, on Shia jurisprudence (Curtis 2013) and, arguably, on Shia understandings of halal. While the Sunni undertake a more literal reading of the Quran, Shi'ites look more to the spirit of the Quran and to Allah's teachings as disseminated through the Imams. In Arabic, these differences are often referred to as the *al-dhaher* (the apparent) and *al-baten* (the hidden) meanings of the Quran (Bassiouni 2012) – what Tabatabai (1979) refers to its outward and inward aspects. The implication of this interpretation is that there are deeper levels of meaning to the Quran that can only be comprehended by members of the spiritual elite. With a central role interpreting the Quran for each generation, the Shia religious hierarchy thus has a much greater influence on society than could ever be possible in a Sunni state.

Shia jurisprudence and halal

Much like the Hanafi, Hanbali, Maliki and Shafi'i schools of jurisprudence in Sunni Islam, the divisions within Shia Islam – between Zaydism, Ismailism, Batinis, Nizaris, Mustalis, Druzes and Muqanna'ah – could be categorized in line with their legal orientation. However, Nasr (2004) suggests a better understanding of Shia jurisprudence can be gained by looking at the different positions each school takes on the Imams. In general, Islamic (*Shari'ah*) law is based on a hierarchy of Quran, Sunnah and Hadith. It was from these three sources that an elaborate methodology was developed to create a body of Islamic laws, with the science underpinning the decision-making process facilitating the rise of legal principles and Islamic schools of jurisprudence. The intellectual process of deriving laws from the three sources is called *ijtihad* (independent thinking) and is conducted by *mujtahids* (men of learning) (Tabatabai 1979; Nasr 2004).

Sunnis decided a millennium ago that submission to one of the four schools was allowed and that *ijtihad* or imitation of any other school was not permissible; it is only recently that the Sunni world has turned away from consensus and started to enable *ijtihad* in line with wider global concerns (Tabatabai 1979; Nasr 2004). In Shi'ism, however, *mujtahids* have taken part in *ijtihad* throughout history, thus embodying in every generation what Ahmed (2002) calls the seeds of 'renewal and revolution'. Nasr (2004) confirms the historical difference between Sunni and Shia on this matter in the following way:

> In the Sunni world, the 'the gate of ijti' closed after the tenth and eleventh centuries, when the major schools were established, whereas in the Shi'ite world it has remained open to this day and in each generation the *mujtahids* have derived the laws from the established principles and sources.
>
> *(Nasr 2004, 123)*

Arguably it is this difference that has kept Shi'ite jurisprudence dynamic and fresh throughout the ages. Indeed, for the Shia, the act of seeking guidance by following a living *mujtahid* is central to everyday practice – anything more is forbidden. Leadership, in this sense, is a central aspect of Shi'ism.

These issues are directly related to Shia understandings of halal. In his first days as caliph, Ali gave several sermons in which he described the importance of the Quran and provided guidance on what is halal (permitted/inherently good) and haram (not allowed/forbidden). Ali's views are outlined in a collection of sermons, letters and sayings that Shia consider the most valuable text after the Quran (see Abu-Talib 2009). In sermon 176, Ali explains the spiritual dimension of halal and haram as acts that are liked and disliked by God, respectively. The implication is that by performing halal actions and avoiding haram actions a person will move closer to God and become a better person. Halal and haram, in this sense, from a Shia perspective, are the rationale behind almost every decision-making process, establishing an awareness of how to manage all one's actions.

Ali was an exponent of leading by example. When questioned about his poor diet he answered that he would continue to eat what the masses ate at least once a day until better food was available for all, and not just the elite; it is in this sense that the qualities of leadership can also be considered halal or haram. On this account, the food we eat has a profound impact on our spiritual as well as our physical health. The Quran explicitly allows the consumption of meat from certain animals on the condition that they are slaughtered in a specified way. The Quran also places high emphasis on the humane treatment of animals in over 200 verses. In verse 6:38, for example, it is stated that: 'There is not an animal (that lives) on earth, nor a being that flies on its wings, but (forms part of) communities like you'. Akhtar (2012) makes a similar point today. She argues that there is mounting evidence of a very real and often very direct relationship between animal and human welfare, most specifically in relation to human and environmental health. Food production companies, on this account, thus have a direct responsibility to produce food in ways that is good for animal, human and environmental health. Parallels can therefore be drawn between the understanding of halal we are putting forward and organic methods of food production (Friedlander 2014), and therefore with the global assemblage of alternative food ethics (Goodman and Sage 2013).

Although the rise of Islamic and un-Islamic food can be traced back to the Iranian revolution and the origins of political Islam, it is only recently – in line with the rise in demand for halal products in Muslim and non-Muslim countries (Lever and Miele 2012) – that halal has emerged as an internally and externally linked issue in Iran. In addition to national standards governing animal slaughter, principles of hygiene, food safety, food labelling and packaging, the authorities have introduced a national Iranian halal standard in line with the development of global halal discourses. In September 2009, the Institute of Standards and Industrial Research of Iran (ISIRI) passed a proposal for the standardization of halal by launching the Halal Food: General guidelines ISIR 12000. Fifteen national food standards are considered alongside this new halal standard, which covers a wide variety of issues and provides a detailed and in-depth account of what is considered to be halal or haram.

The jurisprudence of the standard, including the provisions of food, beverages, animal slaughter (Zebh) and fishing is aligned with Jafari (Shi'ite) jurisprudence. Everything that Jafari jurisprudence considers halal is also considered halal by the four Sunni schools (with one exception), whereas the reverse is not true. In the introduction to the guidelines it is stated that steps have been taken to ensure that there should be coordination between the Iranian national standard and the standards of other Islamic countries whenever this is possible. Although halal certification is not yet obligatory in Iran, over recent years Iran has participated in the Malaysian International Halal Showcase (MIHAS) in order to extend its influence (*Iran Daily* 2014). A number of Iranian food products have also been recognized by the Halal World Institute, which is linked directly to the Organisation of Islamic Cooperation (OIC) (Halal Focus 2014). While these links give Iranian 'halal' products authenticity and credibility within the emerging assemblage of halal at the global level, our case study poultry farm provides important insights into a production process that challenges the authenticity of these Iranian 'halal' products. Despite the continuing threat of disease, and a range of production problems linked to the mismanagement of the industry by the state, we argue that the farm has stayed disease free for a considerable period of time because of innovatory management practices that remember and remain closer to the true spirit of halal.

The Iranian poultry industry: past and present

To have a clear understanding of halal in Iran in general and within the poultry industry in particular, it is necessary to examine the socio-political and economic changes that took place before and after the Iranian revolution of 1979. Between 1941 and 1979, the head of the monarchy, the late Shah of Iran, introduced steady and gradual changes in line with the economic and technological tenets of Western modernity. Educated in Switzerland, the Shah attempted to bring about widespread social and economic change through controversial policy reforms in a number of areas. What he called *The White Revolution* was to include land reforms, the introduction of voting rights for women, the elimination of illiteracy and the industrialization of small-scale industries such as poultry production. However, the changes introduced were seen by many to undermine the cultural and institutional foundations of society, thus provoking fear amongst religious leaders that they were losing their traditional authority. This culminated in the revolutionary uprising of 1979 (Mirsepassi 2000; Ansari 2001).

The poultry industry started to feel the force of the changes being introduced by the Shah from the 1950s onwards. There was a transition from small-scale production focused on indigenous breeds grown for local consumption towards a process of commercialization based on the importation of new breeding lines and production technologies from the West. However, the arrival of industrial breeds such as Truman, Plymouth Rock, Rhode Island Red and New Hampshire (Anon 1994) was accompanied by the arrival of Newcastle disease – one of the major contagious diseases affecting the poultry industry worldwide (Fazel et al. 2012) – which wiped out Iran's native breeding stock. As a consequence, throughout the 1960s there was a gradual increase in the number of poultry breeding and production farms. With the production of day-old broiler chicks subsequently increasing, imports started to decline and the domestic market grew rapidly throughout the 1960s.

Between 1965 and 1975 Iran's population grew by 15 million to reach 45 million. At the same time, there was mass migration from rural villages to large cities and urban areas as people looked for work and searched for a better way of life. The effect of this migration on poultry production was twofold. First, as the demographics of rural society changed, traditional ways of poultry production also declined, thus facilitating an increase in demand more generally (Anon 1995). Second, this reduction in agricultural produce increased Iran's dependency on imports, which in turn contributed to the rapid expansion of the poultry industry after the revolution. At the time, the halal–haram dichotomy was most evident in the slaughter process, although the availability of pork meat was also problematic. A limited number of pig farms were providing meat for minority groups (Axworthy 2010), but the risk of contamination was minimal; pork meat was only sold in particular shops and it did not enter the mainstream food supply chain or the national meat market.

After coming close to agricultural self-sufficiency in the 1960s, by 1979 Iran was importing 65 per cent of its food. Declining productivity was blamed on the use of modern fertilizers that had inadvertently scorched Iranian soil. Unresolved land reforms, lack of economic incentives to raise surplus crops and low profit ratios combined to drive increasingly large segments of the rural population into urban areas (Ansari 2001). The 1979 revolution sought self-sufficiency in foodstuffs as part of its overall goal of decreased economic dependence on the West. In line with demands for 'Islamic authenticity' and a 'novel political interpretation of Shia doctrine' (Zubaida 2002, 60), Ayatollah Khomeini banned all imported meats and declared them '*un-Islamic*' (*Washington Post* 1979). Higher government subsidies for grain and other staples, expanded short-term credit and tax exemptions for farmers complying with government quotas were all intended by the new regime to promote self-sufficiency. However, although the poultry industry continued to grow in the post-revolutionary period, it was affected by the Iran–Iraq war (1980–87) in different ways. The state focus in this period was on maintaining the growth of the domestic market to reduce the volume of imports and reduce foreign currency expenditure. Nevertheless, the strategic decision to limit the import of breeding stock was to affect Iran's poultry industry for the next decade. Stock was reduced to only one breeding line in order to strengthen the domestic market, create a sustainable environment and allow the state to gain greater control over production. The policy was controversial and opposed on scientific grounds because of the dangers of limiting production to one breeding line, diversity of breeding stock giving some protection from the increased threat of disease. Not surprisingly, contrary to what might be seen by the late 1990s, Iran became more dependent on agricultural imports (Shariatmadari 2000).

Another decision that affected the industry in this way was the Poultry Industry Liberalization Act 1998, which was implemented in two phases. In the first phase in 1998, the government relinquished control of stock but retained control of price regulation. In the second phase seven years later, the state attempted to introduce a supply-and-demand pricing scheme to provide the industry with a degree of economic freedom. The second phase also set out to improve management, reduce waste and increase productivity by making more efficient use of resources, credit and foreign currency, thus getting poultry meat and eggs to the same quality as imported products. The hope was that this would enable exports of poultry products in line with the development of non-oil products export policy to provide a secure environment for investment and a reduction in the role of government. The Fourth Development Programme for 2005 (Mustafavi 2012) outlined similar plans to peruse macro socioeconomic and agricultural development. Poultry producers received the programme enthusiastically, as it raised the hope that as the industry became more self-sufficient they would be able to export their products without added customs and excise duties. In line with this renewed enthusiasm, the targets and milestones set for the industry in the programme were met in full and in some cases exceeded recommended national targets.

The global poultry industry made significant advances in the 1970s and 1980s through the use of new technology, including buildings with better ventilation and lighting, as well as improvements in disease control and innovations in animal feed science (Delgado et al. 1999). In 1996, Iran joined the World Poultry Science Association (WPSA) and participated in educational activities in accordance with WPSA rules and requirements in order to promote greater awareness amongst Iranian farmers. A study of over 13 poultry meat-producing countries over the past 40 years illustrates the improved position of Iran in poultry production during this period (Mustafavi 2012). Between 1969 and 2009 Iran rose from twenty-seventh to sixth in the league of global poultry meat producers, and from fifty-sixth to twelfth in the league of egg-producing countries (USDA 2011). Between 1997 and 2009, per capita consumption of poultry meat in Iran increased from 8.6 kilograms to 11.5 kilograms, with egg consumption increasing from 8 kilograms to 9.8 kilograms during the same period. Compared with global poultry meat consumption, Iran's is 10 kilograms higher than the global per capita average; egg consumption per capita is slightly higher than the world average. However, despite these seemingly positive trends, the industry faces some very significant challenges, many of which are arguably driven or enhanced by state policies, mismanagement of the industry and international sanctions.

Challenges facing the poultry industry

The poultry industry's share of national gross domestic product (GDP) in Iran is 1.2 per cent and it currently employs around 600,000 people. Although the phenomenal quantitative growth in production over recent decades has pushed Iran up the global league of poultry meat and egg producers, the industry continues to face many challenges. One of the most significant problems is the supply and production of poultry feed. Corn is the most important energy source in poultry feed and it constitutes approximately 60 per cent of the feed ration. The cost of feed is one of the most serious challenges for the industry. Iran imports around 4.5 million tonnes of corn annually, a figure that has been increasing year on year for the past ten years. In 2011, the price quickly rose from $100 per tonne to $320 per tonne. Soymeal is another important protein source that constitutes 30 per cent of the feed ration and Iran requires 2.3 million tonnes of this vital protein feed per year. However, the increased global demand for soymeal has almost doubled its usual price and since 2007 imports have increased from 1 million to 2 million tonnes per year.

The large increase in poultry farms has also led to an increase in demand for different types of vaccines to comply with the Vetinary Ministry's policy for the prevention of disease. This has been a significant challenge. Domestic production could not meet the increasing demand for vaccines and huge volumes had to be imported from abroad, which were then restricted by economic sanctions. As a result, the industry suffered heavy fatalities amongst broiler chickens and laying birds and there were serious financial implications. The lack of a vaccination policy and the inability of domestic laboratories to identify new strains of disease took their toll on farms across the country, causing the loss of 20 million layer chickens and over a million broiler chickens. Another related challenge is the lack of adequate farm biosecurity to reduce cross-contamination and disease transmission in poultry processing plants. This is an area where progress has been slow. The recent outbreaks of the H9N2 virus in Iran, H7N9 in China and H7N3 in Mexico have heightened both the awareness and need for an effective biosecurity programme (VAG 2008).

The Poultry Industry Liberalization Act of 1998 removed the foreign exchange rate subsidies afforded to poultry producers and the rate of exchange for poultry producers was increased sixfold. In order to finance the sudden rise in expenditure most farmers resorted to heavy borrowing from state banks and financial houses. As raw materials, vaccines and technology-related items have to be imported by producers and paid for in foreign currency, the exchange rate rise significantly increased the costs of production, which were not reflected in market value as determined by the state. It has also become much easier to get an operating licence and set up a poultry farm; farms are now often run by people with little or no knowledge and experience in taking up such a responsibility. Obtaining a licence to set up a farm also facilitates securing a favourable bank loan and credit facilities, which places a significant burden on these new farmers when the enterprise fails; debt amongst poultry farmers is substantial and on the increase.

The poultry industry is mainly private; some services are provided by cooperatives and there are few poultry farms owned and managed by the government. There are currently more than 23,000 poultry farms in Iran, including 450 parent stock broiler farms, 160 hatcheries and 1,500 egg laying farms. There are also 600 feed factories and 200 slaughter plants. The market is heavily regulated and controlled by the government, but if prices drop the government rarely intervenes. Interventions are conducted solely for the purpose of restocking, which often results in a glut of new birds and a price crash. In the absence of a professionally tailored export strategy, surplus production will continue to disturb the market balance for the foreseeable future and it is estimated that there is a surplus of 20,000 tonnes of poultry meat being produced every month (Mustafavi 2012). One of the objectives of the Fourth Development Programme was to avoid imposing export duties on the export of poultry meat and eggs, but this was later disregarded and duties were introduced after production had increased.

At the same time, a 25 per cent reduction in export duties was being offered to poultry exporters in Turkey (Iran's neighbour), where mortality rates amongst broiler chicks are almost four times lower than they are in Iran (Mustafavi 2012). If the output of an Iranian poultry farmer is compared with his Turkish counterpart, the Turkish farmer will fare 35 per cent better. This is not all down to poor performance or a lack of enthusiasm on the part of the Iranian farmer; it highlights a combination of factors impacting on the industry, including poor strategic planning, contradictory government policies, both domestic and trade related, mismanagement and poor decision making.

Another blow to the industry came in 2011 when the state imposed a 40 per cent import duty on the already expensive corn imports. This caused the price of corn to reach unprecedented levels and the industry suffered greatly. At the same time, the government made the astonishing decision to reduce import duties on poultry meat from 10 to 4 per cent (Mustafavi 2012). When the price of poultry meat is reduced in the market by such actions there is a domino effect on the price of day-old broiler chicks, which has knock-on effects throughout the industry as all types of breeding stock (first parent stock and then grandparent stock) have to be taken out of the production cycle. Under these conditions, it is the private sector that bears the brunt of the government's mismanagement and their disparate attempts to keep control of production.

Increases in poultry production to feed a restless population and avoid social unrest in the face of international sanctions are paramount (Gyton 2014). The price of poultry products has to be kept at an affordable level, regardless of the cost of production and the problems government policy creates for producers, if the status quo is to be maintained. Taken in its entirety, the preceding analysis draws attention to the state's wide-ranging attempts to control the poultry industry for its own political purposes. Arguably the recent development of national halal legislation and Iran's engagement in global halal networks is another way for those in power to govern effectively. We now turn to our case study farm in north-eastern Iran to examine an alternative approach to poultry production that can arguably be aligned with the true spirit of halal from a Shia perspective.

Innovation in the poultry industry: remembering the spirit of halal

In this section, we present a case study of an innovative poultry farm in the north east of Iran. Despite the many problems faced by the poultry industry, we argue that the farm has managed to stay disease free for a considerable period of time because of innovatory management practices that remain close to the true spirit of halal. The case study farm backs on to the Binalood Mountains on a large plot of land. On arrival, four very large buildings separated from each other by quite large distances catch the eye. On entering the courtyard there is a designated area for parking and a point at which it is not possible to drive beyond. The farm has been under the same management for the past 20 years; home to more than 100,000 laying hens, it has been disease free for the last 15 years.

The manager of the farm has won an award for innovation based on the design and introduction of the first cages for layer and breeder chickens in Iran. The supplies used are the best available; the water supply, for example, comes from a deep well in the mountains. Asked how the farm has managed to stay disease free for so long, the manager replied:

> The short answer is good management, adequate buildings, proper nutrition and sanitation ... [and] management support is required not only in terms of resources but also in acting as role models, you have to get your set of priorities right. Priorities must be set around the reduction of the risk of disease transmission and that is what we have tried to achieve here and we have also enjoyed the good luck of the nature by being far away from any other poultry farm. This poultry farm enjoys the mountainous fresh air and the land is quite elevated, the buildings are almost free from any feces or ammonia smell. Chickens are intelligent animals. We recognise this fact and try to treat them that way. We are not on the path of any migrating birds. We have tried to follow and apply this principal rule of keeping what is

inside the farm (bacterial or viral populations) inside the farm and keeping what is outside the farm outside.

(Interview with managing director and farm manager, May 2012)

The manager explained that this had been achieved by following a number of interrelated management practices. All employees on the farm have their own living quarters on the site and there is no interaction with employees from the neighbouring farms; although there is no farm nearby this is part of the culture. No poultry products are allowed on to the farm from premises outside the farm and employees are allowed to consume as much chicken, meat and eggs as they need on site. There is a policy of no equipment sharing with any other farm. Vehicles delivering or collecting products have a designated area and they cannot enter the inner part of the farm. For this reason, there is a special building for storing feed deliveries and collecting boxes of packed eggs. The equipment used for transport between this building and the main farm area is regularly cleaned and disinfected.

The buildings have also been designed to keep the chicken population healthy. The farm buildings are constructed on two floors so that bird droppings are collected at the lower level in a deep pit system about 3–4 metres high. The cages are monitored and cleaned regularly. Each building is well ventilated on both floors and each house is home to 30–35,000 laying chickens. All the staff are trained and experienced, with the average length of employee service being over 15 years. There are CCTV cameras in every part of the farm, which facilitates remote monitoring of all the buildings for the farm manager. Because the buildings are well ventilated, the chicken manure collected in the pits is dry and can be used as valuable compost and byproduct.

A number of management lessons can be drawn from this case study. Within the organizational literature, it has long been assumed that a primary condition for the adoption of innovations is managerial support. Jassaawalla and Sashittal (2001) note that the successful adoption of an innovation is inherently dependent upon the ability of the management team to create an environment of trust, creativity and collaboration. Benson and Palaskas (2006) emphasize the responsibility placed upon senior management for fostering an organizational culture and climate that is supportive and encouraging in ways that motivate staff. The research on which this chapter draws clearly illustrates that senior management support is pivotal to the successful diffusion of innovatory practice. As Rudnyckyj's (2013) work illustrates, Islamic ethics and management principles can be brought together effectively in ways that help to create more ethical and disciplined employees. On this account, religion is not seen as a retreat *from* or as a form of resistance *to* global capitalism; it is closely aligned with capitalism in ways that enable Islamic virtues to address the challenges of globalization within a 'spiritual economy'.

The analysis of technical change in poultry production shows that innovation is a complex economic and social phenomenon. Bryant (1998) argues that for a single firm innovation can be defined as applying ideas new to the firm in products, processes, services, organization, management and/or marketing. However, the concept of innovation is not restricted to technological innovations. Schumpeter (1939) defined innovation as setting up a new production function. In other words, if we vary the production function by changing factors of production instead of quantities of factors, we have an innovation. Technology transfer is not merely an exchange of documents or reports embodying the details of an innovation; it is a process whereby the transfer of knowledge takes place from one person to another (Ratnasiri 1984). In poultry farming, innovation dissemination is a collaborative activity involving a set of actors, activities, organizations and institutions. As they interact with each other in order to gain, develop and exchange various kinds of knowledge and information, communication channels play an important role. Rogers (1995) defines diffusion as the process by which an innovation is communicated through certain channels over time amongst the members of a social system. In reality, innovation diffusion in poultry production is an economic and social process, with interdependencies between various actors such as farmers and researchers playing a crucial role as determinants of innovation.

Discussion

Over recent decades, the key drivers shaping the poultry industry worldwide have been shifts in consumer demand, changes in government policies, environmental concerns, technological advances, innovation and an increasing demand for animal-friendly food products (Akhtar 2012; Miele and Lever 2013, 2014). The rise and growth of alternative methods of production such as organic and free range illustrate the growth of consumer concerns about the way animals are reared (Lang and Heasman 2004). Consumers now want food that is antibiotic free, ethically packaged, fairly traded, tasty, nutritious and halal (Abdul-Matin 2010). In traditional poultry farming, tacit knowledge played an important role in production. Chickens were kept in small coops with free access to outdoors where they could exercise their natural behaviour, but with the advent of factory farming the ability to engage in instinctive behaviour has been lost (Akhtar 2012). There are many dictums in the Quran that prohibit cruelty to animals. Animals are referred to as being part of communities like human beings and it is our understanding that the application of the halal concept covers the whole life cycle of animals up to the point of slaughter. Halal should not, in this sense, simply be a confirmation of the fact that an animal died well.

In line with Ong and Collier's (2005) work on global assemblages, we could say that Iran's poultry industry is currently based on a range of discourses that cut across debates in theology, politics and regulation in a national and global context. As noted in the introduction to this volume, the proliferation of global markets for halal products signifies broader changes within regimes of exchange, ethics and values. The mobile and dynamic qualities at work within these exchanges are helping to reconstitute 'society', 'culture' and 'economy' simultaneously, subjecting individuals, groups and collectives to reflections on questions of value and morality

(Ong and Collier 2005). Although primarily used as a means of maintaining the status quo within Iran, the notion of 'Iranian halal' has, we would argue, in this context, now become inherently global as the state looks to enhance the authenticity of Iranian products. In this instance, as in many others, a local epistemology has become ubiquitous by extension (Mol and Law 2005) within the global assemblage of halal.

We can observe throughout this book a number of competing definitions of halal at work within national and global contexts. Iran is a unique case in many ways. Instrumental in the rise of political Islam, ostracized by the international community, the ruling elite is starting to use global halal for its own political purposes, much as it has previously used the poultry industry. The Shia perspective we are putting forward presents an opportunity for Iran to take a more central and leading role at the global level in this sense. Viewed alongside emerging debates about food security and sustainability at the global level (Marsden and Morley 2014), our case study farm presents an alternative and more significant notion of what Iranian halal can and should be. Linked to changing regimes of exchange, ethics and values within the global assemblage of alternative food ethics (Goodman and Sage 2013), halal is, under certain conditions, slowly being aligned with a range of inclusive environmental qualities (Lever 2013) linked to 'a new, more mobile, global philosophy' (Haenni 2010, 335). In this context, innovation and leadership are the key if Iran is to play a more central role in global poultry production in a way that can be aligned with the true spirit of halal within a spiritual economy.

Conclusion

The poultry sector is one of the fastest growing parts of the food industry. If the industry is to move forward effectively, technological innovation is required to satisfy new demands in the supply chain. This presents a historical opportunity for halal advocates in general and Iran in particular to take the lead and make up for lost opportunities by following the clearly drawn boundaries between humans and animals in Quranic dictums. The Shi'ite belief teaches us that halal as a concept must be fully encapsulated within the construct of a product. Halal reaches much further into the disciplines of the management of a company, its organizational behaviour and the inherent relationships between management and workers, workers and animals: it is a spiritual endeavour.

As the poultry industry in Iran and other developing Islamic countries has moved from a traditional to an industrialized system of production, there have been many missed opportunities by *mujtahids* to encourage and improve animal welfare. Although the Iranian poultry industry is not under any great pressure from consumers about animal welfare and genetically modified organisms in feed at this time, the industry will no doubt be confronted with these additional challenges in the near future. Consumer concerns over food safety, product quality and the environmental impact of the industrial production system are already emerging.

However, if production costs are to be kept at a level that can encourage innovation and address these emerging concerns, sustainable supply chain management is an absolute necessity. Our study of an award-winning farm in north-eastern Iran clearly illustrates the need for leadership and innovation if the Iranian poultry industry is to become a producer of poultry products for external as well as for internal markets – a recurring theme in state policy. This can only be done by encouraging collaborative practice between decision-making bodies and by developing better governance arrangements. A scientific approach to data collection and analysis for educational purposes is also crucial if the industry is to innovate and lead the halal industry by example in the manner encouraged by Ali ibn Abi Talib.

Bibliography

Abdul-Matin, I. (2010) *Green Deen: What Islam Teaches About Protecting the Planet*, San Francisco, CA: Berrett-Koehler Publishers, Inc.
Ahmed, A. (2002) *Discovering Islam: Making Sense of Muslim History and Society* (2nd edn.), London and New York: Routledge.
Akbar, A. (2002) *Discovering Islam: Making Sense of Muslim History and Society*, London: Routledge.
Akhtar, A. (2012) *Animals and Public Health: Why Treating Animals Better Is Critical to Human Welfare*, New York: Palgrave Macmillan.
Anon (1994) Evaluation of the poultry industry in Iran, *Cheakavak*, 3: 1–10.
——(1995) The history of the poultry production industry in Iran, *Cheakavak*, 3: 1–10.
Ansari, A. (2001) The myth of the white revolution: Mohammad Reza Shah, 'modernization' and the consolidation of power, *Middle Eastern Studies*, 37 (3): 1–24, http://maxwellsci.com/print/ijava/v4-389-393.pdf.
Axworthy, M. (2010) *A History of Iran: Empire of the Mind*, London: Basic Books, Perseus Books Group.
Bassiouni, M. C. (2012) *Schools of Thought in Islam*, Middle Eastern Institute, www.mei.edu/content/schools-thought-islam.
Benson, R. and Palaskas, T. (2006) Introducing a new learning management system: an institutional case study, *Australasian Journal of Education Technology*, 22 (4): 548–67.
Bryant, K. (1998) *Evolutionary Systems: Their Origins and Emergence as a New Economic Paradigm*, Cheltenham: Edward Elgar Publishing Ltd.
Curtis, M. F. (2013) Fiqh, the science of Islamic jurisprudence, in Bennett, C. (ed.), *The Bloomsbury Companion to Islamic Studies*, London and New York: Bloomsbury.
Delgado, C., Rosegrant, M., Steinfeld, H., Ehui, S. and Courbois, C. (1999) Livestock to 2020: the next food revolution, IFPRI, Food, Agriculture, and the Environment Discussion Paper 28, Washington, DC: IFPRI.
Fazel, D., Khoobyar, S., Mehrabanpour, M. J. and Rahimian, A. (2012) Isolation and differentiation of virulent and non-virulent strains of Newcastle Disease Virus by polymerase chain reaction from commercial broiler chicken flocks in Shiraz-Iran, *International Journal of Animal and Veterinary Advances*, 4 (6): 389–93.
Friedlander, N. (2014) *Beyond Halal*, website accessed on 14 September, http://beyondhalal.com.
Goodman, M. and Sage, C. (2013) Food transgressions: ethics, governance and geographies, in Goodman, M. and Sage, C. (eds.), *Food Transgressions: Making Sense of Contemporary Food Politics*, Aldershot: Ashgate.
Gyton, G. (2014) *Iran increases poultry production to avoid social unrest*, Global Meat News, www.globalmeatnews.com/Industry-Markets/Iran-increases-poultry-production-to-avoid-social-unrest.

Haenni, P. (2010) The economic politics of Muslim consumption, in Pink, J. (ed.), *Politics, Culture and Identity between the Local and the Global*, Newcastle: Cambridge Scholars Publishing.

Halal Focus (2014) Iran: major Iranian food products receive Halal food standard label, 14 August, http://halalfocus.net/iran-print-version-major-iranian-food-products-receive-halal-food-standard-label.

Iran Daily (2014) Iranians to participate in MIHAS 2014, Iran Chamber of Commerce, Industries, Mines and Agriculture, http://en.iccima.ir/news/iccima-news-bulletin/iran-economy-bulletin/item/8147-iranians-to-participate-in-mihas-2014.html.

Jassaawalla, A. and Sashittal, H. (2001) The role of senior management and team leaders in building collaborative new product teams, *Engineering Management Journal*, 13 (2): 33–39.

Lang, T. and Heasman, M. (2004) Food Wars: The Global Battle for Mouths, Minds and Markets, London and New York: Routledge.

Lever, J. (2013) The postliberal politics of halal: new trajectories in the civilizing process?, special issue of *Human Figurations*, 2 (3): November.

Lever, J. and Miele, M. (2012) The growth of halal meat markets in Europe: an exploration of the supply side theory of religion, *Journal of Rural Studies*, 28 (4): 528–37.

Lindgreen, A., Maon, F., Vanhamme, J. and Sankar, S. (2013) *Sustainable Value Chain Management: A Research Anthology*, Aldershot: Gower.

Marsden, T. and Morley, A. (2014) *Sustainable Food Systems: Building a New Paradigm*, London: Earthscan.

Masri, A. B. A. (2007) Animal Welfare in Islam, The Islamic Foundation.

Miele, M. and Lever, J. (2013) Civilizing the market for welfare friendly products in Europe? The techno-ethics of the welfare quality assessment, *Geoforum*, 48: 63–72.

——(2014) Improving animal welfare in Europe: cases of comparative bio-sustainabilities, in Marsden, T. and Morley, A. (eds.), *Sustainable Food Systems: Building a New Paradigm*, London: Earthscan.

Mirsepassi, A. (2000) *Intellectual Discourse and the Politics of Modernization: Negotiating Modernity in Iran*, Cambridge: Cambridge University Press.

Mol, A. and Law, J. (2005) Editorial: boundary variations: an introduction, *Environment and Planning D: Society and Space*, 23: 637–42.

Mustafavi, M. (2012) *Challenges Facing Poultry Industry in Iran and Solutions to Overcome These Challenges*, Centre for Strategic Studies Report 148.

Nasr, S. H. (2004) *The Heart of Islam: Enduring Values for Humanity*, San Francisco: Harper One.

——(2010) *Ideals and Realities of Islam*, Kazi Productions, Inc.

Ong, A. and Collier, S. J. (2005) *Global Assemblages: Technology, Politics, and Ethics as Anthropological Problems*, Oxford: Wiley-Blackwell.

Ratnasiri, P. A. J. (1984) *Technology Development and Transfer*, Report of a Seminar, Physical Science Section, Sri Lankan Association for the Advancement of Science, 28 March, Colombo, Sri Lanka.

Rogers, E. (1995) *Diffusion of Innovations*, New York: Free Press.

Rudnyckyj, D. (2013) *Spiritual Economies: Islam, Globalization, and the Afterlife of Development*, Ithaca: Cornell University Press.

Schumpeter, J. A. (1939) *A Theoretical, Historical, and Statistical Analysis of the Capitalist Process*, New York: McGraw-Hill.

Shariatmadari, F. (2000) Poultry production and the industry in Iran, *World's Poultry Science Journal*, 56 (1): 55–65.

Tabatabai, A. S. M. H. (1979) *Shi'ite Islam*, ed. Nasr, S. H., University of New York Press.

Talib, Abu-. I. A. (2009) *Peak of Eloquence Nahjul-Balagha*, Tahrike Tarsile Qur'an, Inc, New York, www.duas.org/pdfs/Nahjul-Balagha.pdf.

USDA (2011) *United States Department of Agriculture, International Egg and Poultry Review*, 12 (28).

VAG (2008) *Biosecurity Incidents: Planning and Risk Management for Livestock Diseases*, November, Victorian Auditor General.

Washington Post (1979) *Khomeini power play: Iran meat imports banned*, http://news.google.com/newspapers?nid=1314&dat=19790303&id=8PVLAAAAIBAJ&sjid=8O0DAAAAIBAJ&pg=3342,1084219.

Yaqubi (1992) "Tarikh Yakubi" in *History of Yaqubi*, Scientific and Cultural Publications, Tehran.

Zubaida, S. (2002) Trajectories of political Islam: Egypt, Iran and Turkey, *The Political Quarterly*, 71, August: 60–78.

5

BELDI MATTERS: NEGOTIATING PROPER FOOD IN URBAN MOROCCAN FOOD CONSUMPTION AND PREPARATION

Katharina Graf

Introduction

In urban Moroccan open-air markets,[1] halal labels are rare. Instead, the lawfulness of meat and other food products is taken for granted by the mainly lower income consumers shopping in them. Furthermore, dietary laws are never elaborated on nor part of popular discourses, as they are in multi-faith (e.g. Kanafani-Zahar 1999, Fischer 2008, Sauvegrain 2012) or Muslim minority societies (e.g. Bergeaud-Blackler 2004, Fischer 2011). None the less, the propriety of food products matters greatly to Moroccan consumers, and it does so according to locally conceived standards of food quality, which take into account a product's provenance, taste, safety and ethics. In this chapter, I focus on female consumers' consumption practices in the open-air market places that make up Marrakech's food spaces in the *medina* (pre-colonial quarter). I explore in particular how, in the absence of halal labelling, domestic cooks as consumers negotiate what they consider licit, good or simply 'proper' food, and how their daily practices of selecting and processing food products speak to broader issues of standards in food production and consumption.

As a Muslim majority society, the Moroccan case argues for a situated conceptualization of food standards. I contend that it is not the halal-haram pair that helps Marrakchi cooks make consumption decisions, but the bodily practices of choosing these by means of the local indices *beldi* (literally 'from the country', and by extension, 'home-made') and *rumi* ('foreign', and by extension, 'industrial'). At the same time, these indices are not restricted to scriptural foods, but include many more. The ethnography of Marrakchi cooks' consumption practices and their use of local standards allows the researcher to explore the central role played by a consumer's knowledge of and degree of control over the food system, which stands in contrast to an increasingly disembodied label such as that of global halal. I argue that trust in proper food moves along a continuum from a consumer's bodily knowledge to an anonymous, disembodied form of information of food products. By exploring trust in proper food from the perspective of Marrakchi female consumers, I seek to show how the definition of food standards is also an epistemological question of bodily knowledge. This chapter thus widens the approach taken in this book and in other studies of alternative food consumption (e.g. Carrier & Luetchford 2012, Goodman et al. 2012) by nuancing commonly held understanding of standards and consumer choice within the global food system.

In the introduction to this book, the editors ask how and by whom, for whom, and for what reasons are objects, discourses and practices called 'halal' or 'haram'? Within the urban Moroccan context I worked in, this question needs to be reversed. In a context where the lawfulness of food products is taken for granted and the claim to knowledge lies with the cook as consumer, how do urban consumers identify what they consider proper food, and what alternative indices exist to denote proper food? In short, why are halal and haram largely absent as markers of food objects, discourses or practices in this Muslim market context? The key argument I make is that in the absence of nationally institutionalized standards and an overall lack of trust in the broader food system, Marrakchi consumers rely on their own bodily and knowledgeable practices of self-certification to identify and name what they consider proper food (see West 2013). I seek to illustrate how the abstracted, and hence for a Marrakchi consumer initially unknowable, global is interacting with the embodied, and thus knowable, local in everyday practices of food consumption and preparation.

In order to relate everyday negotiations of food consumption and preparation to such bodily assessed food standards, I think of food consumption and preparation through a phenomenological interpretation of practice theory (Merleau-Ponty 2001 [1962], de Certeau 1984, Jackson 1996). I maintain that knowledge emerges through/in bodily practice and that especially the identification of food quality emerges through a cook's multisensory engagement with food products (see Ingold 2011 [2001]), rather than through disembodied national or international agencies of certification. By looking at the everyday practices of consuming and indexing food, I relate the Moroccan case to this book's focus on how globalized markets of halal products are setting new global standards for halal food production, handling and certification. In line with a conceptualization of halal markets as global assemblages (see Collier & Ong 2005), I understand these new standards as being able to de- or re-contextualize and thus to be abstractable and mobile, whereas beldi is a highly contextual and situated phenomenon. I argue that it is based on the knowledge a consumer can have of food production, handling and distribution that one or the other prevails.

The remainder of the chapter is structured as follows: I first introduce the research context and methodology upon which this chapter is based. In the next section, I unpack the notion of standards in relation to food consumption in Marrakech to introduce the role of halal certification on a national and consumer level, and propose this chapter's conceptual frame and theoretical argument. In the section on consumption practices, I describe Marrakchi food spaces, consumers' relations with shopkeepers and relatives in the countryside and how consumers contextualize food consumption to illustrate through what bodily practices domestic cooks source proper food products on a daily basis. I then describe how foods are processed at home to be made proper and what ethical considerations are involved in such practices. In the last section, I explore how the resulting standards are indexed by defining the terms beldi and rumi, and explain how these are used in practice. This leads to my concluding argument for a situated, embodied standard of food products in interaction with a global food system.

Research context and methodology

This contribution is based on 12 months of ethnographic research, which I carried out between 2012 and 2013 in the medina of Marrakech, in southern Morocco, living and working with three women and their families. All three families belong to the lower income group that makes up the majority of the medina population (Wilbaux 2001). Though each family is unique in many respects, they had a common uncertain, yet not dismal, financial situation, which makes them reasonably representative of a large socioeconomic section of urban Moroccan society. The first family I worked and lived with was that of 45-year-old unmarried Arab Fatima, her mother and two unmarried adult brothers, all of whom I got to know as neighbours during my first stay in Marrakech in 2007. During fieldwork, Fatima had no permanent occupation and shared kitchen work with her widowed mother. The second family was that of 40-year-old Ranya, who upon marriage migrated to Marrakech from her Berber village, her unemployed Arab husband and her 15- and 20-year-old daughters, who during fieldwork attended secondary school and university. Despite being the main cook, Ranya worked five to six days a week as a cleaning lady. I met her at one of her private clients. The last family was that of 30-year-old Aiya, who is also Berber, but came to Marrakech in search for work as a teenager and later married a Marrakchi Berber, with whom she had two small daughters, aged one and four during fieldwork. She worked part time as a cleaning lady in a nearby bed and breakfast. I have also known her since 2007, before she was married.

My methodological approach rested mainly on participant observation as an assistant cook, of which bodily experience and learning to prepare food alongside my research participants were essential components. Theory thus merges with methodology (see Harris 2007) and the presented ethnography should be read in this light. While shopping, processing and preparing foods with these women and eating within their family circle, I also informally interviewed each member and their extended kin. Furthermore, to capture the many non-verbal aspects of food consumption and preparation, I employed photography, video and audio recordings. Observation of shops and markets, and interviews with shopkeepers, food professionals and other experts complemented this micro-ethnography and extended its scope beyond these families.

Unpacking standards

As stated in the introduction to this book, standards are 'ideas of appropriateness', 'the generally accepted, normal and best way' to say or do something. Especially in the form of institutionalized standards, the editors argue, audit and inspection systems 'generate comfort and reassurance' or, what Kjaernes et al. (2007) call, 'institutional trust'. I agree that in all types of food markets the function of standards is to generate consumer trust. Yet I also argue they function on different scales and are equally a question of knowledge. The negotiation of standards hinges on various scales of trust, which are based on familiarity, traceability or proximity of food products, and therefore closely relates to questions of knowledge and control. The closer, more local a product's trajectory is perceived to be, the less likely a consumer relies on an abstracted norm. By unpacking what standards mean for Moroccan consumers, I conceptually ground their claim to food knowledge to then demonstrate how their bodily practices of identifying and naming proper food reflect in fact epistemological questions of knowing in practice.

Halal certification in Morocco

In Morocco, standards function on two extreme levels. Whereas halal certification has existed for a few years on the national level, this does not include food products sold in the open-air markets that dominate both urban and rural food markets. Here, other standards prevail. Before conceptualizing these alternative standards, I briefly sketch the current landscape of certification.

National standardization and certification of halal production and distribution is a fairly recent phenomenon and is relevant mainly to food chains that generate food products such as ready-meals, packaged snacks and export products (Imanor 2014a). The first halal norm (NM 08.0.018) for food products was issued in 2010 by the independent body of the Institut Marocain de Normalisation (Imanor), but in its revised form (NM 08.0.800) it has been certifying national and international food companies since 2012 (*Saphir News* 2013). It was developed based on international food production and handling standards such as the HACCP (Hazard Analysis and Critical Control Points) and by the Organisation of Islamic Cooperation (OIC).

Although recently much national attention has been given to the growing global halal market through fairs and professional reporting (e.g. Amor 2012), only few national food companies have adopted halal certification by Imanor (Imanor 2014b). During fieldwork, labelled halal food products were rare in the open-air markets of Marrakech's medina. Yet, in the absence of labels, how do Moroccan consumers identify lawful food? Where does their trust in food as proper stem from?

The consumer's concern with good food

In the current Moroccan landscape of certification, and as literature on alternative food movements from other non-Western regions has shown (e.g. Jung et al. 2014), regulation systems such as halal do not have a central role in generating comfort and trust in food. Similar to these voices, I found that standards of judging food as proper were context specific and relative, and that the consumer played a crucial role in determining what is considered good and trustworthy (see Bergeaud-Blackler 2004, Nestle 2010).

Benkheira (2000) argued that for Muslim societies a food is licit if it is good (Arabic: *tayyib*) and gives pleasure to the senses (*tyb*), and, in the North African context in particular, *tyyb* also means cooking itself, and *tâb* refers to cooked, ripe, mature or edible. In other words, a carefully cooked item of food is considered good, proper food and I extend this observation to argue that also a carefully selected, processed and hence tasty product is considered good. This broader concern with 'goodness' takes the lawfulness of food for granted, assuming that both producer and consumer share the same belief in the divine order as elaborated in Islamic scriptures (see Bergeaud-Blackler 2006). The consumer does not question that the producer follows a divine order to produce lawful food, just as the consumer trusts that all food she sources in Moroccan markets is lawful.

Nevertheless, the women I worked with had a clear sense of the meaning of halal. For instance, while eating lunch with Aiya, I asked whether all foods in Morocco were halal. She replied, 'well, only those that need to be, like meat'. I enquired whether all butchers were producing their meat in a halal way and she confidently responded 'they are all'. I insisted, 'if they don't have a halal label, how do you know it is lawful?' She replied that all animals are subjected to a veterinary check,[2] stressing that only healthy animals are permitted for slaughter. She added that at the moment of slaughter the butcher makes a ritual blessing. Aiya indeed stressed the quality control more than the ritual aspect of the process.

Dimensions of proper food

In the Moroccan context, a communitarian logic – i.e. a community that takes Islam and thereby halal food as a shared marker of identity (Bergeaud-Blackler 2006) – prevails with respect to the lawfulness of food, which is non-explicit and non-institutionalized. Beyond halal, however, the identification of proper food is less taken for granted and consumers are critical about the foods they buy. Consumers interrogate much broader concepts in order to identify proper food products and hence rely on other standards than halal. Taken beyond the underlying religious frame, food quality in Marrakech is primarily judged based on the consumer's knowledge that the food she buys is good (*tayyib*) for her family. The definition of what 'good' food means is flexible, relates to various dimensions and has multiple meanings, in particular the following.

First, Marrakchi consumers want to know where food products come from. The closer a food product's origin is to the origin of the respective consumer, the better and tastier it is considered to be, as its provenance and trajectory through the food system can be more easily traced. Second, from a health and safety perspective, a Marrakchi cook considers what treatment and processing a food product has undergone before she identifies it as proper to buy and eat, including consideration of a food's own transformation from raw to rotten. Proper food is furthermore not just food that entails little health risks from the consumer's perspective (see Nestle 2010), but is, by contrast, doing the body good by supporting its different functions. Third, from an ethical perspective, proper food products are those that have been handled with respect along the production, distribution, consumption and processing chain. Ethically proper food also refers to food security, and the ability to share food with those who have less. In a country that has historically been marked by frequent droughts and food shortages, which gave legitimacy to a government that was able to provide food in times of need (see Davis 2006, Holden 2009), the ethics of food include the popular expectation that the state provides food to all citizens.

Negotiating standards through bodily knowledge

As I seek to show in this chapter, it is not the institutionalized certification of proper food that a Marrakchi consumer trusts, but her own bodily practices of negotiating consumption and preparation in daily life (see Merleau-Ponty 2001 [1962], de Certeau 1984, Jackson 1996). In other words, only food that can be *known* by the consumer herself is considered trustworthy and this knowledge is based on a cook's bodily experience. I document how a cook relies on her hands, nose, eyes, ears and taste – and crucially, their interaction – to 'sense' food and to critically evaluate whether it fulfils her standards of proper food. From this perspective, categories of near/safe/good and far/risky/bad foods are experienced and embodied rather than externally imposed on the individual consumer; the expertise lies with the cook as consumer who through repeated experience develops her own bodily standards.

Similar to my argument, Jung (2014: 109), in her study of Bulgarian organic certification, called this ability to identify or know proper foods as 'consumer competence'. A consumer in this case is not passively consuming but actively engaging with food and people implicated in food consumption. By relying on her own experiential knowledge of sourcing, processing and eating food, a cook thus 'self-certifies' food products (West 2013: 216). How does this focus on consumption as an embodied and situated practice fit into the overall framework of global assemblages adopted in this book? Most local practices, discourses and ideas are shaped by and shape global processes in intricate ways in both long- and short-term interaction. Collier and Ong (2005: 13) called this interaction between global forms and 'specific substance or value orders', in this case the Moroccan concept of beldi, the 'actual global' or a 'global assemblage'. I consider the embodied, local standard of beldi to be such an actual global. We can understand global halal better if we also look at complementary local indices.

Practices of consumption

There are two main practices of consumption that help a skilled cook identify and define food as proper. First, sourcing food products in local markets, from trusted shopkeepers and through rural family connections. Second, processing through cleaning, sorting, portioning and to some degree also cooking food products in the home. Broader ethical considerations underlie both practices.

I refer mainly to fresh foods, although other food products are equally concerned. Most fresh food products are produced within Morocco and pass through a short commodity chain. Distribution is organized around terminal wholesale markets, with only limited supermarket retailing and contract buying. Food production remains seasonal, dependent on annual precipitation, and is little standardized (Codron et al. 2004). Consequently, food products on sale in the medina are not packaged, labelled or portioned and daily prices and availability depend on external factors, such as season, weather, transport and globally driven developments in import and export. All of these require a consumer to develop a plethora of skills to identify proper food.

Sourcing in Marrakech's food spaces

Practices of sourcing refer to tactics of identifying proper food, from how to and what to choose, to where to and from whom to source foods. The women I worked with chose between small temporary stalls and shops lining the main thoroughfare street and proper open-air markets. Non-storable food items like milk products were sourced from small corner shops at the entrance of most dead end streets (Arabic: *derbs*). Along the main thoroughfare, into which most derbs lead, shops sold fresh vegetables, fruit and meat, often complemented by temporary stalls selling one or two types of vegetables, fruit or herbs. At junctions with other neighbourhoods proper markets offered a larger, clustered arrangement of similar shops, which allowed for direct comparison and had lower prices than neighbourhood shops. These markets also offered dry food goods, which were bought in larger quantities on a weekly basis, like flour, oil and spices.

Except for butchers, who had the kilogram prices of meats visibly displayed and offered similar prices across the medina, most vegetable or fruit shops had no signs indicating prices, due to weekly and monthly fluctuation of wholesale prices. Even though the price per kilogram varied between shops and stalls, shopkeepers do not haggle over prices. For instance, with every shopping trip, even when out for leisure, Aiya compared prices by enquiring at several shops before assessing qualities and choosing a produce. She remembered these details for comparison with the next shops or over the course of several days, to monitor when it was cheapest to buy a specific item that could be stocked up.

The women I worked with inspected every single item before choosing one, by picking them up and looking at them from all sides, while touching, squeezing, smelling and tasting them. For white meat, like chicken, the women preferred to buy a live chicken and listened to it before it was slaughtered on the spot. The more

FIGURE 5.1 Vegetable and fruit shop display in Marrakech's medina. Photograph by the author

vehemently it protested, the better the chicken's health was deemed to be. Red meat, like lamb or beef, was assessed by the colour it had when on display, but also in how it responded to further processing at home. Generally, dry and pink meat was considered safe. Klein (2013) observed similarly how Chinese consumers judge risk by assessing food's appearance. In France, Bergeaud-Blackler (2004) also noted how it is consumers who thus control and 'label' what is considered halal food.

Overall, women preferred to buy from shops or stalls that allowed them to directly engage with food products. In most shops, indeed, especially fresh foods were displayed within reach of the customer (Figure 5.1). Thus, if a shop's products were, due to the layout of the shop, pre-selected by the shopkeeper, most women assumed the quality was low and avoided such shops. Although meat shops did not encourage the customer to touch their products, they still displayed their offer close enough to the customer to allow for visual or, in the case of chicken, audible inspection. Consumers thus imposed those preferences of representation and layout onto shopkeepers (see Bergeaud-Blackler 2004), which allowed them best to bodily assess food quality.[3]

Establishing relations of trust

If a shopkeeper offered fresh produce on a regular basis and of consistently high quality, Fatima, Ranya and Aiya returned regularly. With these shopkeepers, all three women had established relations of trust (see Jung 2014, who argued similarly for urban Bulgaria). By showing their loyalty as reliant customers, they were in

FIGURE 5.2 White meat shop in Marrakech's medina. Photograph by the author

turn treated to the best available products or received higher quantities per price. Over time, all women knew and enquired about these shopkeepers' respective families and spent more time tending the relationship than choosing produce. Both Aiya and Ranya relied moreover on a common rural Berber identity to establish such a relation and enacted this commonality by speaking Berber with the shopkeeper.

However, none of these women were ever off guard, they still thoroughly inspected each item and were willing to question a relation of trust anytime that they were dissatisfied with a product (see Klein 2013). For instance, when I was once sent by Fatima to buy chicken from her regular butcher who by then knew me well, she instructed me to be sure he picked a male chicken, with sparkling eyes and a high pitched voice of complaint (Figure 5.2). This meat, she assured me, would not only be healthier, it would also not shrink like a female chicken when cooked.

Similarly, if a shopkeeper was unknown, all three women took careful precautions not to be cheated. For instance, one day, Fatima's mother Hajja sent me to a red meat butcher, whom she did not know personally. She told me to look out for the right colour of the minced meat she sought by showing me a leftover piece and warned me to only accept meat that came straight from the fridge. I should also tell him not to add onions, as that was a way of cheating with the quantities. She further instructed me to ask the butcher to empty the mincing machine from leftover pieces before fine-mincing my order, to avoid contamination with less fresh meat. Hajja finally sent me off by saying, 'whatever he does, watch it carefully!'

Sourcing from the countryside

Another way of controlling the source of proper food was by drawing on family connections with the rural hinterlands of Marrakech. As a regional trade hub since its foundation in the eleventh century (Deverdun 1959), Marrakech's economy has always been based on the relations it kept with its agricultural hinterlands (Pascon 1977). Even today most medina inhabitants are migrants and maintain ties with their extended family in the countryside, often still owning shares of agriculturally used land (Crawford 2008).

Hajja, for instance, grew up in the Souss Valley south of Marrakech and as part of her inheritance owned lemon and olive trees, which were attended to by one of her brothers. When the annual harvest was large enough, he would send her several bags of lemons or olives. Alternatively, visiting relatives would bring food as gifts. One day, Fatima proudly told me that an aunt from the Souss had brought fresh milk from her small herd of cows. For Fatima this milk was 'the best', because 'you know what's in there'.

Even when Marrakchis did not have direct control over agricultural land, like Aiya and Ranya, they still accessed agricultural products through their parents or siblings living in the countryside. Thus, whenever Aiya received visits by her mother or brothers, they brought seasonal products with them. Aiya was especially keen on sourcing mutton meat from her home village (Arabic: *bled*), which for her was of superior quality to the mutton available in Marrakech, because she knew where the mutton was herded and fed, and who bred and slaughtered it.

Comparable concerns were brought up before 'Id al-Kabir, the annual feast of the great sacrifice. Women discussed with their male household members, who source the live animals, what qualities to look out for in a ram, centring on the provenance of the animal. Although rams were sold in temporary markets throughout the city, many consumers preferred to source the ram in the breeding regions. I was told by one male family member that the choice of region depended on what feed the animals get in the different pastoral zones. Especially Berber consumers claimed to prefer animals grazing on rough terrain and feeding on mountain pasture.

Fatima, Ranya and Aiya were thus using their intimate knowledge of a place as a way to certify products themselves. This reminds of the scriptural idea that the consumer knows and trusts the trajectory a halal meat takes from pasture to butcher. By thus tending connections with the countryside, Marrakchi consumers, similar to Bulgarian (Jung 2014) or Chinese (Klein 2014) ones, are ensured a more direct and traceable access to agricultural produce.

Knowing the food context

Apart from these various ways of controlling food sources, most consumers had a clear idea of the relation of food products to broader ecological, economic and political issues. They were aware of the seasonality of fresh foods and knew when specific harvests would reach the markets. For instance, during the winter months, heavy rains could foreclose the harvest of staples like potatoes or storms could prevent sardine fishing off the Moroccan coast. Consumers knew this would reduce availability and drive up prices and often anticipated when certain productions seemed less readily available than usual by expanding their sources, for instance, by using social relations in another agricultural region.

Furthermore, I was told that when global wheat prices rose to unprecedented spikes in 2008 and 2011, owing to a globally poor cereal harvest, the Moroccan wheat price was protected by government subsidies. Although the government announced to reform the increasingly financially untenable subsidies (Royaume du Maroc 2013), most women assured me that it would never dare to abandon them as this would result in riots. The women concluded that bread was just too important for Moroccans. Discussing and sharing such economic and political knowledge was part of women's daily conversations and played a determinative role in what produce was sourced at which quantities at specific times in the week or year.

Processing food to make it proper

Practices of food processing, such as cleaning, sorting, trimming, portioning and stocking, refer to both another way of assessing food's qualities when undergoing transformation in the home and to the bodily knowledge a cook possesses in order to *make* food proper. A cook not only assumes that food is not necessarily good when she sources it, she also improves it by preparing food in an adequate way. All cooks I worked with admitted that processing was time intensive and required physical effort. Yet all three women preferred to buy foods in an unprocessed stage to be able to control food's transformation, thereby enhancing its qualities.

Often, cooking also served as an indicator of the food's qualities. This was particularly the case for meats, where its reactions to heat were closely observed by eyesight, touch, hearing and taste. For instance, if it shrank and hardened fast it was considered to contain too much water and, from an ethical perspective, the animal was possibly grown under inappropriate circumstances. If the meat sizzled in a crackly, noisy way, it consisted of the right balance of lean and fat parts.

Or, for the sake of a fresher, more intense taste, especially Fatima preferred to buy whole spices and roots and ground them at home whenever needed. When food products were suspected of being treated with *duwa* (Arabic for: medicine, here: chemicals), Hajja in particular went to great lengths to peel most vegetables and fruit, from tomatoes to grapes, even though she knew that many micronutrients are contained in the skin. Different bits of knowledge are thus carefully considered and weighed against risks.

Another striking example is the processing of durum wheat for the daily preparation of bread. All three women I worked with sourced Moroccan grown durum wheat in the form of grains in 10–20 kg bags from the wholesale market or through relatives in their respective bled. They cleaned and dried the grains before

FIGURE 5.3 Sorting beldi lentils in a Marrakchi home. Photograph by the author

milling them at the neighbourhood miller and then sieved them into different densities. This allowed them to determine the refinement of all parts of the grain. Especially the resulting wholemeal bran was considered to be full of vitamins, flavour and texture and help digestion. Most commercially processed durum flours, they said, do not contain enough bran and are less tasty and less healthy.

Therefore, although food safety is not of high national political priority as in more industrialized food systems like those in Europe or the US (Lien & Nerlich 2004, Nestle 2010), Marrakchi consumers were aware of food-borne risks and treated food products accordingly. Even when foods were bought in pre-packaged bags, like couscous or lentils, they were still sorted and thereby quality controlled at home (Figure 5.3).

Ethical dimensions of food consumption

While the halalness of food products was taken for granted in this Muslim majority context, the religious dimensions of food consumption were engaged with in much broader ethical terms in the everyday, ordinary context (see Lambek 2010, Carrier & Luetchford 2012). Yet engagement with food products and reflection on its ethical dimensions took place through and with the body and did not make sense as an abstract, disembodied norm. Ethical considerations were often part of women's decision-making, both in sourcing and even more so in processing foods. Consumers and shopkeepers constantly invoked the spirituality of food.

For many of the people I worked with, food in particular contained God's blessing (Arabic: *baraka*) (Westermarck 1968 [1926]). Baraka is only bestowed upon a person, animal, object or action if deserved. Most notably, a cook was said to have baraka when a dish turned out to be delicious, referring to the effort she invested into preparing a dish, which is in turn ascribed to baraka. The outcome of skilled preparation and care is thus twofold: it has a qualitative and an ethical dimension.

Food is furthermore considered to be a gift (Arabic: *ni'ama*) from God and as such has to be treated with respect. Bread or bread-like foods, including couscous or flat cakes, were never thrown out but always redirected to feeding other creatures. Bread in particular is considered to be the essence of food and is treated with reverence. For instance, cooks and shopkeepers retained the remains of bread and gave it to poor men who collected and resold it as animal feed. Alternatively, it was dipped in water and fed to birds on one's rooftop or, in Marrakech, it was used for a lentil dish called *terda*.

Respect for food, for what God has given (ni'ama), is also closely related to respect for animals. One day, when I showed the video I had made of the ram's slaughter for 'Id al-Kabir to Hajja after she returned from the pilgrimage to Mecca (Arabic: *al-haj*), she said with tears in her eyes 'the soul [of the ram] had no time to leave the body'. When I enquired, she explained that the butcher who performed the ritual slaughter had not taken enough time to bleed out the dying animal before proceeding. He did not pay the ram and thus God the due respect. Only ethically treated food can be fully good food.

Local standards of food consumption

As described above, and following the proposed phenomenological reading of practice theory, markers of quality are identified through a cook's bodily, multi-sensory and even ethical assessment of food products and relate to taste, provenance, health and well-being, safety and food security. While standards are thus assessed experientially, they are named by the concept of beldi and rumi. This index exists throughout Morocco and is not limited to food, it also refers to humans or other objects (Rachik 1997). They are used in both urban and rural Morocco.

Defining beldi and rumi

For a first definition beldi means from the country and rumi means Roman, i.e. foreign. However, not only are these terms charged with ambivalence, oscillating between changing valuations and imageries of the rural person, place or object as backward and uncivilized or as unspoiled and authentic (see Bessière 1998, West 2014), they also acquire differing and sometimes contradictory meanings with respect to food. They are neither in opposition to one another (Rachik 1997), nor do they have a fixed meaning. Their contextual meaning depends not only on urban or rural perspective, but also on each person's past and present life context. Beldi and rumi allow to index food quality based on at least three dimensions.

First, they refer to origin or provenance of a food product. For instance, beldi broad beans, from the perspective of a Marrakchi consumer, are grown in the agricultural area around Marrakech, the Haouz. Rumi beans are grown in any other region than the Haouz. This definition relates to the terms more literally: beldi refers to one's own hometown or region (Arabic: *bled*) and thus, from the perspective of the individual consumer, most produce that is sourced from one's home region is referred to as beldi, whereas foods grown outside of that region are referred to as 'from Rome' (Arabic: *rum*, i.e. foreign). Second, they refer to taste or flavour. For instance, beldi cumin is considered strong and intense in flavour, whereas rumi cumin is associated with a less strong, more average flavour. Often, though not forcibly, cumin that is named beldi is grown in Morocco, while rumi cumin tends to be imported. Third, they refer to the context of production. For instance, beldi chicken is an artisanal, small-scale farmed animal that can be identified by multi-coloured feathers and a skinny, tall body. Rumi chicken, by contrast, is an industrially grown animal that is white, small and rather fat. Vegetables and fruit of a beldi context of production are marked by their diverse shapes and tend to be smaller than rumi varieties, which as a consequence of their streamlined production are larger and uniform in appearance.

Indexing in practice

In practice, one of the three dimensions can outweigh another. For instance, once Aiya's mother brought rumi nectarines from her hometown. They were industrially produced by a European-run farm on which Aiya's mother worked as a seasonal picker. When tasting the fruit, we discussed how perfectly shaped, yet how tasteless the nectarines were in contrast to the small and rather ugly beldi ones Aiya had bought earlier from a temporary fruit stall. Our bodily senses confirmed this distinction. Generally, an unappealing or less standardized outer appearance of fresh foods led consumers to assume these were beldi, whereas pretty and uniform products tended to be associated with rumi, i.e. industrial production. The latter were often suspected of being treated chemically and considered a potential health risk (see Klein 2013).

Furthermore, while a distinction of quality in terms of taste was made, this was not necessarily in favour of beldi. For instance, beldi butter, usually home-made, was considered too liquid and strong in taste to be used for preparing sweets. It was instead reserved for dipping bread. Industrially produced rumi butter, firmer and with a predictable flavour, was preferred for daily food preparation. True beldi butter could not be purchased, but in production was comparatively cheaper than rumi butter. Similarly costlier, yet also more labour intensive, home-made bread with durum flour was preferred over cheaper commercially produced tender flour bread.

For yet different reasons, the Marrakchi consumers I worked with exclusively bought rumi chicken. In this case, rumi chicken was not only double the price of beldi chicken, all three women also considered it to have more meat and taste.

Interestingly, the term rumi was altogether omitted when Fatima, Ranya or Aiya referred to chicken and none ever bought beldi chicken during my stay. However, research participants with more purchasing power told me they buy beldi chicken for special meals, asserting its more flavourful taste. Cost of foods is thus not easily associable with a beldi or rumi standard.

As I described above, through reference to a shared regional or ethnic origin, Marrakchi consumers employed beldi furthermore as a way to establish a relation of trust with shopkeepers. Fatima, for instance, preferred to buy from Omar, a spice and dry foods seller whose family also originated in the Souss Valley. In this case, the regional origin outweighed the ethnic one, as Fatima is Arab, whereas Omar is Berber. For Ranya, her trusted chicken butcher is beldi, simply because he is Berber like her.

A situated index of food standards

Since it is a highly situated index that depends on the bodily knowledge and context of each cook, not all food products in Marrakech were divided into a beldi and rumi variety in everyday usage. When no beldi variety was available, which was more likely in an urban than a rural market setting, rumi food products would not be named as such. Yet potentially they could be. For instance, when Ranya visited her parents in the nearby countryside, where potatoes from both a neighbour's garden and mass produced ones were available, the distinction between beldi and rumi potatoes would again be made.[4]

A cook's memories of past efforts involved in food processing were also bound up with these terms. Beldi couscous,[5] which is hand-made and nowadays, if at all, produced in rural areas, was associated with hard work and patience, which especially older cooks like Hajja resented. Most urban consumers preferred to use the rumi version, which is industrially produced, often by transnational firms. Among my younger research participants, who have never made the couscous grains themselves, I noted a tendency of nostalgic reverence for beldi couscous. Yet, as they had no bodily memory of making couscous, they perceived no difference in quality or taste.

Thus, while beldi and rumi constitute a local norm of food provenance, flavour and context of production, neither of the two refers to just good or just bad quality. Their meanings are multiple and vary with each spatial and bodily context, sometimes contradicting one another. While beldi could in many ways also be said to embody a specific 'taste of place' (Trubek 2008), it does so in a highly contextual way. For instance, for Aiya a piece of meat from a mutton grown and butchered in her hometown embodied a 'taste of the bled', which she considered better and tastier than meat of unknown provenance. That same meat, however, would not taste remarkable to Ranya or Fatima. For them, beldi meat came from their own respective home region and had a different, equally unique taste.

Yet, overall, there is a tendency to associate industrial, mass-produced rumi products, which tend to be imported, with lower quality. This is further reinforced with a lack of trust in packaging and food safety. For instance, whereas at the beginning of fieldwork I still assumed that packaged foods were clean, requiring no further sorting in contrast to loose and individually packaged products – what is called 'institutional trust' by Kjaernes et al. (2007) – my growing experience soon proved that my trust in neat packages and labels was indeed misplaced in the Moroccan market context.

Conclusion: beldi matters

Throughout my research, I found that several characteristics of food matter greatly to local ideas of proper food: where it comes from, how it is processed, who sells it, what is in it. The more knowledge and hence control a cook has over the process of food consumption and preparation, the more it *becomes* proper food. A cook as consumer does not assume food to be intrinsically good, it has to be *made* good through her careful and ethical engagement in shopping and processing each item. A cook uses her bodily senses to identify what she considers good food and the terms she uses to distinguish proper from improper products are equally embodied, assuming relevance only from within the position of the consumer. Beldi matters differently to different consumers and, if abstracted and disembodied in the form of a label, loses its meaning altogether.

The terms themselves, beldi as from the country or home-made and rumi as foreign or industrial, signal a gradation based on the long-term embeddedness of the Moroccan food system in globalizing processes. Though situated and contextualized in the consumer's body and life trajectory, this index works along a complex, sometimes contradictory continuum of proximity and distance. The local only assumes relevance in relation to the global. In Morocco, food is indexed through terms that imply the 'ability to know': where it comes from, who produced it and what it tastes like. A beldi product is proximate and can be known, whereas a rumi product is less proximate, less traceable and hence less known.

In the daily practices of food consumption and preparation, by using touch, smell, sight, hearing and taste for either choosing or rejecting foods, the global is literally incorporated by the knowing body of the cook as consumer, who is always also implicated in globally determined processes of food production and distribution: beldi and rumi are the 'actualization' (Collier & Ong 2005: 12) of this relation of proximity and distance. A consumer bodily engages and thereby critically assesses markers of quality against a broader economy of food. Stark (cited in Collier & Ong 2005: 7) called this 'reflexive practices'.

By inversion, a uniformly valid certification of standards such as halal can only attain relevance when this bodiliness of food products is absent, when the process of bodily standardization and certification is no longer in its place (Trubek 2008) and when proper food cannot be identified or known other than through a label (West 2013). Beldi standards distinguish what is knowable from what is unknowable, and attribute value accordingly, while halal certification makes knowable what is unknowable in a global food system.

Notes

1 By this term I refer to food markets that include both indoor and outdoor as well as permanent and temporary shops or stalls, as opposed to supermarkets or covered, fully licensed markets.
2 Aiya referred to the animal sanitary checks supervised by the Office National de Securité Sanitaire des Produits Alimentaires (ONSSA).
3 Interestingly, supermarkets attempted to resemble open-air markets in displaying fresh food products in a similarly tangible way. I often observed customers ripping open flour bags, to touch and smell flours, before deciding which one to buy. This was tolerated by supermarket staff and in some stores even encouraged.
4 Recently, some national supermarkets like Marjane started to market beldi products, especially fruit, like lemons or apples, as long as they were grown on Moroccan territory and had a distinct, smaller shape. Other products that could potentially be labelled beldi, such as honey or olive oil, however, were marketed as organic. Interestingly, the women I worked with did distinguish both honey and olive oil as beldi or rumi, based on the context of production and their provenance.
5 Couscous generally refers both to the final dish that includes a sauce and vegetables and the raw product of various types of cereals, typically durum wheat, which are processed into small chunks ready to be steamed. In this case, I refer to the raw grains.

References

Amor, A. (2012) Halal: une carte à jouer à l'export. *Food Magazine*, October–November. http://issuu.com/fclair/docs/food48. Accessed 01 August 2014.
Benkheira, M. H. (2000) *Islam et interdits alimentaires: juguler l'animalité*. Presses Universitaires de France, Paris.
Bergeaud-Blackler, F. (2004) Social definitions of halal quality: the case of Maghrebi Muslims in France. In: Harvey, M., McMeekin, A. & Warde, A. (eds.) *Qualities of food*. Manchester University Press, Manchester, pp. 94–107.
——(2006) Halal: d'une norme communautaire à une norme institutionelle. *Le Journal des Anthropologues* **106–7**, 77–103.
Bessière, J. (1998) Local development and heritage: traditional food and cuisine as tourist attractions in rural areas. *Sociologia Ruralis* **38** (1), 21–34.
Carrier, J. G. & Luetchford, P. (eds.) (2012) *Ethical consumption: social value and economic practice*. Berghahn, London.
Certeau, M. de (1984) *The practice of everyday life*. University of California Press, Berkeley.
Codron, J.-M., Bouhsina, Z., Fort, F., Coudel, E. & Puech, A. (2004) Supermarkets in low-income Mediterranean countries: impact on horticulture systems. *Development Policy Review* **22** (5), 587–602.
Collier, S. J. & Ong, A. (2005) Global assemblages, anthropological problems. In: Ong, A. & Collier, S. J. (eds.) *Global assemblages: technology, politics, and ethics as anthropological problems*. Blackwell, Oxford, pp. 3–21.
Crawford, D. (2008) *Moroccan households in the world economy: labor and inequality in a Berber village*. Louisiana State University Press, Baton Rouge.
Davis, D. K. (2006) Neoliberalism, environmentalism, and agricultural restructuring in Morocco. *The Geographical Journal* **172** (2), 88–105.
Deverdun, G. (1959) *Marrakech: des origines à 1912*. Editions Techniques Nord-Africaines, Rabat.
Fischer, J. (2008) *Proper Islamic consumption: shopping among the Malays in modern Malaysia*. NIAS, Copenhagen.
——(2011) *The halal frontier: Muslim consumers in a globalized market*. Palgrave Macmillan, New York.

Goodman, D., DuPuis, E. M. & Goodman, M. K. (2012) *Alternative food networks: knowledge, practice and politics*. Routledge, London.

Harris, M. (2007) Introduction. In: Harris, M. (ed.) *Ways of knowing: anthropological approaches to crafting experience and knowledge*. Berghahn, Oxford, pp. 1–24.

Harvey, M., McMeekin, A. & Warde, A. (2004) Introduction. In: Harvey, M., McMeekin, A. & Warde, A. (eds.) *Qualities of food*. Manchester University Press, Manchester, pp. 1–18.

Holden, S. E. (2009) *The politics of food in modern Morocco*. University Press of Florida, Gainesville.

Imanor (2014a) Label national halal. www.imanor.ma/index.php/Certification/LABEL-NATIONAL-HALAL. Accessed 01 August 2014.

——(2014b) LLH05: liste des titulaires du label halal. www.imanor.ma/index.php/content/download/21065/300318/file/LLH05-%20Liste%20des%20titulaires%20du%20label%20HALAL.pdf. Accessed 30 June 2014.

Ingold, T. (2011 [2001]) *The perception of the environment: essays on livelihood, dwelling and skill*. Routledge, London.

Jackson, M. (ed.) (1996) *Things as they are: new directions in phenomenological anthropology*. Indiana University Press, Bloomington.

Jung, Y. (2014) Ambivalent consumers and the limits of certification: organic foods in postsocialist Bulgaria. In: Jung, Y., Klein, J. A. & Caldwell, M. L. (eds.) *Ethical eating in the postsocialist and socialist world*. University of California Press, Berkeley, pp. 93–115.

Jung, Y., Klein, J. A. & Caldwell, M. L. (eds.) (2014) *Ethical eating in the postsocialist and socialist world*. University of California Press, Berkeley.

Kanafani-Zahar, A. (1999) Du divin à l'humain, du religieux au social: les repas sacrificiels au Liban. In: Bonte, P., Brisebarre, A.-M. & Gokalp, A. (eds.) *Sacrifices en Islam: espaces et temps d'un rituel*. CNRS Editions, Paris, pp. 199–213.

Kjaernes, U., Harvey, M. & Warde, A. (2007) *Trust in food: a comparative and institutional analysis*. Palgrave Macmillan, Basingstoke.

Klein, J. A. (2013) Everyday approaches to food safety in Kunming. *The China Quarterly* **214**, 376–93.

——(2014) Connecting with the countryside? 'Alternative' food movements with Chinese characteristics. In: Jung, Y., Klein, J. A. & Caldwell, M. L. (eds.) *Ethical eating in the postsocialist and socialist world*. University of California Press, Berkeley, pp. 116–43.

Lambek, M. (2010) Introduction. In: Lambek, M. (ed.) *Ordinary ethics: anthropology, language, and action*. Fordham University Press, New York, pp. 1–36.

Lien, M. E. & Nerlich, B. (eds.) (2004) *The politics of food*. Berg, Oxford.

Merleau-Ponty, M. (2001 [1962]) *Phenomenology of perception*. Routledge, London.

Nestle, M. (2010) *Safe food: the politics of food safety*, revised edition. University of California Press, Berkeley.

Pascon, P. (1977) *Le Haouz de Marrakech: Volume 1*. Unknown publisher, Rabat.

Rachik, H. (1997) Roumi et beldi: Réflexions sur la perception de l'occidental à travers une dichotomie locale. *Égypte/Monde Arabe* Première Série (30–1), 293–302.

Royaume du Maroc (2013) *La réforme du système de compensation se fera de manière progressive*. www.maroc.ma/fr/actualites/chef-du-gouvernement-la-reforme-du-systeme-de-compensation-se-fera-de-maniere-progressive. Accessed 1 August 2014.

Saphir News (2013) Maroc: la nouvelle norme du halal a du succès. *Saphir News*, 13 January. www.saphirnews.com/Maroc-la-nouvelle-norme-halal-a-du-succes_a16155.html. Accessed 30 June 2014.

Sauvegrain, S. A. (2012) Cuisines et temps de partage à Alep … , OCHA. www.lemangeur-ocha.com/texte/cuisines-et-temps-de-partage-a-alep/. Accessed 14 March 2014.

Trubek, A. (2008) *The taste of place: a cultural journey into terroir*. University of California Press, Berkeley.

West, H. G. (2013) Appellations and indications of origin, *terroir*, and the social construction and contestation of place-named foods. In: Murcott, A., Belasco, W. & Jackson, P. (eds.) *The handbook of food research*. Bloomsbury, London, pp. 209–28.

——(2014) Bringing it all back home: Reconnecting the country and the city through heritage tourism in the French Auvergne. In: Domingos, N., Sobral, J. M. & West, H. G. (eds.) *Food between the country and the city: ethnographies of a changing global foodscape.* Bloomsbury, London, pp. 73–88.

Westermarck, E. (1968 [1926]) *Ritual and belief in Morocco: Vol. 1.* University Books, New York.

Wilbaux, Q. (2001) *La médina de Marrakech: formations des espaces urbains d'une ancienne capitale.* L'Harmattan, Paris.

6

ISLAMIZING FOOD: THE ENCOUNTER OF MARKET AND DIASPORIC DYNAMICS

Florence Bergeaud-Blackler

Throughout the world, in Muslim countries and in countries with minority Muslim populations, halal markets are flourishing. This growth generates a mixture of scepticism and envy. According to trade agencies, there is no longer any reason to scorn this market. In a report entitled *Addressing the Muslim Market: Can You Afford Not To?* (2010), the American agency AT Kearney calls on the agrifood, pharmaceutical, cosmetic, clothing, banking and tourism industries to consider halal to be one of the most promising global markets. Can manufacturing and financial corporations remain indifferent to a $632 billion per year market representing 17 per cent of the global food industry? Can they ignore the performance of Nestlé, a food industry giant and the main promoter of halal products in Asia, the continent where the majority of Muslims reside?

This call to jump into the throes of the Islamic market signals a change in the attitude of the business community towards the Muslim world in the post-9/11 period. Ten years after the destruction of the Twin Towers, the 'Islamic world' – a symbol of 'other' from a Huntingtonian perspective in the West – may now be seen in a 'positive' light as a large market to initiate, build and develop. On this civilizational divide, which has been used to justify the oil wars (Afghanistan, Iraq), forward-looking agents now seek to do away with the old hostilities and promote a *pax economica* by active participation in sharia compliant markets. There has been a gradual extinction of food rituals in secular industrial societies, and the growth of the halal market is viewed with scepticism. But the recent interest in halal has revealed the existence of a market that is already well structured.

To understand the halal market phenomenon, we need to investigate its origins. We do not need to look to the mosques, the preachers or to the Muslim militants. The halal market was born in Western industrial countries to supply Muslim countries with sharia compatible meat, foods and an expanding range of commodities. I propose to break with the marketing message that showcases the primacy of religion and suspicious theories that consider the halal market as a venal and unscrupulous way of targeting gullible Muslims. The truth probably lies somewhere in between.

I propose to consider the 'halal' concept as a 'quality' in a French context. As conventionalists understand it, quality emerges as an on-going process of qualification.[1] By 'halal market' I mean an exchange of qualified and reputable 'halal' products, defined not by a manufacturing process, but by the qualification process itself, operating according to logic, rules and negotiated opportunities. The chapter calls for avoidance of the pitfalls of 'theological' approaches to this market. It shows how the dynamic norms concurrent to the market, both diasporic and religious, interfere and combine to produce religious products. It describes the impact of this production on the redefinition of religious norms and the relational conditions of those who produce and consume them. Therefore, the more general aim is to shed new light on the relations between the political, religious and economic spheres and to examine theories of secularization at the interface of these dynamics.

Scholar Muslims rather than Muslim scholars

Rare are the works that describe and analyse the industrial production conditions of halal food; rarer still are works that question the foundations and the religious arrangements of production (Marei 2001; Bergeaud-Blackler 2005; Fischer 2011). Most of the literature related to the industrial production of halal comes from consultants and food scientists in the form of 'manufacturing guidelines'. One of the authors of reference for this type of work is the American of Pakistani origin Muhammad Munir Chaudry, founding member and president of the Islamic Food and Nutrition Council of America (IFANCA), the oldest halal certification agency in the United States.

This agribusiness consultant's first article attempted to align industrial processes with religious laws (Chaudry 1992: 92, 93, 104). Completed with Mian N. Riaz, an American expert on food protein of Pakistani origin, and largely inspired by the work of the Jewish American Joe Regenstein[2] – a pioneer in the industrialization of kosher – the article gave rise to a book that today constitutes one of the main reference points for those entering the halal business (Riaz and Chaudry 2004). This type of book illustrates the emergence of a new domain of expertise consisting of 'scholar Muslims' (food scientists and veterinarians qualified through their authority in the scientific field) rather than 'Muslim' or 'Islamic scholars' (qualified in the religious field). In this type of book, the reader can find advice on the selection of animals, seasonings, colourants, packaging, the compatibility between halal and kosher, halal and genetically modified organisms (GMOs), and halal and organic products – all of which are compliant with selected and vulgarised Islamic rules.

Most of these experts are rather unfamiliar with the complexities of Islamic reasoning, and they do not bear any recognition or legitimacy in the religious field. But they get around this lack of religious knowledge and legitimacy by relying on the most accessible fatwa (opinion concerning Islamic law issued by an Islamic scholar) on the market, that is to say, ritualistic and fundamentalist 'off the shelf' Islamic handbooks available in the cyberspace fatwa banks or in a local Islamic bookstore. For example, a section dedicated to religious rules in the Riaz and Chaudry book is based on a synthesis of a chapter of the best seller *The Lawful and Prohibited in Islam* (1984) by the famous TV preacher of Al-Jazeera, and theological reference of the Muslim Brotherhood, Youssef Al-Qaradawi.

This lack of religious knowledge is compensated by a reverential and apologetic style that blurs the complexity of century-old debates on dietary laws in Islamic history.[3] But due to their academic background, these experts publish in scientific and technical food science journals where their selective choice of religious laws taken out of context does not raise any particular objection on the part of non-Muslim colleagues who do not necessarily differentiate between Muslim identity and theological competence. Those contributions 'sound' religious and they play their role: to provide a religious rationale for a lucrative commerce.

Indeed, to sell a halal product, the industry needs an input that it is unable to produce: religious legitimacy. It must ensure the constant and sustainable supply of this input. Fortunately for the industry, due to the current global crisis of Islamic authority in the Muslim world (Mandaville 2001), Muslim expertise seems to be an inexhaustible resource. The Ummah is re-imagined through migrations, the development of the Internet and social networks that allow for an intense discursive activity (Mandaville 2001). As Bunt points out: 'traditional structures of authority and power can be reconfigured within Cyber Islamic Environments, and new forces of authority are emerging' (Bunt 2000). This intense activity leads to religious questions on new issues linked to modernity in a liberal and globalized world. Each day, Muslim community websites publish commentaries on everything that relates to halal food: the food chain; identity and consumption; industry and animal welfare; the relationship between man and his environment; and the globalization of production systems.

By questioning what is halal and haram, the major themes of modernity are discussed and reviewed. But the market is a complex undertaking; it is not enough for a seller to simply find a buyer. And certainly not when it comes to halal, which crosses three dimensions: the rise of quality schemes in the agrifood market, the internal transformation of contemporary Islam and the ongoing dynamics of diaspora.

To summarize, born in the 1980s,[4] the halal market has two origins. The emigration of Muslims towards non-Muslim countries and the development of the commercial food trade between Muslim and non-Muslim countries was made possible by technological progress, and the universalization of the principle of 'free trade'. The birth of this market over the last quarter of the twenty-first century essentially concerned meat products, but it has since been extended to all products and commercial services over the last few years (Bergeaud-Blackler and Bernard 2010). The markets for halal products were therefore not born in Muslim countries. If it is possible to find halal products in the stalls of butchers' shops, grocery stores and supermarkets in the major cities of Muslim countries such as Casablanca, Algiers, Tunis or Ankara; often this is because they have been imported, or, as in Jakarta or Kuala Lumpur, because their spread is part of a national and nationalist strategy of the 'moralization' of economic development (Fischer 2012). The halal mark on the labelling of products sold in Europe, the United States, Brazil or Australia is contemporaneous to Muslim immigration, but it is also part of a broader strategy to reassure consumers after the food crises of the 1990s, a strategy that has led to a proliferation of labels and health claims on foods. This dominant confidence-building model is based not on direct knowledge of the processes involved, but on access to the information provided to the final consumer (Kjærnes, Harvey and Warde 2007).

The edible space

The global halal assemblage is the result of congruence between two dynamics – the extrinsic dynamic of the market and the intrinsic dynamic and innovation of the diaspora. I now develop this argument further. Halal draws a line around that which is edible by Muslim emigrants outside of Dar al-Islâm (literally, 'Islamic territory'). Food prohibitions are found in the meeting or confrontation with another realm of edible food. The need for distinction and separation originates from the presence of a discriminant in one that does not exist in the other. As Mary Douglas made clear, a missing discrimination in the 'edible realm' is experienced as a source of confusion, disorder, filthiness or impurity (Douglas 2001). Before the globalization of halal trade, 'halal foods' were unknown in Muslim countries; organizations and food supply structures excluded illicit products de facto. The wine consumed by Jews and the pork eaten by Christians were kept at a distance, well differentiated by systems of specific supply. It was up to the minorities to name, produce, organize and separate their own foods. The Muslim majority was not required to identify its own food, and to name the obvious. 'Halal' is an appellation of the diaspora in contradistinction with 'haram', a word often used to qualify the forbidden foods in the new environment; it was then used by economic actors.

When the first Muslim migrants arrived in Europe they organized the separation of meat to enhance or consolidate their Muslim identity: being a Muslim is 'to cut sheep!' (Brisebarre 1998a). The technical procedure for slaughter was no different from that of the local French butcher and the ritual was mostly a ceremonial devotion to God: orientation towards Mecca and pronouncing the *tasmiyya* (In the name of Allah). The link between food and devotion, eating and religious identity thus became explicit. Yet, in a seminal article on halal butchers, Benkheira (1995) noted that Muslims open their own butchers's shops in spite of the absence of directives set by the Islamic authorities. The Ulema (religious functionaries), according to this anthropologist, did not formally forbid the consumption of food of the 'people of the Book', that is to say Christians and Jews and their traditions.

How then do we explain why Muslims submit to rules and to strict rituals that religious scholars neither justify nor require?

Taboo

Food is far from being only the expression of a choice; its emotional dimensions make it a social habit most profound and resistant to change. The disgust and the revulsion expressed towards *halouf* (pork) and any food declared haram is the biological expression of a social taboo passed down over the centuries. These emotions become accentuated in social or group situations to survive social change. For Mary Douglas, the existence of a taboo is the intelligible concern to protect society against behaviour that could put it in danger (2001: 191). Therefore, it is useless to question the rationality of the taboo itself and better to rely on what it expresses. It is preferable to question the changes induced by its transgression. In other words, to try to understand the social dynamics of taboos through what is violated rather than what is prohibited. How does the transgression concern the mind of Muslims in the diaspora? Who and/or what is accused of transgression?

> Meat is brought to us in dishes but we do not know if it is lawful or prohibited; it is a source of torment for me; I think about it night and day and I must be told what my current situation is with respect to God. Know well, my dear father, and I swear by God and by what is sacred, that I will never stop praying, that I will never lose my faith.
>
> *(Meynier 1981: 456)*

This letter from a soldier posted in France during the First World War, addressed to his father in Algeria, could have been written today. It has been recorded many times in literature on migrants and more generally in anthropological contributions that food transgressions run the risk of a break with one's identity, a break in the chain of passing on one's heritage. Taking in an illicit substance is like becoming someone else, 'a Christian' in this case. It is an act of self-denial and group-denial, all the more serious in that it also affects one physically (Simoons 1994).

This identity/food relationship is not automatic: one can feel fully Jewish without eating kosher food exclusively and fully French without eating frogs' legs. The link between food and identity is only valid if continuously invested with meaning, verified and re-verified collectively by the group or beyond the group. Children of Muslim families do not restrict their food choices after receiving a progressive and rational religious education by specialists. The taboo of what is unlawful is not taught, but is 'transmitted' emotionally, sometimes 'brutally',[5] by a vigilant warning concerning this evil and prohibited pig flesh. It is around this taboo that a collective imagination of a corrupt world and food restrictions have emerged, a view that goes much further than the mere transmission of religion, and which is intended to unify and preserve the integrity of the group and its reproduction. Halal marketing, widespread today, also helps to strengthen and confirm diaspora Muslims of the bond that they have built between Islamic identity and diet.

Eating pork flesh is the main prohibition of the Islamic food taboo in the Koran, which is the primary source of Islamic law: 'You are forbidden the dead, blood, the flesh of swine, what hath been invoked by a name other than that of Allah' (Hamidullah 1963: 107). However, there is no need to return to the observance of an Islamic practice to explain the almost total absence of pork consumption among Muslims, since this pre-Islamic prohibition seems to have been internalized, 'digested' from generation to generation. Anthropologists have compared its nature and its intensity to the prohibition of incest (Benkheira 1995).

The other guilty party of the Muslim diaspora is blood. Meat not properly slaughtered would be unlawful because it would be similar to carrion, or derived from bludgeoned animals and 'full of blood'. While pork is most often dismissed without any justification other than the emotional, the justification for the prohibition of the meat of the 'Christians' is based on various arguments: impurity of blood and residue, health risks, disrespect for the animal, industrialization, etc. Although industrial halal meat is derived from animals that have been bled and emptied of their blood in the same way as conventional meat, this fear persists.

Before the private slaughter of animals was formally prohibited, Muslims shared the meat of the animals they slaughtered themselves. Throughout the twentieth century, isolated families tended to abandon this practice, while situations of communal living perpetuated them. In the homes of the military or workers, the task of slaughtering poultry, sheep or young cattle was entrusted to a Muslim so that it would be done 'according to custom'. The Harkis immigration of the 1960s, the family migrations of the 1980s and the birth of French Muslims confirmed the pork taboo and the separation of ritual and conventional slaughter. Up until the 1990s, the separation of meat was largely carried out without the intervention of Islamic authorities, free of any publicity, through direct transactions between immigrant families and farmers.

The prohibition of private slaughter, and the requirement to kill all animals for slaughter in slaughterhouses controlled by the veterinary services, inaugurated the 'institutionalization of halal' as a political response to market dynamics and the diaspora.

Industrialization of halal slaughtering

What I call the industrialization phase of Muslim slaughtering corresponds to the organization and setting of production and identification rules for halal meat by accountable authorities. As I mentioned previously, the Muslim family slaughter ritual is almost identical technically to the conditions of traditional European slaughter. The differences, without minimizing their impact on the perception of the quality of the meat, can be described as 'symbolic'. As the ceremonial aspects are untranslatable industrially, the industrial and Islamic certifiers attempt to technically differentiate industrial slaughter methods just enough to create a specific quality; the 'stunning exemption' then becomes an 'industrial proof' of the validity of 'Islamic slaughter'.

Slaughtering outside a controlled slaughterhouse was banned in France by a decree issued in 1971 for all slaughter, except slaughter carried out in an emergency and with ruminants bred for personal consumption. To continue ritual slaughtering, Muslims initially invoked the right to slaughter for 'personal consumption'. But the 1980 decree explicitly prohibits any direct ritual slaughter regardless of its destination. It targeted, in particular, the massive ritual slaughter carried out on the occasion of Eid el Adha, where each family slaughters an animal for personal consumption. This type of slaughter was a source of considerable financial loss for slaughterhouses, the government and the local communities that levied a tax on each carcass. In order to promote standardization, open new markets and ensure 'public safety' the French government put in place legal requirements to establish 'ritual Islamic slaughter' (Brisebarre 1998b; Bergeaud 1999). Once ritual slaughter was institutionalized, Muslim families lost control of the short-circuit channels of production and distribution. Three solutions were left open: defy the prohibition, buy from Jewish butchers or open Muslim butchers's shops. Kosher butchers, themselves in decline, thus saw a slight resurgence in demand for about a decade, before halal supply chains were organized. In the 1980s, no 'halal meat' could be marketed as such if it was not derived from an industrial process. Butcher shops proliferated and the 'halal' (or 'hallal') label in Latin lettering flourished on shop fronts.

The invention of an industrial ritual

How does one industrialize a ritual, especially if this ritual is no different from traditional non-religious slaughtering? The government used the conditions that applied to *shechita* (Jewish slaughter ritual) as a model, and granted the Muslim community clearances identical to those granted to the Jewish community for its *shokhatim* (ritual slaughterers). In the same way that it had granted authority to the Inter-community Rabbinical Commission of Paris to license slaughterers in 1982, the French government authorized first one, then two other Great Mosques to distribute Muslim slaughterer licences.

By giving mosques this power the government introduced a 'religious' aspect into the production of halal meat previously organized by families, farmers and local slaughterhouses. This legal decision was mainly done for economic and political reasons. Economic because unregulated halal slaughter would be a net loss for the slaughter industry, and also because halal meat was a promising export sector. Political because successive French governments were obsessed with controlling French Islam in a period marked by threats and Islamist attacks on French territory. Charles Pasqua, Interior Minister, thought that setting up an 'Islamic kashrut' entrusted to the Mosque of Paris would provide the means to assert his authority on the Muslim population living in France (Kepel 1987). The choice of the Mosque of Paris was all the more surprising because for Algerian dignitaries of the Mosque, halal slaughter, including that organized during the feast of sacrifice, was seen only as a 'tradition and superstition falling within popular beliefs'.[6]

The government contributed directly to specifying and setting the rules of Islamic slaughter. It drafted the ministerial circulars and supporting sketches to explain the procedure to slaughterers: the orientation towards Mecca, the identification of the carotid, jugular and oesophagus and the way to sever them. The French government played an important role in modelling Islamic slaughter modus operandi, as well as Islamizing the function of the slaughter by raising to the rank of 'sacrificator'[7] workers of Muslim faith or identity who had, for the most part, no specific religious training.[8]

By expanding Muslim worship to include the right to slaughter without stunning,[9] while no Islamic authority actually made the request, the State participated in the setting up of an industrial religious rite for Muslims.

The 'industrial proof'

Before the 1990s, the majority of Muftis showed no particular hostility towards 'Western' slaughter methods that they ascribed as 'Christian', particularly with respect to the stunning of animals in slaughterhouses. One of the first to officially comment on this matter in Europe was the Imam of the Woking mosque in the United Kingdom. In 1928 he formally authorized the stunning of animals before having their throats slit.[10] In 1964, the Mufti of Jordan went further by lambasting the 'scrupulous' who ask the people of the Book how they slaughter their animals:

> The jurists have agreed that a Muslim is allowed to eat meat offered by a man of the People of the Book. It is not right for him to suspect the method of their slaughtering, whether or not the name of God has been invoked at the time of slaughtering. It is not even good to make an enquiry on that matter, because the verses in the Qur'an are absolute without any restrictions (mutlaq). A considerable number of religious doctors have said that animals cut by a man of the 'People of the Book' are permitted for Muslims to eat, whatever may be the method of slaughtering […]. Those who do not eat their meat in Europe and USA, according to opinions held by some who are against the above-mentioned opinion, have no reason for doing so, save illusion (wahm). This opinion goes against the majority view, which allows meat cut by Christians and Jews for Muslims.
>
> (Masri 2007: 144)[11]

From the 1990s onwards, a battle ensued between the proponents of this interpretation and those who believed that stunning did not meet the criteria of Islamic validity. The latter based their argument on the following religious prohibitions:

1. The mayta prohibition (consumption of carrion) – when an animal is killed by stunning and not by bleeding it is forbidden to eat the meat;
2. The shirk ('associationism') – the risk that animals may be sacrificed to someone other than God;
3. The prohibition of blood – blood does not drain well out of the carcass of an animal stunned before bleeding.

The argument in favour of 'un-stunned' halal constitutes an element of differentiation and of commercial valuation for the halal certification agencies. In the 2000s, opposition to pro-stunning began to organize. Slaughter without stunning became a marketing argument in the increasingly competitive halal certification market. Mirroring animal rights campaigns, halal certification agencies advocating the authenticity of halal meat from animals that are not stunned before slaughter broadcast frightening pictures of animals violently shot by pistols. Muslim Consumer Associations[12] declared stunning 'anti-Islamic'. Hunting for pig DNA and 'illicit stunning' become a mantra against the corruption of a halal market that was estimated to be 80 or 90 per cent fraudulent. Judging by the emotion aroused among Internet users on community website forums, the impact of these campaigns was strong; and it was very effective in France. The three mosques approved by the government for the licensing of slaughterers, who engaged in the halal market certification with this advantage, were rather tolerant of stunning practices. As a result, they began to face attacks and pressure from Muslim consumers who strongly rejected stunning and they thus developed a much stricter interpretation. Up until this point they never dared to condemn stunning, but during a consultation carried under 'Animals and Society' framework meetings, and during a consultation with the European Dialrel project funded by the European Commission (EC), the three Great Mosques of Paris, Lyon and Évry aligned their position with that of the Jewish Consistory of Paris that were invariably hostile to stunning.

Halal as a religious resource

In the 2000s, the battle between true and false halal drew a line between the 'righteous' and the 'corrupt'. Controversies on the legality of the chicken produced by the chicken company Doux and the halal Knacki sausages produced by Nestlé provided a specific opportunity to challenge the religious monopoly of the Grand Mosques. This helped to facilitate a Muslim conscience to face the Islamophobic threat, or even formulate a modern Islamic ethics based on the criticism of production systems.

'Fait social total': to borrow the famous expression of Marcel Mauss, food is an inexhaustible subject of discussion and of Islamization for the diaspora. Food helps to address all the major themes of modernity, morality and corruption and links them to the yardstick of the Islamic normative rules of lawful and wrongful acts. All the major French Muslim web forums (Ummah, Saphirnews, Mejliss and Al-Kanz) intensively discuss halal in their editorials, opinion columns and testimonies. Ritual monitoring becomes a place of contestation towards the institutions that represent the 'Islam of France', including the French Council of Muslim Worship (CFCM), the French Muslim umbrella group who gather the main official Islamic trends of the country. Up until the late 1990s, French Islamic officials had never seriously believed that they were able to even play a role in the development of the halal market. Neither the Mosque of Paris nor the Muslim Brotherhood of the Union of Islamic Organizations of France (UOIF) attempted to make halal a serious resource or a tool for the control of the community.[13] This was because their interpretations of religious texts did not bind them to do so (the meat of Christians and Jews was permitted), because economic actors deprived them of all initiatives in this area, and probably because of their own position as educated migrants. As 'religious diplomats' close to the Moroccan Maghzen, the Algerian State or the Muslim World League, they were not confronted, as were the majority of Muslims born in France, with a choice of identity. While young Muslims adopted the food taboos of their parents, officials of Islam considered themselves as emigrants and modern. Even the most radical of them did not refuse the meat (of the people of the Book) regardless of its provenance except if it was obviously pork meat. However, after the 2000s, and the anti-stunning campaign, it was no longer possible for them to be publicly seen eating in a non-halal restaurant.

Halal has now become a public issue. Economic actors, producers and distributors communicate more openly about halal. It has also become a political issue, with groups of the extreme right wing (the National Front party) taking hold of the issue to denounce the 'Islamization of France'. This publicizing of halal has allowed the independent certification agencies of the mosques, the most famous being AVS,[14] and groups representing 'Muslim consumers' to disseminate their conceptions of lawful and unlawful food. Groups of 'young Muslims' saw this as an opportunity to challenge the older generation of Muslims who had held power over the Muslim community for decades (Kepel 2011, 2012). Through halal it became possible to climb the steps of the governance of Islam in France through a bottom-up strategy of conquest exalting the religious values of piety, endurance and resistance.

Conclusion

The global halal market has developed unimaginably over the last 15 years. As I have attempted to demonstrate, by considering halal as a negotiated quality we can see how this development resulted from the interaction between the dynamics of the market and the dynamics of the diaspora.

Until now, the halal market has drawn more on the diasporic dynamics of global capitalism than on the complex exegesis of scholarly Islam. First, because those to whom it is addressed expect Islam to be a recognition of identity, food safety and ethics; and second because the proper functioning of a market requires that the protagonists agree on relatively simple productive, harmonized rules. The definition of what is lawful has been overtaken by the combined force of the diasporic and market dynamics. Religious authorities and their challengers are now thinking of the opportunity of jumping on a moving train, either by espousing the movement or by proposing a different model, while surfing on the tremendous wave opened up by this market. In France, a 'Petition to (support) the respect of the principles underlying the halal' published through the social networks and relayed in the French Muslim cyberspace succeeded for the first time to gather and unite the various oppositions to the representative authority of 'the Conseil Français du Culte Musulman'. The French Muslim brothers of the second generation seem to have seen the importance of capturing the symbolic and financial benefits of controlling halal. They are supported in this way by a discourse coming from the Muslim world and a growing hostility to the Western control of what is deemed to belong to the Ummah. In an interview given to the Muslim consumer association ASIDCOM, Hani Al-Mazeedi, the Kuwaiti specialist given the Halal Award for 2009 for achievements in the halal industry, and organizer of the first halal Gulf conference in 2011 in Kuwait, said: 'the current interest for the world halal is mainly due to the desire to protect the trade of the West and not the protection of the Muslim consumer […] if we want to change the situation, the work must be done by consumers'.[15] It seems that the liberties taken with standards by the market have indeed dug a gaping hole in the religious field, leading various religious actors with the opportunity to redefine what is halal and haram in the name of the 'Muslim consumer'. In France, and in Europe, it seems that the halal market fuelled by diasporic dynamics is just starting to play a role in Islamic normativities as well as in Islamic governance.

Notes

1 According to conventionalists, quality does not exist before the product and is always the result of a negotiated qualification process. Quality is defined in a social context that goes beyond that of the market, it 'is determined according to rules and conventions that are not limited only to coordination methods between the market and the firm, but are also part of a more vast social space composed of collective knowledge, standards and conventions' (Isaac 1998). See also Bergeaud-Blackler (2005).
2 Professor at Cornell University and founder of Cornell's Kosher Food Initiative programme. He is the author of an article published in 1979 (Regenstein and Regenstein 1979).
3 The debates are numerous – see for example Benkheira (2000).
4 See Chapter 7 in this book, 'The halal certification market in Europe and in the world: a first panorama'.
5 'When I was 11, at school, I ate … I remember, I ate in the cafeteria, I ate a cordon-blue [sic]. And my mother, she yelled at me, she said: "You'll go to hell"' (Zaina, 20 years' old, discussion group organized in Bobigny, 2005). For other accounts, see also Harrami (2000).
6 'In 1987, the late rector of the Grand Mosque of Paris, Sheikh Abbas, pointed out that performing the sacrifice of sheep in France offended the majority of non-Muslims and

drew a negative judgement on the Islamic religion in the name of a non-compulsory practice [...], under which he saw too much tradition and superstition relating to popular beliefs' (Brisebarre 1998b: 59).
7 The name of 'sacrificator' or 'sacrificer' is traditionally unknown in Islamic vocabulary for butcher.
8 Unlike shokhatim of the kashrut, these are slaughterers who have a function and a defined religious status (Nizard 1998).
9 What other countries, such as Germany, have not done, due to their belief that this derogation granted to the Jews for kosher food was not justified in the case of halal.
10 The leaders of some sections of the Islamic faith, notably the Imams of the Woking and East London mosques, have agreed that preliminary stunning does not invalidate the carcass as lawful food (Slaughter of Animals Bill 1962: 28).
11 A shared view at the time across several continents, including the Indian theologian Maulana Sa'id Ahmad Akbarabadi, already expressed in 1949 by the Egyptian theologian Shaikh 'Abd al-Wahlab Khallaf (1949), quoted by Masri (2007: 144). The scholars of the reformist tradition such as Sheikh Muhammad 'Abduh; Sheikh Rashid Rida; Sheikh Mahmud Shaltut and Sheikh al-Qaradawi also defend this position.
12 Al-Kanz, ASIDCOM (Association for the Defence of Muslim Consumers), UFCM (French Union of Muslim Consumers).
13 Even now the Mosque of Paris continues to doubt its capacity to play an active role in its control and even more so in its development. The rector of the Grand Mosque of Paris, Dalil Boubaker, was speaking on the 8 o'clock news on channel France 2 on 22 July 2012: 'We will never be able to guarantee [that the meat is halal], neither by our structures, nor by our mosques, our imams, or by our slaughterers ... ' Ensuring halalness is a 'community' responsibility, he goes on: 'There is the internet, all the information of the community, which can pick out the black sheep'.
14 'At Your Service' (AVS) was created in 1991 by young Muslims of Saint-Denis, France, close to the Union of Young Muslims and the Tawhid bookstore, author of a book (Brahami and Otmani 2010).
15 Source: ASIDCOM website, www.asidcom.org/Interview-avec-Dr-Hani-Mansour-M. html.

Bibliography

Académie vétérinaire de France (2006) Rapport au Ministre de l'agriculture et de la pêche sur le degré de réversibilité de l'étourdissement des animaux d'abattoir tel qu'il est pratiqué en France, Académie vétérinaire de France, December.
Anil, M. H., Yesildere, T., Aksu, H., Matur, E., McKinstry, J. L., Erdogan, O., Hughes, S. and Mason, C. (2004) Comparison of religious slaughter of sheep with methods that include preslaughter stunning and the lack of differences in exsanguination, packed cell volume and quality parameters, *Animal Welfare*, 13: 387–92.
Bauer, J. (1996) *La Nourriture cacher*. Paris: PUF.
Benkheira, M. H. (1995) La nourriture carnée comme frontière rituelle: les boucheries musulmanes en France, *Archives de Sciences Sociales des Religions*, 92: 67–88.
——(2000) *Islam et interdits alimentaires juguler l'animalité*. Paris: PUF.
Bergeaud, F. (1999) *L'institutionnalisation de l'Islam dans un espace urbain (Bordeaux)*, Thèse de doctorat en sociologie-anthropologie, Université Victor Segalen de Bordeaux.
Bergeaud-Blackler, F. (2004) Social definitions of halal quality: the case of Maghrebi Muslims in France. In M. Harvey, A. McMeekin and Warde, A. (eds.) *The Qualities of Food. Alternative Theories and Empirical Approaches*. Manchester: Manchester University Press: 94–107.
——(2005) De la viande halal au halal food: comment le halal sest développé en France, *Revue Européenne des Migrations Internationales*, 21(3): 125–47.
Bergeaud-Blackler, F. and Bernard, B. (2010) *Comprendre le halal*. Liège: Edipro.
Boubekeur, A. (2006) L'européanisation de l'islam de crise, *Confluences Méditerranée*, 57: 9–23.

———(2007) Islam militant et nouvelles formes de mobilisation culturelle, *Archives de sciences sociales des religions*, 139: 119–38.
Bouzar, D. (2004) *Monsieur Islam n'existe pas: Pour une désislamisation des débats*. Paris: Hachette.
Brahami, M. and Otmani, F. (2010) *Le marché du halal entre références religieuses et contraintes industrielles*. Paris: AVS Tawhid.
Bras, J.-P., Amghar, S., Fournier, L., Marongiu, O. and Godard, B. (2010) *L'enseignement de l'Islam dans les écoles coraniques les institutions de formation islamique et les écoles privées*. Rapport de l'IISMM et EHESS.
Brisebarre, A.-M. (1998a) Une demande étrangère comme relais de la clientèle locale: les débouchés de l'élevage traditionnel cévenol, *Anthropozoologica*, special edition: 181–89.
———(1998b) *La fête du mouton. Un sacrifice musulman dans l'espace urbain*. Paris: CNRS.
Bunt, G. (2000) *Virtually Islamic: Computer-mediated Communication and Cyber Islamic Environments*. Cardiff: University of Wales Press.
Chapellière, I. (2009) *Éthique et finance en Islam*. Paris: Éditions Koutoubia.
Chaudry, M. M. (1992) Islamic food laws: philosophical basis and practical implications, *Food Technology*, 46(10): 92–104.
Douglas, M. (2001) *De la souillure. Essai sur les notions de pollution et de tabou*. Paris: La Découverte.
EBLEX (2010) *The Halal Meat Market: Specialist Supply Chain Structures And Consumer Purchase And Consumption Profiles in England*. Report. www.eblex.org.uk/documents/content/news/n_en.halal_report191110.pdf.
Endelstein, L. (2006) Les Juifs originaires d'Afrique du Nord, acteurs du développement du commerce cacher aujourd'hui. In A. S. Bruno and C. Zalc (eds.) *Petites entreprises et petits entrepreneurs étrangers en France, 19e-20e siècles*. Paris: Publibook.
Fauzi, A. and Abdul, H. (2007) Patterns of state interaction with Islamic movements in Malaysia during the formative years of Islamic resurgence, *Southeast Asian Studies*, 44(4): 444–65.
Fischer, J. (2005) Feeding secularism: consuming halal among the Malays in London, *Diaspora: A Journal of Transnational Studies*, 14(2/3): 275–97.
———(2011) *The Halal Frontier: Muslim Consumers in a Globalized Market*. New York: Palgrave Macmillan.
———(2012) Branding halal: a photographic essay on global Muslim markets, *Anthropology Today*, 28(4): 18–39.
Frégosi, F. (2008) *Penser l'islam dans la laïcité*. Paris: Fayar.
Garine, I. de (1988) Anthropologie de l'alimentation et pluridisciplinarité, *Ecologie Humaine*, 6(2): 21–40.
Hamidullah, M. (1963) *Le Saint Coran*. Paris: Imprimerie de Carthage.
Harrami, N. (2000) *Les jeunes issus de l'immigration marocaine dans la région de Bordeaux: étude de quelques aspects de leur participation à la culture parentale*. Villeneuve d'Ascq: Presses Universitaires du Septentrion.
Isaac, H. (1998) Les normes de qualité dans les services professionnels: une lecture des pratiques à travers la théorie des conventions, *Finance Contrôle Stratégie*, 1(2): 112–21.
Kepel, G. (1987) *Les banlieues de l'Islam: Naissance d'une religion en France*. Paris: Éditions du Seuil.
———(2011) *Banlieue de la République*. Paris: Institut Montaigne.
———(2012) *Quatre vingt treize. Banlieues de la République*. Paris: Gallimard.
Kjærnes, U., Harvey, M. and Warde, A. (2007) *Trust in Food: A Comparative and Institutional Analysis*. London: Palgrave Macmillan.
Mandaville, P. (2001) *Transnational Muslim Politics: Reimagining the Umma*. London: Routledge.
Marei, M. H. (2001) *A Rising Star? Halal Consumer Protection Laws*. Working Paper. Harvard Law School.
Masri, B. A. (2007) *Animal Welfare in Islam*. Leicestershire: Islamic Foundation.
Méchin, C. (1997) La symbolique de la viande. In M. Paillat (ed.) *Le mangeur et l'animal. Mutations de l'élevage et de la consommation*. Paris: Autrement, Coll. Mutations/Mangeurs, No 172.
Meynier, G. (1981) *L'Algérie révélée. La guerre de 1914–18 et le premier quart du XXème siècle*. Genève: Librairie Droz, xix–793.

Mintz, S. and Du Bois, C. (2002) The anthropology of food and eating, *Annual Review of Anthropology*, 31: 99–119.

Nasr, S. (2001) *Islamic Leviathan and the Making of State Power*. Oxford: Oxford University Press.

Nizard, S. (1998) L'abattage dans la tradition juive – Symbolique et textualisation, *Études rurales*, 147–48: 49–64.

Noor, F. (2001) Islam et Politique en Malaisie: une trajectoire singulière, *Critique internationale*, 2001/4.

Picaudou, N. (2010) *L'islam entre religion et idéologie: essai sur la modernité musulmane*. Paris: Gallimard.

Poulain, J. P. (2002) *Sociologies de l'alimentation*. Paris: PUF.

Al-Qaradawi, Y. (1984) *The Lawful and Prohibited in Islam*. Beirut: The Holy Quran Publishing House.

Ramadan, T. (2008) *Islam, la réforme radicale: éthique et libération*. Paris: Presses du Châtelet.

Regenstein, J. M. and Regenstein, C. E. (1979) An introduction to the Kosher dietary laws for food scientists and food processors, *Food Technology*, 33(1): 89–99.

Riaz, M. N. and Chaudry, M. M. (2004) *Halal Food Production*. Boca Raton: CRC Press.

Rougier, P. (2008) (ed.) *Qu'est-ce que le salafisme?* Paris: Presses Universitaires de France.

Roy, O. (2002) *L'Islam mondialisé*. Paris: Seuil.

Scholliers, P. (2001) *Food, Drink and Identity: Cooking, Eating and Drinking in Europe since the Middle Ages*. Berg: Oxford.

Simoons, F. J. (1994) *Eat Not This Flesh: Food Avoidances from Prehistory to the Present*. Madison and London: The University of Wisconsin Press.

Slaughter of Animals Bill (1962): Private Member's Bill presented by Lord Somers, December 1962.

The Halal Journal (2006) Nestlé Group's Halal Excellence Centre in Malaysia, No 186.

7

THE HALAL CERTIFICATION MARKET IN EUROPE AND THE WORLD: A FIRST PANORAMA

Florence Bergeaud-Blackler

Introduction

In the second half of the 1990s, the emergence of halal, and its expansion from meat and food to other commodities, led to the birth of a highly competitive 'global market for halal certification', with each certifier wanting to appear 'more halal' than its competitors.[1] This rivalry has been running for over two decades on all continents, mostly in industrial countries without Muslim traditions, and also in a few exporting Muslim countries predominantly located in Southeast Asia. This chapter provides an initial overview of the market for halal certification in some of the main countries involved in the trade of Islamic-compliant products, and provides an initial classification. Particular attention is paid to the contentious issue of stunning,[2] which is pivotal in the competition between certifiers. Analyses produced here are based on surveys conducted over the past five years with experts and industry players in the global market for halal certification during professional events in Europe (Paris, Brussels), Africa (Meknes, Casablanca) and Asia (Tokyo). This approach is supplemented with Internet-based documentary research.[3]

From 'Islamic compatibility' to a 'market for halal certification'

The existence of a 'halal market' requires at least a demand for a 'halal quality'. This demand can only exist in a context where such quality is not obvious any more, that is, outside of the *Muslim world*.[4] The quest for halal is rather recent. It was first formalized in the 1980s when Muslim importers required non-Muslim countries to set up specific Islamic processes in their plants. Before the 1980s, trade between Muslim and non-Muslim countries existed but no one used the term 'halal', not because it was not Islamic, but because the halalness of products was not an issue. Products sold to Islamic countries were, as I call them, 'Islamic-compatible'.

Each importing country assured itself of the compatibility of imported products in line with their own requirements; trade was based on trust. There was no control, and as long as the issue of fraud was not raised, the goods were deemed compliant. Major meat exporters from Australia, New Zealand and Europe provided customers with the required conformity assessments. Only Saudi Arabia and Egypt required the countersignature of their own embassies to satisfy the most religious segments of their population, but this precaution was not accompanied by direct controls on the plants. Under this system, if fraud was suspected, once the goods were imported customers could either dispose of the commodities or ignore the problem, as the issue of religious legitimacy was less important than the economies of developing countries.

The advent of the Islamic Republic of Iran in 1979 was a major step in the shift from Islamic compatibility to halal certification. Ayatollah Khomeini pronounced a ban on all imported meats, which were declared *non-Islamic*[5] and immediately destroyed. Initially this measure appeared to be very damaging, as Iran did not produce enough meat to feed the population; the ban was actually followed by a rise in meat imports from New Zealand and Australia. To overcome this problem, the Iranian government decided to Islamize the production process at its source. Iranian workers and inspectors were sent to Australasian and European slaughterhouses to adapt the chain to Iranian requirements and ensure the compliance of imported meat with Islamic principles. This expensive system did not last very long, but it inspired the one we know today: certification by an independent third party.

At the time, Saudi Arabia, a great political and religious rival of Iran, was also importing Western meat. After the declaration of Khomeini, the Saudis were not going to be seen as 'less halal' than their Iranian rivals and they turned to the Sunni Muslim minorities living in exporting countries.[6] In exchange for their benediction, and petro-dollars for local Islamic associations, the Saudis received supervision from local Muslims who controlled meat for export to Saudi Arabia. The operation was both economic and religious. The Islamic World League, the world body preaching Saudi Wahhabism, played a particularly active role in the institutionalization of these intermediaries. Applicants for halal certification – and for grants from generous Saudi donors – were required to show commitment and overcome ethnic and cultural divisions for the sake of the Ummah, thus becoming detached from their original allegiances.

For leaders of the numerous and rival Islamic associations, the battle for the control of halal was seen as an opportunity to impose their leadership on the Islamic community. They could fuse the religious legitimacy given by the guardians of Islam's holy places with their petro-dollars and the money made from meat certification. Several Islamic associations started to offer training, recruitment and supervision services and eventually opened the first halal certification business agencies. Since the 1980s, this model of third-party certification expanded rapidly in Australia, New Zealand and Europe to the point that companies wishing to export to some Muslim countries were no longer able to avoid halal certification. To escape this dependency on Islamic associations, some big companies created their 'own independent Islamic certification agencies', either by recruiting Muslim workers, or by supporting moribund or inactive so-called Muslim associations. To summarize, the birth of the halal market started from the moment responsibility for quality – and therefore the possibility of fraud – moved from the client (the importer) to the seller.

Today there are more than a hundred halal certification agencies[7] of various sizes within the global assemblage. In countries with an Islamic majority, where there are very few such agencies, certification is closely tied with the state institutions in charge of religious affairs. They are found mainly in Southeast Asia, but exporters of food and cosmetics are now proliferating in the Arab world in countries such as Morocco and Tunisia. Most certification agencies are located in countries with Muslim minorities. Being cheap and open access, the market for halal certification has become very competitive. Halal guarantees and logos have multiplied, fuelling distrust and demand for further guarantees.

In the 2000s, increasingly wary consumers pushed the market for halal certification to a logic of religious one-upmanship. To avoid the looping effect of distrust, countries involved in the halal trade engaged in international regulation initiatives hoping for the formalization of a single 'halal' standard that would help to regulate the market and provide consumer confidence. However, in many Muslim majority countries engagement in the halal certification market is a matter of national socio-economic development, while for the Muslim minorities living in Western countries the halal market is a da'wa tool that plays an increasing role influencing religious trends and ideas, and organizations in the religious field.

Halal certification as a tool for economic development in Muslim countries

By the 1980s, Muslim countries in Southeast Asia began to show an interest in the development of the halal industry, both to improve their competitiveness in regional and global markets and to accelerate and render the modernization of their economies more acceptable to their populations. Companies in Malaysia, Thailand, the Philippines, Brunei and Singapore were among the first to invest in the halal sector with the direct support of their individual states. Halal certification policy (what Johan Fischer (2011) terms 'halalization') provided a systematic way of strengthening food security and safety while enhancing international competition in the most heavily populated Muslim region in the world.[8]

Established in 1978, the Islamic Religious Council of Singapore (MUIS[9]) is one of the oldest agencies for halal certification. In 1989, the Majelis Ulama Indonesia (MUI), or Indonesian Ulema Council, set up the 'Lembaga Pengkajian Pangan Obat-obatan dan Kosmetika'[10] to protect Muslims consuming food, drug and cosmetic products. However, one of the most successful initiatives is the Malaysian agenda, which is now described in more detail.

In Malaysia especially, the halal trade is an affair of the state. Embarrassed by his growing Islamist opposition, one of the responses of Prime Minister Mahathir

Mohamad in the 1980s was to make the country a modern and efficient 'global Halal hub'. The *halalization* of the economy was also a way of getting support for modernization. Malaysia was the first country to provide a working definition of halal in the Trade Descriptions Act 1975. This gave the Malaysian Islamic Development Department (Jabatan Kemajuan Islam Malaysia or JAKIM)[11] the authority to issue halal certificates to businesses. All commodities imported into Malaysia require the approval of JAKIM, which is known for its strict halal guidelines. In the unregulated global market for halal certification of the early twenty-first century, JAKIM accreditation became the default global standard for halal guarantees.

The halalization policy of Malaysia primarily had a regional goal, to attract investors from the Association of Southeast Asian Nations (ASEAN[12]). In 2004, Malaysia organized an international exhibition of halal (MIHAS: Malaysian International Halal Showcase). This brought together hundreds of stakeholders, among them the giants of food and retail industries such as Nestlé, Tesco and McDonald's.[13] Malaysia's aims were subsequently expanded through the creation of the World Halal Forum, organized by KasehDia[14] with the support of the Malaysian government. In 2006 the Halal Industry Development Corporation was launched under the authority of the Ministry of International Trade and Industry to further global expansion.

Malaysian experts are invited to share their expertise at the many halal international exhibitions that have flourished around the world. Through this renowned expertise, Malaysia attempts to impose its standard as a global halal standard by focusing on 'halal excellence' and 'halal science', and by developing detection techniques for monitoring labelled halal products. The Malaysian halal vision is inclusive. It defends a halal concept that is compatible with all religions and cultures. At the first World Halal Forum, Dato' Seri Abdullah Ahmad Badawi, Prime Minister of Malaysia and Chairman of the Organization of the Islamic Conference (OIC) stated that: 'Halal (...) represents values that are held in high regard by all peoples, cultures and religions'.[15] On this account, halal should not only be a symbol of quality for food:[16] 'The halal business must ... be respectful of animal welfare and the environment. Halal embodies social justice, welfare and protection of the poorest and weakest'.[17]

However, Malaysia's halal vision is not shared by all. Since the early 2010s, Malaysian aspirational hegemony has been increasingly questioned. Its leading position in the global halal market, coveted by the richest and most powerful, is now under threat. If Malaysia is a leader in technical certification, it lacks the most desired resource of the market: religious legitimacy. Arab countries, especially the rich Gulf states, are now trying to promote a more restrictive and less ecumenical model – in other words, a notion of halal integrated with a global Islamic economy. Another attack came from Turkey, who claims legitimacy in the leadership of halal within the OIC, despite the fact that Malaysia was the first to suggest the creation of an OIC halal universal standard.[18] Turkey asked the Standing Committee for Economic and Commercial Cooperation of the Organization of the Islamic Cooperation (COMCEC)[19] to accelerate the creation of the Standards and

Metrology Institute for Islamic Countries (SMIIC)[20] (two institutions of the OIC based in Istanbul) that would look after halal matters. Turkey then proposed the creation of a halal standard through the SMIIC. The propensity of Malaysia to remain the global halal hub may now be severely tarnished even though the country has played and still plays a central role in the inclusion on the agenda of the OIC halal standard.

The Moroccan government, which introduced a first regulation inspired by the Malaysian model in 2010, has since retreated. According to the journal *La Vie Eco*, 'the fact that Moroccan Ulemas did not take part in drafting the norm means that it never gained credibility. [...] Since it came into force, not one single business has attempted to have itself certified according to this norm'. A few months later, Morocco decided to adopt the model of the OIC, involving the Ulema of the kingdom,[21] thus becoming one of the first Arab countries to establish a national standard for halal food and cosmetics. In 2014, four years after the creation of the Moroccan standardization body IMANOR, and one year after the new IMANOR halal norm in 2013, 16 companies have received this certification including Koutoubia, the largest producer of meat and sausage, and Nestlé. As in Malaysia, halalization is a way of promoting exports while lifting local businesses and economies. To obtain the halal standard of IMANOR,[22] companies must implement the Hazard Analysis and Critical Control Points (HACCP) protocol for food security. Once certified, a routine check is conducted annually to ensure compliance with procedures.

Tunisia also developed its halal label to conquer foreign markets. The national halal label INNORPI[23] applies to dates, spices, dried fruits, vegetables, olive oil and tuna. Again, the labelling policy encourages the modernization of the sector. The halal label INNORPI requires the prior corporate compliance with the ISO 22000 standard, which guarantees the safety of the product. Companies receive annual accreditation from INNORPI once the Muftis of Dar El IFTA agree. Halal has thus become, quite recently, a stake within intra-Muslim international trade. It is a tool of industrial and economic development at the national level and, increasingly, a religious legitimacy issue, much as it is in non-Muslim countries.

Halal certifications in non-Muslim countries: economic and religious issues

In secular countries, halal certification initiatives are organized by private organizations. Halal labelling of consumer products is not mandatory and, with the exception of some states in the United States, no secular law applies to production labelled as halal. This does not mean that secular states are not interested in the development of the halal market, but because halal has a religious meaning, their support can only appear as indirect. There is currently no exhaustive list of halal certification bodies, because of the instability of this fairly large new market, because of an opacity maintained by market players for competitive reasons, and also because of nervousness with respect to public opinion. In what follows I provide a review of some of the most relevant forms of certification in the Pacific, the

United States and Europe, which are among the most important or significant in terms of seniority and renown within the global assemblage. They are notable for their illustrative (symbolic?) value, not necessarily for their economic performance, which is still very difficult to assess.[24]

The pioneers of the Pacific

Some of the oldest halal certification agencies are found in New Zealand and Australia. Both countries are historical meat exporters to the Muslim world.

New Zealand

New Zealand is located in the southern hemisphere. With 50,000 Muslims in a population of 4.3 million, the country has a relatively small Muslim minority[25] comprising immigrants from Somalia, the Middle East, central Europe (former Yugoslavia, Albania, Bulgaria) and Fiji. Most arrived in the 1970s and 1980s, joining a small Chinese Muslim minority established in the territory from the late nineteenth century. New Zealand is the largest global exporter of sheep meat and a major exporter of beef. This agricultural land has always been very dependent on foreign trade and the economy has always been dependent on the sale of wool, meat and dairy products, which ensured economic prosperity throughout the twentieth century. Exports of meat to the Middle East and Southeast Asia began in the 1960s, growing significantly from the start of the 1980s when halal became a major global opportunity.

At the forefront of the industry for halal slaughter, New Zealand has developed a stunning method called 'reversible' that does not kill the animal before it dies of bleeding. Although this method is now challenged by the recent 'no-stunning' campaigns launched by what I am calling the second generation certification industries (see infra), this 'head only stunning' method has been widely accepted by New Zealand's Muslim business partners and has allowed the country to become the biggest halal lamb exporter. The two major agencies for halal certification share most of the market. New Zealand Islamic Meat Management (NZIMM) and the Federation of Islamic Associations of New Zealand (FIANZ) both emerged in the 1980s. Initially connected to the meat industry, NZIMM became officially independent with the arrival of its competitor FIANZ. Led initially by Egyptian Abdel-Al, NZIMM is best known for its role in the development and use of head only stunning, which is accepted both by animal welfare organizations and Muslims.

The Federation of Islamic Associations of New Zealand (FIANZ) is a federation of several local Islamic associations created between the 1960s and 1970s. From its inception in 1980, its president, an ethnic Albanian businessman, Mazhar Krasniqi, supported by the Muslim World League, endowed FIANZ with a 'halal department' to compete with NZIMM. Despite the hostility of the meat industry, FIANZ has emerged as a certifier with the support of major clients in the Gulf countries (Saudi Arabia and Kuwait). While NZIMM is only dealing with meat products, FIANZ applies halal certification to food in all its forms, as well as to beverages, non-food products such as cosmetics, drugs, additives, supplements, dietary supplements, and at places of halal food distribution: canteens, restaurants and butchers. Its board of directors consists of both religious experts and professionals in the food industry. It employs its own personal slaughterer who is selected jointly by FIANZ and the Meat Industry Association of New Zealand. The hegemonic position of FIANZ has attracted criticism. It is regularly challenged on its choice of slaughter personnel who, according to its detractors, are not 'religious enough'. Thus in 2004, the Muslim Association of Canterbury said that FIANZ slaughterers failed to perform their five daily prayers. These disputes, which mostly targeted Somali workers, led the slaughterers to form a union in 2004, the New Zealand Halal Union Incorporated (NZHUI), which is responsible for defending the interests of halal slaughterers (also called the Halal Slaughtermen Union) and regulating relations between workers and their employers. In New Zealand, conflicts around the certification of halal meat have been occurring for several years, creating significant tensions between different Muslim groups. Both FIANZ and NZIMM are today seeking closer collaboration, but other Islamic associations are emerging to challenge them, arguing that the practices of these two agencies are not transparent enough and require the intervention of public authorities to regulate halal.

This current situation between these two pro-stunning agencies is good for the meat industry of New Zealand. The country has made its system of halal slaughter with 'reversible stunning' a selling point and an exportable model.[26] In New Zealand the state does not need to be involved in the regulation of a halal standard, unlike neighbouring Australia.

Australia

Unlike New Zealand, Australia is a country of Muslim immigration. The number of Muslims living in the country is estimated at 540,000 out of a population of 22.3 million.[27] Most Muslim immigrants have arrived over the last 30 years from, at first, Lebanon and Turkey, followed by immigrants from Pakistan, India, Indonesia, Malaysia, Bangladesh, Fiji, Albania, the former Yugoslavia, Greece and South Africa.

As a large agricultural country, Australia has exported carcasses and live animals to several Muslim countries including Egypt, Indonesia, Malaysia and Saudi Arabia since the 1970s; Meat Export Australia currently claims to export beef, sheep meat and goat meat to over 40 Islamic countries.[28] Australia provides stunning before halal slaughter but is more tolerant towards shechita (Jewish ritual slaughter) in line with the European and US derogation legislation. To boost exports to Muslim countries, Australia has developed a centralized halal policy based on the principle of dual control of government and Islamic halal slaughter. In 1983, the country adopted a programme of public accreditation for certification under the Australian Quarantine and Inspection Service (AQIS) (the equivalent of veterinary services); in 2009, the Australian Government Supervised Muslim Slaughter Program

(AGSMS) became the Australian Government Authorised Halal Program (AGAHP). The programme is implemented in the framework of the Export Meat Orders-Export Control Act (1982) for products to butchers and is aimed in principle only at exporters.

This unique programme in the non-Muslim world is based on shared responsibility between three actors: the government, which guarantees the AQIS AGSGM programme; the producer via accreditation from AQIM in the place of production ensuring the execution of the AGSGM on-site; and the certification body responsible for Islamic religious issues. Islamic organizations may be accredited to AQIS, who provide training for slaughterers, and controls on slaughter are conducted by both the Islamic organization and AQIS. Animals must be stunned by reversible stunning methods. Halal stamps are officially recognized by the government and delivered by staff accredited by AQIS. Even if production is almost entirely halal, the halal stamping operation after slaughter is not mandatory. However, carcasses must show a stamp if they are to be sold as halal. The disadvantage of this system is that it does not identify as such the meat of animals slaughtered according to a religious rite, which may deceive consumers who do not want to consume any ritual or religious products.

Another peculiarity of Australia is the existence of an 'objective alliance' between Islamic associations, such as the biggest member, the Australian Federation of Islamic Councils (AFIC), animal welfare organizations and the Australian Meat Industry Employee Union (AMIEU). In other countries, these three actors – religion, welfare and the meat industry – are often in strong disagreement about religious slaughter. In Australia, these actors unite to promote the export of meat rather than the export of live animals.[29] Like welfarists, Islamic leaders speak out against 'cruelty in the live export trade', highlighting the fact that chilled meat exports are 'widely accepted in importing countries'. The meat industry thus promotes meat slaughtered in compliance with 'Islamic laws' in Australia.[30]

United States

The United States has a relatively large domestic halal market. As in Europe, although to a lesser extent, the presence of 2.7 million Muslims out of 310 million Americans has a big impact on the halal certification market, which is directly controlled by consumers. There have been waves of Muslim migration to the United States throughout the twentieth century, which increased significantly during the 1960s with the arrival of Muslims from India, Pakistan, Indonesia and Afghanistan. During the mid-twentieth century Islam inspired political activism such as Nation of Islam, which was created in 1930 by the Afro-Americans Wallace Fard Muhammad and Elijah Muhammad, and the Muslim Students Association, created by students from the Egypt-based Muslim Brotherhood and from the Pakistan-based Jamaati Islami movements.

In the domestic market, halal is very much inspired by the success of kosher.[31] Although they come from diverse backgrounds, Muslims in the United States are not defined by religious practices or by the Hanafi, Maliki, Shafi'i and Hanbali schools of jurisprudence (*madhhab*). In a liberal US context, the understanding of halal is plural and promotes the growth of business intermediaries. Since the start of the new millennium, dozens of new bodies have been established.[32] Some are attached to Islamic centres, others come from independent individuals and some are non-profit organizations.

The market for halal certification is totally free except in the states of New Jersey, Minnesota, Illinois, California, Michigan, Texas and Virginia, which have Halal Food Laws.[33] In these states, ritual meat must be labelled under conditions approved by the government. The aim is to ensure fair practices and to protect consumers against fraud and any abuses they might suffer. It is illegal to advertise or sell products labelled as halal unless they comply with the processes involved. In principle, Halal Food Laws are aligned with Kosher Food Laws, the first of which was initiated by the state of New York in 1915.[34] The first Halal Food Bills or Halal Consumer Protection Acts emerged in the 1990s. The first was established in New Jersey. The New Jersey model differs from that of New York in that no definition of kosher and halal terms is given *a priori* by the state. In New Jersey, the state monitors the compliance of products based on definitions developed by retailers themselves.[35] Since the state cannot define the religious norm, economic actors define standards following the religious model of their choice. These food laws raised considerable criticism almost immediately after being enacted, including the accusation of state interference in religious affairs.[36] But the procedures requesting abolition were dismissed based on the grounds that they were not hostile to religious freedom but instead guaranteed its possibility.[37]

Among other Muslim countries, the United States exports meat, food and other consumable products to Egypt, Saudi Arabia, Oman, Qatar, the United Arab Emirates, Pakistan, Indonesia and Malaysia. The US halal certification market is dominated by three major certification agencies: the Islamic Food and Nutrition Council of America (IFANCA); the Islamic Society of North America (ISNA); and the Islamic Services of America (ISA). Established in 1980, the Islamic Food and Nutrition Council of America (IFANCA[38]) is based in Chicago (Illinois) and is dedicated to the promotion and certification of halal in the food, cosmetic, chemical and packaging industries. It claims monopoly over US products for Malaysian certification, and accreditation of certification for all the other major importers from Southeast Asia such as Indonesia, Singapore, Thailand, the Phillipines, and also the Arab World League (Saudi Arabia).

Because of its current president Muhammad Chaudry, who is also an OIE[39] expert on issues of slaughter and animal welfare, and whose books on halal are seen as a halal benchmark in the agro-industrial sector, IFANCA became the most famous US certification agency. Chaudry advocates dual skilled certification, with expertise in religion and food technology. IFANCA also has a reputation for adapting to the constraints of the agro-industrial sector. It is one of the first to have developed a certification procedure for slaughtering plants and food processing. On slaughter, IFANCA accepts stunning, although it does not communicate on this sensitive issue. While in theory it accepts halal slaughter carried out by a Jew or a Christian, in practice it highlights the need to employ Muslims so that an Islamic blessing is given to the slaughtered animal. IFANCA initially communicated to producers and regulators of the halal market through technology and marketing conferences attended by religious leaders, academic experts and policy makers. It is only recently that they have developed communication tools directed at consumers through a website.

Established in 1981, the Islamic Society of North America (ISNA[40]) describes itself as the largest religious organization and Islamic educator in the United States. Its accreditation process, similar to IFANCA's, is considered strict and rigorous. Much like IFANCA, it claims the approval of JAKIM Malaysia. After a period of hard competition and conflict, ISNA now campaigns with IFANCA for the development of US halal standards and an accreditation body. The Islamic Services of America (ISA[41]), founded in 1975, claims to be the oldest certifying agency of the United States. Located in Iowa, this agency claims seniority in an area of high Muslim immigration, most notably Syrian, where the first Islamic mosque and Islamic cemetery in the United States were established. The Halal Food Council USA presents itself as the leading grassroots community organization providing international halal certification in North America. Its certification has governmental recognition from MUIS of Singapore and MUI of Indonesia. It is part of the Halal Food Council, an international network with linkages to other local Muslim organizations around the world (cf. infra).

European examples

Halal guarantees are varied in Europe. This plurality is related to the structural characteristics of markets, but also to the different status accorded by each country to religion and religious practices, the acceptability of religious visibility in general and Islam in particular, the level of Islamic organization activism and the population's sensitivity on animal welfare issues. European countries have been linked to the Muslim world since colonial times. The 1960s post-colonial period was marked by the growth of trade relations between European countries and their ex-colonies or protectorates (France with Maghreb and African countries, the United Kingdom with the Indian subcontinent and Egypt, the Netherlands with Indonesia etc.).

After the 1970s, the 'Islamization of food trade' by Iran and Saudi Arabia (cf. supra) was followed by other Muslim countries and became an emergent trade issue. Because of, or in spite of, their commitment to the separation of public and religious affairs, Europeans have been reluctant to regulate the market for halal certification. They have largely ignored the impact that battles for control of the market have on the organization of the religious field in their territories. Until the 1990s, the income of the halal market mainly benefited the industry. But with Islam emerging as the second religion in Europe, where millions of European

Union (EU) citizens are Muslims, the capture of economic and symbolic revenues from this expanding halal market presented a new challenge for Islamic groups. If the cultural, ethnic and linguistic diversity of European Muslims has often been considered by experts and researchers to be a major obstacle to the creation of a European Muslim diaspora, and therefore a barrier to a pan-Islamist activism, the growth of the halal market presents a significant challenge, as the new Islamic consumer culture promoted by the market through Islamic consumerism is fuelling the idea of a transnational Ummah. This is why the Islamic groups fighting for leadership are increasingly involved in a battle over halal certification. After a review of the main agencies of several western European countries, I propose a first classification of these agencies.

United Kingdom

Islam has had a long-established presence in the United Kingdom since the nineteenth century (Ansari 2004). After the latest main wave of immigration in the 1970s and 1980s from the Indian subcontinent, Africa, the Caribbean, and more recently the Balkans and the Middle East, Islam became the major non-Christian religion in the United Kingdom. Almost 3 million Muslims live in the United Kingdom, around 4.6 per cent of the total population, with nearly three-quarters coming from the subcontinent.

The United Kingdom does not fund religion, although the Anglican Church benefits from indirect public funding for the maintenance of religious buildings. Benefiting from a flexible legal framework, hundreds of Muslim organizations develop their activities through large organizations such as the British Muslim Parliament. The state contributes financially to the cost of maintenance of Muslim chaplains in prisons, hospitals and schools, and the Education Act 1944 recognizes the possibility of student absences for religious holidays.

Ritual slaughter is permitted through an exemption from the requirement for all animals to be stunned prior to killing, as is defined by the Slaughter of Poultry Act 1967 and the Slaughterhouse Act 1974. There are many organizations involved in the halal guarantee, but until relatively recently two dominated the market: the Halal Food Authority (HFA) and the Halal Monitoring Committee (HMC).[42]

The Halal Food Authority (HFA[43]) is a non-profit organization created in 1994, aiming to monitor and regulate the market for halal meat in the United Kingdom. It provides annual certification to meat producers, distributors and processors as well as for non-food products. It conducts audits and claims to have worked with the Food Standards Agency and the Department for Environment, Food and Rural Affairs (DEFRA). The Halal Monitoring Committee (HMC[44]) is based in Leicester and presents itself as a certification agency following strict Islamic requirements, including a guarantee of manual slaughter without stunning. The agency certifies several points along the chain of production and distribution of halal: slaughterhouse, processing plant, butcher, retailer and restaurants. It claims to distinguish itself from its main competitor HFA by sending inspectors to various sites for monitoring purposes to ensure compliance with their procedures.

France

France is the country with the largest number of Muslims in western Europe with about 4.7 million Muslims out of a total population of 66 million.[45] Muslims in France come mainly from North Africa (43.2 per cent in Algeria, 27.5 per cent and 11.4 per cent of Morocco to Tunisia), black Africa (9.3 per cent) and Turkey (8.6 per cent).[46] They arrived in successive waves of migration in the twentieth century, mainly during the 1970s and 1980s. French secularism established a regime of 'laïcité' in the so-called 'law of 1905' which 'guarantees the free exercise of religious worship' but 'does not recognize, pay, or subsidize any worship'. The tension between these two measures makes the French model unstable, going from open support of religion to strict unrecognition. France regulates ritual slaughter to allow Muslims to practise their religion, but refuses to regulate halal products in order to comply with its neutrality in religious matters.[47]

Associations linked to three great mosques (the Ritual Association of the Grand Mosque of Lyon, the Halal Certification of the Mosque of Évry, the French Society for Control of Halal Meat at the Mosque of Paris) dominate the market for halal certification in France alongside the independent association At Your Service (AVS). There are also dozens of minor associations. The three halal agencies linked to the mosques were created following the decision by the French government to grant these three mosques the power of distributing licences for Muslim slaughter. This decision has given them a competitive advantage in the market.

The French Society for Control of Halal Meat (SFCVH[48]) is empowered by the Great Mosque of Paris. It presents itself as a society for the control and certification of products along the production and distribution chain, outlining what is required to obtain a certificate. The SFCVH is a commercial enterprise[49] directed by Cherif Kriouche, an Algerian member of the Institute of the Mosque of Paris. It is the only company that declares its turnover publicly, estimated at €1,317,900 per year.[50]

Halal Certification at the Mosque of Évry[51] offers control through an annual inspection performed by a controller selected by mutual agreement by the mosque and the producer.

The Ritual Association of the Grand Mosque of Lyon (ARGML[52]) was created in 1995. ARGML is the only one of the three mosques that proposes permanent controls of the halal procedure. This costly choice brings some credibility in the certification market, as it is closer to the approach of the 'second-generation agencies' (cf. infra the classification). ARGML is opposed to stunning but tolerates it in some instances for poultry.

A Votre Service – At Your Service (AVS[53]) was created in 1991 by Youssef Baouendi, a computer engineer and a member of the Muslim World League, Lahcène Belatoui, a French Algerian, and Jean-Jacques Megaides Moussa, a French merchant, born a Jew who converted to Islam. The association was made up from volunteers who were primarily concerned with the origins of the meat sold as Islamic in the first halal butcheries. The association was the first European agency to develop control along the production chain to the butcher shop, a method inspired by the traceability of kashrut. Within a few years the association expanded across France and other European countries. It now draws its legitimacy from its seniority on the halal certification market, and also from its methods of control, which until recently were considered the strictest. Without religious or state support, AVS has established itself as a major player in halal certification in France, and has developed a unique (although somewhat partial) expertise.[54] The association knows very well how to showcase its market independence through a comprehensive website that very clearly informs visitors about the group's activities, putting equal emphasis on the religious, structural and functional parts of the agency. However, there is little transparency and AVS does not publicly declare its turnover. On stunning, AVS is like all second-generation agencies – hostile to stunning before slaughter as a selling point to attract consumers.

Spain

Out of a population of approximately 47 million there are almost 1 million Muslims in Spain. They are mainly from Morocco and to a lesser extent from the Middle East (Syria, Lebanon, Jordan and Iraq),[55] mostly from a relatively recent period of immigration dating back to the 1970s. For historical reasons, there is also a community of Spanish Muslims who have converted to Islam, some of whom are actively involved in Islamic organizations in Spain.

The Spanish Constitution of 1978, 'based on the principle of a democratic and pluralistic state', abolished the idea of 'state religion' and established the principle of religious freedom. In 1992, the Spanish parliament signed agreements of cooperation between the Spanish state and Muslims, recognizing the Islamic Commission of Spain (founded in 1991) as the sole representative of the Muslims in Spain. The Commission is represented by Muslims, including a number of Spanish converts; it preaches a liberal form of Islam and has issued a fatwa calling for the excommunication of the head of the attacks of 11 September 2001 in New York and Washington, Osama bin Laden. One of its members, also leader of the Junta Islamica Cordoba, has opened a debate on gay marriage.

The Islamic Commission of Spain has adopted a single regulator and certification of food products and services called 'Instituto Halal' (IH[56]). Although other European halal certificates are evident in Spain, IH has a quasi monopoly and is led by a woman of Spanish origin who converted to Islam (the presence of women is rare enough to be mentioned). The agency offers two distinct services: accreditation to companies wishing to sell halal branded Islamic Council warranted products and accreditation of consumption sites and their services. IH has adopted a fairly liberal view on stunning, which is permitted and considered positively. The slaughterer can be a woman, and can be Jewish or Christian (although a Muslim is preferred). This liberal position has not prevented IH from obtaining approval from the Indonesian Ulema Council (MUI Halal) and the United Arab Emirates (UAE). But, to date, IH is not recognized by JAKIM Malaysia. According to an interview conducted in 2009 with the head of the organization, the acceptance of systematic stunning before slaughter can be explained by the relatively high level of outdoor slaughter in Spain.

Netherlands

The number of Muslims in the Netherlands is estimated at 1 million[57] out of a total population of 16.8 million. Muslims in the Netherlands come from Surinam (with Indian or Indonesian roots), Indonesia, Turkey, Morocco, Iraq, Iran and various African countries. Mostly concentrated in big cities such as Amsterdam, The Hague, Rotterdam and Utrecht, Islam is the first non-Christian religion and the fourth in the country after Catholicism, Protestantism and Dutch Calvinism. Islam received direct funding from the state until 1983, when a separation between church and state was imposed. However, while the state no longer funds religious institutions, it still finances educational, social, cultural, charitable or spiritual activities, including the work of chaplains in prisons and other state institutions.

The Netherlands has maintained economic and cultural relations with its former colonial empire, especially within Southeast Asia. Its coastal location and historical ties with Indonesia have the potential to make Rotterdam the bridgehead of halal trade in western Europe. This is what motivated the port of Rotterdam to create the first distribution centre of halal products in western Europe in 2006, which now imports halal products from Indonesia and Malaysia by sea and distributes them across Europe.

The certification market is fairly active in the Netherlands and there are more than 30 certification bodies.[58] However, it is dominated by three main organizations: Halal Voeding in Voedsel, the Control Office of Halal Slaughtering and Halal Correct.

Halal Voeding in Voedsel (HVV[59]) is an organization headed by Abdul Qayyoem, a Surinamese chemist. It is controlled by a 'Majlis Al Ifta' (council of fatwas) and by an inspection service – the HFFIA (Halal Feed and Food Inspection Authority). HFFIA staff comprise employees and Muslim volunteers, specialized nutrition scientists, chemists, imams, slaughterers and inspectors; the association accepts some electrical stunning methods. The government regularly consults the HVV foundation and it is also working with industry heavyweights such as Campina, Friesland Foods and Nestlé for halal certification of their products. HFFIA is a member of the World Halal Council, an organization of Indonesian origin that includes certification agencies that operate on the principle of mutual recognition (cf. infra).

The Control Office of Halal Slaughtering or Halal Quality Control (HQC[60]) is based in The Hague. Established in 1980, this organization is one of the oldest in the Netherlands, aiming to provide the industry with Muslim slaughterers. In 1996, HQC established a certification agency, 'European Halal Certification Agency for Food and Nutrition', which issues the certificate 'Halal Quality Control' (HQC) for food for Muslim consumption. The agency is headed by Abdul Munim Al Chaman, an honorary consul of Syria, which has close ties with the embassies of Arab countries. This organization delivers its halal certificate on an annual basis and claims to organize spot checks. The Control Office of Halal Slaughtering is recognized by JAKIM Malaysia.

Halal Correct[61] was established in 1995 in Leiden. It is run by Abdel Fatteh Ben Ali-Salah, a Tunisian who is very critical of older agencies. Halal Correct has links in Belgium, Germany, France, the United Kingdom, Poland and the Czech Republic. It gained credibility in the certification market by opposing HVV and HQC, and by promoting the principle of the necessity of continuous assessment[62] throughout the food chain. Like all 'second-generation' agencies (see below), Halal Correct started out by offering local certification to extend to international certification. Through a website and through the organization of conferences, Halal Correct campaigns against halal audits without continuous control, against stunning and for the moralization of the field of certification.[63]

Austria

Out of a total population of 8.3 million, the number of Muslims in Austria is estimated to be 450,000.[64] Muslims are mostly of European origin from Bosnia, Turkey, Albania and Kosovo. More recent immigrants came from the Middle East, Afghanistan, Iran and Iraq. Austria is a secular republic that grants certain benefits to religious communities, including the freedom to teach in schools and tax benefits. Islamische Glaubensgemeinschaft in Österreich (IIGIO[65]) was recognized in 1979 as a representative body of Muslims by the Office of Religion under the Ministry of Culture and Education, which informally granted them power to ensure the halalness of products sold in Austria. This power was rapidly challenged due to the lack of halal regulations.

The Islamische Informations und Dokumentationszentrum Österreich (IIDZ) is an association that aims to support the Muslim community. Günther Ahmed Rusznak, an agro-food expert, who converted to Islam in 1995, is an outspoken opponent of IIGIO, which he considers a 'dictatorship' (he has taken the institution to court many times). As a supporter of an Austrian Islam, Rusznak was elected General Secretary of the IIDZ in 2005 before chairing the development in 2007 of an Austrian halal standard in collaboration with the Austrian Standards Institute.[66] Halal standard ONR 142000 'Halal Food – requirements of the food chain' was officially launched in 2009 to support the domestic economy in its new markets. To prevent the misuse of the term halal by IIGIO, Günther Ahmed Rusznak registered the term 'halal' within the Austrian Patent Office.[67] Accreditation from major halal customers in Austria, the UAE, Singapore, Malaysia and Turkey has allowed this initiative to succeed. It is a pioneering initiative in Europe in that it brings together leading religious figures, market actors and public regulation. The Austrian Standards Institute (ASI), with the support of Bosnia and Turkey, has asked the CEN[68] to study the feasibility of a European standard regulating the requirements for halal food (cf. infra).

A first classification of halal certification agencies in Europe

In an attempt to bring order to these different expressions of the market for Islamic certification, I distinguish between 'first-generation' and 'second-generation' halal certification agencies. I stick to the western European case that represents a large and diverse space for halal guarantee as outlined above. First and second generations differ on at least four points:

- the boundary of the target market (national or international)
- the method of control (audit or permanent)
- communication
- stunning.

Market

'*First-generation*' agencies address the needs of merchants. They are 'producer led', driven by mass production and naturally oriented towards international trade. The reputation of first generation agencies is built on the basis of accreditation by Muslim importing countries, by membership in international networks, by the size of their order book and/or by recognition from public institutions.

'*Second-generation*' agencies are primarily concerned with addressing consumer needs. They first target the domestic market and then the international market. They attempt to gain the trust of consumers in importing countries by gaining local trust. They promote the idea of a global and transnational consciousness, morality and solidarity among 'Muslim consumers' all around the world. These agencies claim to represent the voice of the Muslim consumer as defenders of the interests of Muslim minorities for the unity of the Ummah.

Halal activism

While first generation agencies proceeded by conducting audits and spot visits, second-generation agencies have introduced permanent quality control on food production. The first exponent of the second-generation model, inspired by the kashrut certification model, has been the French agency AVS (cf. supra). Given the low purchasing power of Muslim minorities in European countries, the approach is costly, but the benefits sought are moral and religious as well as economic. Second-generation agencies are often led by Muslim activists who challenge official Islamic institutions and see the control of halal as a matter of moralization of the religious field. They often denounce the corruption of rival Islamic institutions, and see their linkage with politics and industry players to be for the sake of money rather than religion. Over recent years, as the growth of the unregulated halal market has expanded, second-generation agencies have been quite successful in convincing and attracting increasingly suspicious Muslims.

Communication

The past few decades have been marked by a series of health crises in the agro-food sector. In Europe, self-control and communication to the public have become the primary means of regulating food safety and quality. Responsibility for health and ethics is increasingly aligned with consumers through the proliferation of labels; the consumer has no other option. Food producers and retailers are more often judged on their ability to display their commitment to transparency rather than on their control procedures, which are generally too complex for the consumer to understand. The norm of trust has gradually been replaced by the norm of distrust, which has led to a shift in the way the firms and certification agencies communicate.

Agencies of the first generation depend on institutional support to ensure their credibility. Agencies of the second generation adopt a strategy of 'displaying transparency' that also includes a detailed description of their competitors' fraudulent practices. The second generation is addressing consumers born (or educated) in Europe that have good educational and cultural capital, can read and write, and have developed a sense of criticism towards traditional institutions. They often have links with the Muslim consumer associations that have emerged over the past ten years. Their distrust strategy is also one of a 'pyromaniac fireman' who comes to put out his own fire. This is why second-generation agencies often disappear within a few months, killed off by their own attacks, suspected of the corruptions they denounce.

Second-generation agencies would not exist without the 'enemy', the first generation, while the latter generally ignores the existence of the second generation. The choice of terminology 'first' and 'second' comes from this one-way dependence, but also because the agencies often emerge from second-generation migrants, born or socialized in host countries. The strength of the first generation is its connection with Muslim countries (importers), while the strength of the second generation is cyberspace and communication tools that enable it to reach the consumerist 'Ummah'.

Stunning

Second-generation agencies openly oppose stunning, while the first avoid the issue. The model for these agencies is inspired and legitimized by the status of exception granted to shehita slaughter and kashrut agencies. The comparison is only limited: economic models of halal and kosher are different. The control of kashrut is attached to a local rabbinate, while halal is globalized and not necessarily connected to religious authorities. Nevertheless it is not uncommon to find second-generation agencies that accept a 'dose of stunning'. This is particularly the case in the poultry sector where the use of electrified stun baths before bleeding is widely accepted in order to maintain production speeds and profit margins. But this practice is kept confidential and it is often difficult to detect; slaughterhouses are very protected spaces, difficult to control even for public inspectors.

The differences are tiny and only symbolic between halal and non-halal and in many places halal slaughter is thus very similar to conventional slaughter. The majority of veterinary studies have demonstrated that stunning is less problematic for animals in mass production compared to not stunning.[69] However, by campaigning against stunning, second-generation agencies control the ethical and emotional value of animal killing and draw an ethical line between halal and haram. By making halal a religious, moral and ethical matter rather than an industrial one they reinforce their utility and necessity.

Conclusion: a plethora of certification, a marketing rather than a ritual differentiation

Issues of stunning and mechanization are important divergences between first- and second-generation agencies; most other differences are incidental. All advocate slaughter by a cut to the throat with a sharp tool, and all require that the animal is alive at the time of slaughter. All require the exclusion of pork or exogenous meat products during slaughter in the production process. Some add a number of steps such as the cleaning of the knife that should be out of sight of the animal and that the slaughterer should be a Muslim. But these measures are generally expected in abattoirs and are not subject to competition between agencies.

Finally, distinction points are usually economic and politico-religious issues rather than ritual or cultural differences that merge between Islamic schools of thought.[70] In reality, Islamic concepts of halal/haram can certainly differ among schools, groups or between individuals, but in its marketing application, halal standards are fairly similar with the exception of the issues of stunning, mechanization and the perimeter of controls. One will not find the normative model of halal in the Qur'an or the Sunnah, but rather in the marketing manuals. One can easily compare the standardization of halal to that of organic: issues such as the extent of the application of organic standards, tolerance to a percentage of genetically modified organisms (GMOs), the intervention of humans in the productive model arise in the same way in the case of organic if we replace GMO by pork or alcohol. However, if the comparison between organic and halal is very relevant from a technical point of view, it is much less so when it comes to the implementation of standards. In the case of organic, governments are ultimately responsible for enforcement of organic food in the name of consumer protection. In the case of halal, secular states are unwilling or unable to play this ultimate role of controller because it would infringe the principle of religious freedom.

The battle for halal certification reflects a global economic war that uses the ideological and symbolic resources of religion, wars that secular states hardly understand and are ill prepared to address. Exporting countries may at any time decide to change their standard, and importing countries close their borders to standards that are inconsistent. From the 2000s, we have seen the development of international halal standardization to protect consumers from these uncertainties by introducing regularity and predictability in transactions. What we now observe, behind the Islamic rhetoric about a 'single standard halal' consistent with Islam – highly unlikely given the idea of unified practice – is an ordinary trade war that is extraordinary in its global dimension.[71]

This chapter has attempted to provide an initial overview of the global market for halal certification. With the exception of those developed in Muslim countries, halal certification within the global assemblage comes from non-Muslim countries. These halal guarantees are always contracted on a voluntary basis. They are sold by a multitude of private agencies claiming to represent religious authorities or interests. The most important variations between standards are not due to different legal schools (*madhhab*) but are due to logical marketing differentiation on both economic and religious markets. I have reviewed some of the major certification agencies of the countries involved in the halal trade and stressed the importance of the issue of stunning of animals to distinguish what I called the first- and second-generation agencies.

Notes

1 The available estimations of the world halal market size are based on demographics and not on effective consumption, therefore we will not give these figures. Another indicator of the important progression of the halal market is the number of products launched with the halal claim. According to British marketing agency Mintel, some 12,154 new products and beverages were launched with the halal claim between January 2009 and November 2010 in the world. The trend is similar for cosmetic products (Bergeaud-Blackler forthcoming).
2 Stunning animals at the time of slaughter covers several techniques to immobilize and render the animal unconscious. The modern stunning techniques have progressively replaced old techniques aiming primarily to protect and facilitate the work of the slaughterer. In non-Muslim countries industrial stunning was made mandatory under pressure from animal rights lobbies. Nevertheless the majority of these countries provide exemptions for religious slaughter. See DIALREL European Commission Project, www.dialrel.eu.
3 Some of the references are taken from Bergeaud-Blackler and Bernard (2010).
4 In symbolical, geographical and political senses.
5 'Khomeini power play, Iran banned meat imports', *Washington Post*, 3 March 1979.
6 For demographic reasons, the Saudis could not send their own workers and supervisors anyway.
7 'It is estimated that there are 122 active halal certifying bodies around the world: "Halal in a box"', www.ihialliance.org/hiab.php, first published in 2009.
8 In demographic terms Asia and Southeast Asia focus the strongest Islamic population in the world.
9 www.muis.gov.sg/
10 http://e-lppommui.org/
11 The JAKIM created in 1997 has replaced the BAHEIS (Islamic Affairs Division). It is a religious authority attached to the Prime Minister, www.islam.gov.my.
12 Established in August 1967 in Bangkok, the founding fathers of ASEAN were Indonesia, Malaysia, the Philippines, Singapore and Thailand.
13 www.mihas.com.my/
14 Communication agency.
15 Quote of Prime Minister Abdullah Badawi. Halal menu 'should appeal to all', in BBC News, 8 May 2006, http://news.bbc.co.uk/2/hi/asia-pacific/4752081.stm.
16 *Ibid*.
17 Speech by Yab Dato' Seri Abdullah Haji Ahmad Badawi, Prime Minister of Malaysia at the official launch of the Malaysian International Halal Showcase (MIHAS) 2004, Kuala Lumpur, 16 August 2004, source: www.pmo.gov.my/ucapan/~m=p&p=2880&id=paklah.

18 Proposal made at the conference of foreign ministers of the OIC that took place in Sanaa in 2005, *OIC Journal*, Issue No. 14, August 2010.
19 A multilateral economic and commercial cooperation platform of the Islamic world, www.comcec.org/.
20 Mechanism for harmonization of standards among the Organisation of Islamic Cooperation (OIC).
21 'Food: Morocco, Halal certification regulation ready' 2 May 2014, ANSAm., www.ansamed.info/ansamed/en/news/sections/economics/2012/05/22/Food-Morocco-Halal-certification-regulation-ready–6914352.html.
22 www.imanor.ma/index.php/Certification/LABEL-NATIONAL-HALAL
23 www.innorpi.tn/Fra/produits halal–7–274
24 This would need a systematic survey.
25 Pew Research Center (2010).
26 Meat Industry Association, www.mia.co.nz/industry–information/FAQ-halal/index.htm.
27 Pew Research Center (2010).
28 http://meatexportaustralia.webs.com/
29 Campaigns against live exports have been running since the 1980s, www.banliveexport.com/facts/.
30 Source: www.banliveexport.com/facts/halal.php.
31 Today in the United States, there are more than 10,000 manufacturers of kosher products for 135,000 certified products consumed by more than 12 million American consumers; only 8 per cent of these consumers are religious Jews (Lytton 2013).
32 Marei (2001).
33 The first halal food law was passed on 6 March 2000 in New Jersey. Other Halal Food Laws have followed in Minnesota and Illinois in 2001, in California and Michigan in 2002 and in Texas and Virginia in 2003.
34 The New York initiative has subsequently inspired many other states.
35 *Buying Kosher Food*, 'Regulations Governing the Sale of Food Kosher Represented as Koscher' brochure published by the New Jersey Division of Consumer Affairs, www.njconsumeraffairs.gov/brief/kosher.pdf.
36 Gutman (1999).
37 Masoudi (1993).
38 www.ifanca.org/
39 The OIE is the intergovernmental organization responsible for improving animal health worldwide, www.oie.int.
40 www.isna.net/
41 www.isaiowa.org/
42 For details on the UK halal market: Lever *et al.* (2010); Lever and Miele (2012). For a comparison between HFA and HMC see Harvey (2010).
43 www.halalfoodauthority.co.uk/
44 www.halalhmc.org/
45 Pew Research Center (2010).
46 Tribalat (2004).
47 Cesari (2010).
48 www.sfcvh.com
49 A 'SASU', a 'Société par actions simplifiée à associé unique'.
50 www.societe.com/societe/societe-francaise-de-controle-de-viande-hallal-sfcvh-415223544.html
51 www.mosquee-evry.fr
52 www.hallal.mosquee-lyon.org/
53 www.halal-avs.com/
54 Brahimi and Otmani (2010).
55 Pew Research Center (2010).

56 www.institutohalal.com
57 Pew Research Center (2010).
58 Van der Meulen (2011).
59 www.halal.nl/
60 www.halaloffice.com/
61 www.halalcorrect.com/
62 'The bulk of the European halal market is in the hands of scoundrels', says Abdel Fattah Ben Ali-Salah [...] He goes on to say that 'documents of his certifying bureau are forged en-masse for meat cargoes which don't deserve the title of halal', source: www.volkskrant.nl/vk/nl/2686/Binnenland/article/detail/361160/2009/11/27/Onduidelijke-handel-in-halal certificaten-blijkt-zeer-lucratief.dhtml.
63 Total Quality Halal Correct Certification (TQHCC) held a European Halal Food Conference on 3 December 2012 entitled 'Will it still be possible for the Muslim consumer to eat chicken after January 1, 2013'?
64 Pew Research Center (2010).
65 www.derislam.at/
66 Interview with Günther Ahmed Rusznak, Muslim Markt, 27 October 2009, www.muslim-markt.de/interview/2009/rusznak.htm.
67 Caseau (2010).
68 The European Committee for Standardization (CEN), source: www.cen.eu/.
69 Anil (2012).
70 Often it is said that standards are different because of the plurality of Islamic schools of law, national or ethnic differences between groups of migrant consumers, or personal preferences. This is the preconception of many economic analyses, including one of the most interesting written by van Waarden and van Dalen (2011).
71 Cf. Chapter 12 in this book: Who owns halal? Five international initiatives of halal food regulations by Florence Bergeaud-Blackler.

Bibliography

Anil, H. (2012) 'Religious slaughter: a current controversial animal welfare issue', *Animal Frontiers*, 2 (3): 64–67.
Ansari, H. (2004) *The Infidel within: The History of Muslims in Britain, 1800 to the Present*, London: Hurst and Company.
Bergeaud-Blackler, F. (forthcoming) Le 'Halal World' pour les marchands un conte néo-libéral du XXI siècle? in *Les Sens du Halal*, Editions CNRS.
Bergeaud-Blackler, F. and Bernard, B. (2010) *Comprendre le halal*, Edipro.
Brahimi, M. and Otmani, F. (2010) *Le Marché du Halal – Entre références religieuses & contraintes industrielles*, Editions Tawhid.
Caseau, J. (2010) 'L'économie, porte d'intégration des Musulmans en Occident? Le cas des Musulmans d'Autriche', *EurOrient, Regards croises sur l'Occident*, 31.
Cesari, J. (2010) *Muslims in the West After 9/11: Religion, Law and Politics*, Routledge, p. 254.
Fischer, J. (2011) *The Halal Frontier: Muslim Consumers in a Globalized Market (Contemporary Anthropology of Religion)*, Palgrave Macmillan.
Gutman, B. (1999) 'Ethical eating: applying the kosher food regulatory regime to organic food', *The Yale Law Journal*, 108 (8): 2351–2384.
Harvey, R. (2010) 'Certification of halal meat in the UK', HRH Prince Alwaleed Bin Talal, *Centre of Islamic Studies*, 1 November.
Lever, J. and Miele, M. (2012) 'The growth of halal meat markets in Europe: an exploration of the supply side theory of religion', *Journal of Rural Studies*, 28 (4): 528–37.
Lever, J., Puig, M., Miele, M. and Higgin, M. (2010) 'From the slaughterhouse to the consumer: transparency and information in the distribution of halal and kosher meat', *Dialrel Research Report WP 4.4*, www.dialrel.eu.

Lytton, T. D. (2013) *Kosher: Private Regulation in the Age of Industrial Food*, Harvard University Press.

Marei M. H. (2001) 'A rising star: halal consumer protection laws', Working Paper, Harvard Law School.

Masoudi, S. (1993) 'Kosher food regulation and the religion clauses of the First Amendment', *The University of Chicago Law Review*, 60 (2): 667–96.

Pew Research Center (2010) Pew Research Center's Religion & Public Life Project, www.globalreligiousfutures.org/.

Tribalat, M. (2004) 'The number of Muslims in France, what do we know?' In Y. C. Zarka, S. Taussig and C. Fleury (eds.), *Islam in France*, Paris, PUF, p. 733.

Van der Meulen, J. (2011) 'Private food law Governing food chains through contract law, self-regulation, private standards, audits and certification schemes', *European Institute for Food Law*, Vol. 6.

Van Waarden, F. and van Dalen, R. (2011) *Hallmarking Halal: The Market for Halal Certificates: Competitive Private Regulation*, JPRG Paper No. 33, March.

8

GREEN HALAL: HOW DOES HALAL PRODUCTION FACE ANIMAL SUFFERING?

Manon Istasse

Introduction

In this chapter, I examine the ways in which halal production addresses the ethical debate about animal suffering. Ethics re-emerged as a topic of interest in the social sciences in the 1990s, partly due to the rise of a number of issues linked to social development, including a crisis in values, debates about bio-ethics and the rise of individualism, etc. (Genard, 1992). Ethics – defined as a kind of reflexivity and normativity that, on the basis of the moral principle of Good, proposes ways for human beings to behave – had until this point largely been missing from social science debate. Ethics is however closely linked to responsibility (Genard, ibid.). A close look at ethical matters and human responsibility thus allows us to shed some light on two human features. The first is the attachment of human actors to specific causes and values that allow the evaluation of human situations. This attachment is affective, linked to emotions and passions, and cognitive, in that individuals can explain the reasons for their attachment. Responsibility toward ethical issues then justifies acts according to one's principles or outrage at human and non-human suffering. Second, responsibility sheds light on practical expertise, competences, capacities and knowledge of human actors who take position in a situation, and refer to several kinds of tools in order to act responsibly and appropriately (Genard, ibid.).

In this chapter, I investigate the attachment and the practical expertise of human actors taking part in an ethical issue, namely non-human animal suffering. Scholars and militants think about animal rights, animal welfare, animal cognition or the concept of non-human personhood (Eisnitz, 1997; Al-Hafiz and Masri, 2007; Armstrong and Botzler, 2008). I more particularly address the way Muslims face the issue of stunning animals before slaughter. Stunning challenges the ideal of Muslim ritual slaughter. Alongside the ban on eating pork and drinking alcohol, Muslim ritual slaughter is probably the most notable aspect of the development of halal food standards. In a similar way to halal as a way of life, these standards include rules and express values, like respect for Allah, animals and human health. Halal food standards and their values then closely link to food safety, understood as both the safety of the body and the safety of the soul. Muslims thus give a prime importance to the quality of their food, this quality being material and moral (van Waarden and van Dalen, 2013). Debates about food quality are due to the numerous interpretations of halal standards that have prevented the emergence of clear norms defining quality, which include the issue of stunning before slaughter.

So how do proponents and opponents of ritual slaughtering engage in ethical reflection and practice? In order to answer this question, I take as a case study a Belgian association, Green Halal, which promotes a new Muslim ethic, part of which is ethical halal. Meriem, a Belgian with Moroccan origins, and Gerlando, a Belgian from Sicily, created this association in 2010 because of their concerns about the traceability of halal meat in Belgium, which is available in butchers and supermarkets. Since 2008, supermarket managers have been aware of the importance of the halal business in Belgium and have stocked and sold halal products, particularly during Muslim celebrations (Ramadan, Aïd el-Kebir). Meriem and Gerlando now regularly sell consignments of ethical halal meat – beef and chicken. The halal quality of this meat is not problematic as a Muslim slaughterer enabled by the Belgian Muslim Executive sacrifices the animals. The ethical quality, however, is not so simple to ensure and animal welfare constitutes a cornerstone of the Green Halal ethic.

In investigating this ethical debate, I look closely at the topics and issues this book aims to shed light on, that is to say, practices, discourses and policies that are part of the halal global form. According to Ong and Collier (2006), global forms territorialize in assemblages in specific locations through technologies, politics, economy, religion and ethics. Numerous variables are part of the halal assemblage as it has territorialized in Belgium, including halal rules and religious prescriptions. In this chapter, I first present the assemblage surrounding ethical halal, that is to say, the political, economic and technological variables shaping the global form in Belgium. I continue with a presentation of Green Halal and its approach to ethical halal. I describe the general approach of Green Halal as an ethic promoting the respect for animals, human beings and the environment. I next turn to the specific issue of stunning before slaughter. I take as an example the Belgian society Group of Action for the Interest of Animals (GAIA) that broadcast a radio message in 2013 asking the Belgian government to ban ritual slaughter without stunning one week before the Aïd el-Kebir (Feast of Sacrifice). I also discuss how the members of Green Halal react to campaigns implemented by societies for the prevention of cruelty to animals and how, beyond the legal context, opponents and proponents of stunning and ritual slaughter argue on the basis of scientific research. I finally describe how Green Halal initiators try to reduce sheep's stress during their sacrifice as a glaring example of their ethical enactment.

Before reaching the core of the chapter, let me introduce the methodology underlying the information and research provided. The information I present comes from fieldwork that took place in two main places. I first spent time with Green Halal initiators and Green Halal members during private meetings, two meat sales and the projection of a movie, followed by a debate with the film producer and a day in a slaughterhouse during the Aïd el-Kebir on 17 October 2013. In this first phase, I mainly observed and conducted semi-structured interviews and informal discussions. Second, I used the Internet, and more particularly the GAIA website, the Green Halal blog, its newsletter and websites of Muslims' consumer associations such as Al Kanz. I also browsed the website to find laws related to ritual slaughter, and websites of associations for the protection of animal welfare.

Ethical halal as an assemblage

A focus on ethics should not exclude other variables, that is to say technology, economy, religion and politics. Two main technologies surround the emergence of ethical halal in Belgium. The first of them is the Internet. Turner and Nasir (2013) have shown how the use of new media – web-based information systems – allows the spread of alternative, local opportunities to debate, discuss and spread religious information and issues. The Internet also allows Belgian Muslim consumers to have an idea of the ways of consumption in other European countries. The initiators of Green Halal clearly took inspiration from British associations promoting organic halal food – Abraham Natural Produce and Willowbrook Organic Farm. They moreover encourage the 30 Green Halal members to adopt an 'ethic of consumption' by providing information and advice on the Green Halal blog (http://greenhalal.over-blog.com). The second technology relates to the various ways of stunning animals before slaughter – electric shock and stunbolt gun. The latter however depends on the availability of slaughterhouses allowing Muslims to sacrifice their animals, which links to the religious context in Belgium.

Islam has been an official religion in Belgium since 1974 and the Belgian Muslim Executive is the official interlocutor with the Belgian government. This Executive also receives core funding for the salary of imams, the purchase and the maintaining of mosques, among other things. Although Islamic religious teachers are paid for by the state, private Muslim schools are not funded. The Belgian government also enacts specific rules for Muslims and their rituals. For instance, European Union (EU) legislation does not impose stunning for ritual slaughter. The Directive 93/119/EC requires that animals are spared any avoidable excitement, pain or suffering during slaughter, killing and related operations, both inside and outside slaughterhouses. But the European Convention for the Protection of Animals for Slaughter, article 17, specifies that 'each Contracting Party may authorise derogations from the provisions concerning prior stunning […] in accordance with religious rituals'. Belgium follows this exception. The 14/08/1986 Act for the protection and welfare of animals, article 16, §1, imposes stunning before any slaughter. But article 2, §2 of this same Act introduces derogation for ritual slaughter. The 11/02/1988 Royal Decree then describes the prescriptions in case of ritual slaughter. The Walloon Minister of Animal Welfare is in charge of applying these policies in the French-speaking part of the country – since July 2013 animal welfare has been a regional and not a federal competence.

This Act is important for the halal market in Belgium. There are about 600,000 Muslims in Belgium and the Flemish Department for Agriculture and Fisheries estimated that in 2013 the Belgian halal market was worth around 1.7 billion euros.[1] Muslims in Belgium have access to halal food, halal restaurants, halal beauty products, halal drinks, halal insurance policies, halal travel, etc. The halal food market is growing and is more successful than the organic movement.[2] Halal products produced in Belgium are mainly exported to Muslim countries. Several bodies grant halal certification in Belgium, including Eurohalal and Halal Expertise. In 2010, the Chamber of Commerce in Brussels introduced halal certification for drinks and beauty products in order to help Belgian entrepreneurs operating in the European and international halal market. The abundance of halal certifying bodies is seen by many to be problematic. According to the Belgian Halal Federation, about 60 per cent of all halal commodities sold in Belgium are impure and have fake certification – it is easy to buy a halal certificate. This situation makes the quest for good halal more and more important for consumers.[3] Asked in 2005 if organic halal would be the next big thing, Shaharudin et al. (2010) suggested that organic food is directly related to halal food in Malaysia. Although this link is not yet obvious in Western countries, it is interesting to examine its appearance.

In Belgium, this quest for quality halal is present in the development of organic halal, mainly meat, sold by organic farmers such as Aux Délices du Terroir, Coprosain and Muslim associations such as Green Halal. In their study of the trust that Muslim consumers have in the status of halal meat control in Belgium, Bonne and Verbeke (2006) describe the various places where Muslims buy meat – the supermarket, Muslim butchery, Belgian butchery and farm. Moreover, they found out that Muslims first and foremost trust their butcher. This trust is however declining among younger generations, who prefer buying meat in supermarkets or directly from the farm or the slaughterhouse. Finally, the authors underline that health and respect for animals and religious identity were the three main factors influencing the consumption of halal meat.

As such, a specific political context surrounds the rise of ethical halal in Belgium. Among food movements, Green Halal's concern for ethical food links it to broader political food movements that are creating new markets. The quest for ethical food is not specific to Green Halal. Alternative food networks, such as Slow Food or the agro-ecological movement, also promote ethical food (Holloway et al., 2006). They try to implement solutions to social, economic and political problems. Barnett et al. (2005) define ethical consumption as a mode of political participation, as being an ideological fertile ground for political and identity reactions, and as a way to resist capitalism and industrial food. In a similar way, some social science researchers define citizens as members of resistance movements linked to food activism or social food movements (Levkoe, 2013). However, the approach of Green Halal viewed through this political lens would be too reductive to grasp the general dynamic pursued by this association. The Green Halal initiative is defined by the quest for quality. Since the 1990s, consumers, producers and social science researchers have focused on the quality of food products, after what Goodman (2003) coined the 'quality turn'. Researchers have generally defined food quality as a complex notion with multiple sides whose measure is difficult. Quality has nutritional, health, organoleptic and symbolic aspects and although it is complex quality still influences the choice of consumers. Prigent-Simonin and Hérault-Fournier (2005) highlight the numerous devices assuring consumers about the quality of food. These devices are impersonal – clear information and traceability, brand, label, price – or personal – confidence, face-to-face relations between producers and consumers, and knowledge.

Quality also takes multiple forms: the local, ecological, fairly traded or halal. The latter was and still is at the core of numerous studies about, amongst other things, the socio-technical construction of halal quality (Bonne and Verbeke, 2006) and the dynamics of halal certification (Brahami and Otmani, 2010). It is essential to understand why quality has become so important, how individuals give importance to quality, and more specifically ethical quality. Such investigations allow us to understand the link between global halal assemblages, regimes of ethics and situated practices and discourses. The theory of conventions (Boltanski and Thévenot, 1991) helps me to deal with the multiple forms of ethic present in this article. Ethic appears to be a quality, a worth, and not a world or a justification. This ethical worth may be defined as a kind of reflexivity and normativity that, on the basis of the moral principle of Good, proposes good human behaviour.

Two main consequences stem from the presence of ethic in multiple worlds. First, the ethical worth, or quality, cannot be taken for granted: it does not essentially stick to things but results from a process of qualification. Second, the ethical worth draws both distinction and connections between human collectives. On the one hand, the process of qualification makes ethical food different and collectives claim to be as ethical as possible. On the other hand, ethical concerns link Green Halal with broader food movements – and the human collectives that lead them and are concerned with the quality of food.

Green Halal and the 'ethic of consumption'

Meriem and Gerlando created Green Halal in 2010 after they had seen the documentary 'We feed the world', which is about industrial animal breeding and slaughter. Muslim and former meat-eater Gerlando became aware of a lack of traceability of the meat he ate. He thus decided to buy meat only when he could be sure of its origin. The difficulties of finding traceable halal meat led him and his wife to create their own association in order to provide themselves, their family and their acquaintances with halal meat of traceable origin.

Green Halal is a unique initiative in Belgium. Meriem often evokes the presence of more associations of this kind in the United Kingdom (UK) where, according to her, 'Muslims are better organised than in Belgium'. She finds it regrettable that there is a lack of involvement among Belgian Muslims in questions related to their food, and good food more particularly. Despite great enthusiasm after the creation of the association, no Green Halal member has been willing to get involved in the activities of the association over the long term. Such were the demands and intensity of their work, Meriem and Gerlando had to stop all activities for six months during 2012 in order to rest and to take care of their children because the management of the association was taking up all their free time; Meriem works in a pharmaceutical lab and Gerlando is a sales agent for a firm in Brussels. Green Halal is therefore not as successful as it could be, despite the importance of the Belgian halal market. Meriem and Gerlando have not yet created a group of responsible and involved 'consumer-actors'. There are nonetheless about 30 members in the association from 15 households. All of them live in a city, and none of them consume what they produce. If they cannot be defined as economic elites, these households belong to the middle class, as at least one family member works as an engineer, a civil servant or a teacher. Their interest in ethical halal meat can be directly aligned with an interest for organic food – they buy food in organic shops – and sustainable goods – such as those labelled by Max Havelaar. However, unlike Max Havelaar, Green Halal does not have a label certifying products halal or endorsing the ethical quality of their meat. The measure of these qualities then depends on values, conventions, social relations, sensual and affective perceptions or non-professional knowledge. Meriem and Gerlando, who are by no means meat experts or halal certifiers, rely on confidence and trust. They propose fair prices for their meat; they allow members to attend slaughter; they insist on the importance of direct sales without the intermediary of a butcher; and they provide information about their practices on their blog.

By selling halal and ethical meat, Meriem and Gerlando want to promote a green Islam, a new Islamic ethic. They gather their work around the green of both Islam and ecology. In order to claim and to promote a greener halal, Meriem and Gerlando spread information via their blog. They also organize activities, such as discussion evenings. Their main activity is however the sale of meat – beef and chicken – consignments. For instance, beef consignments are composed of 5 kilos of meat (2.5 kilos of steak and 2.5 kilos of minced meat). The cost is 55 euros and the aim is to provide a couple with two children with meat for one month. Meriem and Gerlando are keen to reduce meat consumption: Meriem says that this is a matter of consuming less, and consuming better, and consuming a 'happy meat'. In opposition to halal viewed in line with the 'spirit of consumption', as a huge market and an industry destroying the environment, Meriem and Gerlando promote an 'ethic of consumption'. The promotion of this ethic however differs from the organic food movement from which Meriem and Gerlando want to distance themselves. For instance, organic and halal meat sold by Bionoor under the label 'Tendre France' does not guarantee the respect for animals during breeding and slaughter. However, respect for animals, as well as religious behaviour and attention given to incorporated food, constitutes the cornerstone of Green Halal's ethic of consumption. This ethic may then be defined as principles that any Muslim has to respect in the context of his or her diet in order to respect the environment, human beings and animals. Meriem and Gerlando gather these principles into three categories.

First of all, Meriem and Gerlando recommend behaving according to religious values and prescriptions. On their blog, they often refer to the Koran and Hadîths to justify the respect for God's creations and the respect for the ecological balance – 'Even if the end of time is upon you and you have a seedling in your hand, plant it!' (Ahmad); 'Whoever kills a sparrow or anything bigger than that without a just cause, Allah will hold him accountable on the Day of Judgement. The listeners asked, O Messenger of Allah, what is a just cause? He replied, That he will kill it to eat, not simply to chop off its head and then throw it away' (an-Naissaï). They explain that in the Koran, God advises behaviour with restriction and moderation, to maintain the balance of creation, to research the happy medium in any behaviour, including food consumption. Green Halal then promotes ecologically aware ablutions (i.e. ablutions using a minimum of water) and a vegan Ramadan. In 2012, Meriem sent out an invitation for members to follow advice for a vegan Ramadan. It was about eating no meat or food products derived from animals. According to her, this practice allows for a better spiritual renewal of the body and the mind by nourishing the body properly and by emptying the mind from any matter linked to the purchase of food and to the preparation of meals. Through these actions, Meriem and Gerlando invite Green Halal members to respect and maintain the ecological balance. These concerns are by no means new. The medieval Arab dietetics is based on the theory of humours inherited from the ancient Greek civilization as a science of balance and measure (Garcia Sanchez, 2007). On this account, in order to work properly, the human body should be in harmony with Nature.

Second, Meriem and Gerlando give advice on eating healthy food to maintain good health. Their blog is full of information about health, such as the World Health Organization (WHO) recommendations for meat consumption – no more than 400 grams per person per week; descriptions of diseases linked to meat (over)-consumption (cardiovascular problems, obesity, high cholesterol, high blood pressure); warnings about the presence of antibiotics in meat that make bacteria resistant in human bodies; assertions that industrial food is dead and contains no nutritional elements. According to Meriem, the abundance of food in Western society goes hand in hand with the bad quality of food products sold in supermarkets. On the blog, she invites readers to follow seven pieces of advice in order to eat 'saintly and cleverly' – it is a word play in French between 'sain', healthy, and 'saint', saintly. The implication is that readers should eat organic and local products in order to help the local economy; buy seasonal products in order to eat food with a good nutritional quality; reduce meat consumption; buy fair-trade products; grow fruits and vegetables (even on the balcony); compost leftovers in order to maintain an ecological balance; cook healthily (e.g. to avoid the use of aggressive modes of cooking such as the pressure cooker). As this advice suggests, 'eating healthily' by selecting food of quality and 'eating saintly' by respecting religious prescriptions are synonyms. Halal and *tayyib* (pure, healthy) go hand in hand.

Finally, Meriem and Gerlando are committed to respecting animals during their breeding and at slaughter. Gerlando chooses animals bred in Belgium and they travel neither before nor after slaughter. They pasture outdoors and are not confined in barns. Moreover, they are fed with food containing no genetically modified organism (GMO) and no animal flour. Furthermore, the absence of antibiotics and hormones in the meat consequently gives it a better taste, according to Gerlando. Meriem and Gerlando prefer the notion of sacrifice to that of slaughter and it appears that they want to return to the Prophet's practice of sacrifice, which could be perceived as a myth. They refer to the passages in the Koran that point out that animals should be killed without pain and undue stress. Mercy Slaughter, an American Muslim slaughterhouse, personifies this approach and its respect for animals. On YouTube, Mercy Slaughter post videos showing how to treat animals before sacrificing them. These videos also highlight the importance of sacrificing animals at home. But this mode of sacrifice is impossible in Belgium where it is unlawful to slaughter animals at home. Since 1952 an expert must evaluate any meat to be sold in a shop and animals can only be slaughtered in a slaughterhouse. Mercy Slaughter's approach also underlines the fact that it is impossible to slaughter high numbers of animals using this approach. As a consequence, Meriem and Gerlando promote slaughterhouse infrastructure designed by Temple Grandin in the United States. This ethologist proposes a method to improve the circulation of animals in slaughterhouses in order to reduce their stress. A corridor in the shape of a snail's shell, for instance, does not allow animals to see what is ahead, that is to say the disappearance of other animals.

At first sight, it appears that Green Halal reduces various uncertainties that Muslim consumers encouter in non-Muslim countries. The various interpretations of halal food standards, long global food chains, new food technologies, multiculturalism, rumours, etc. make halal markets more opaque and increase uncertainties about the quality of food. Green Halal, an association based in a Western multicultural and non-Muslim country, makes the systems of production and distribution more visible to the consumer, who can have direct access to information about the origin of animals and the place of slaughter, if of course they do not attend the slaughter. Green Halal moreover shortens the food chain, as animals are only raised, slaughtered and sold in Belgium. According to van Waarden and van Dalen (2013), Green Halal is part of an 'aunt-and-uncle' market, an informal local domestic market based on networking, trust (and gossip), self-certification and personal reputation. Most non-Muslim Belgians however do not know about this local and informal food chain. In their view, ritual slaughter does not take account of animal welfare and animal suffering before and during slaughter.

Animal suffering: the ethical debate between GAIA and Green Halal

In October 2013, a week before Aïd el-Kebir, GAIA sent an audio message to Belgian politicians to ask them to ban ritual slaughter without stunning. Some days later, national radio stations spread the same audio message:

Masculine voice: 'They have come to take us early this morning. We were still sleeping. I woke up because of the car doors. They shouted at us in this language that none of us understand and they put us in the truck. On the way, I noticed that we haven't taken the usual road. The route was longer than usual. The truck finally stopped in front of a cold and stinking building in which we are now locked up. It is freaky: the cries, the smell and all this red on the ground. I know how it is going to end. I'm not stupid. But what can I do? Except waiting for this guy with a knife and wearing a less-and-less white apron to come and take me.'

Feminine voice: 'Without stunning, animals are aware of what happens in slaughterhouses. Dear politicians, prevent them from fear and pain during sticking without stunning. Improve the law and impose stunning before a ritual slaughtering. More information on gaia.be.'[4]

GAIA intends to give voice to the voiceless and fights against animal suffering. Ritual slaughter is one of its campaigns: 'Slaughter without stunning, suffering for a tradition.' For over five years, GAIA shot movies in Belgian slaughterhouses and temporary slaughter plants during the Aïd el-Kebir to expose animal suffering. It has conducted opinion polls to show that Belgian people are in favour of stunning. It has also implemented actions by mail and e-mail to ask politicians to change the law concerning ritual slaughter and to follow the example of the Netherlands, which has required stunning for any kind of slaughter since June 2011.

GAIA wants all animals slaughtered for meat to have the same protection at the time of killing in order to limit their pain. This protection should be reached by ending the exception authorizing the practice of ritual slaughter without stunning.[5] Undue suffering at slaughter stands at the core of GAIA discourse. For instance, on 29 October 2012 its president Michel Vandenbosch wrote on the GAIA website:[6]

Friday, 26th of October, day of the Feast of Sacrifice, I went to the temporary slaughtering site of Park Spoor Noord in Antwerp. The 1,700 sheep slaughtered from 9 a.m. to 7 p.m. have been sacrificed in the respect of the law but without stunning. [...] Every slaughter or so went wrong and I had to step in in order to prevent animals from even more serious injuries. [...] Was it worth doing? In this context, I did what I could to reduce animal suffering. I could not help but notice that all of them suffered.[7]

In September 2014, a demonstration organized by GAIA attracted about 10,000 people onto the streets of Brussels. The GAIA president asked in a speech 'which politician, which party, which parliamentarian, which minister, which government will finally take responsibility?' Two days later, the Walloon Minister for Animal Welfare, Carlo Di Antonio, called for the banning of ritual slaughter without stunning in Belgium and in Europe.

Many welfare groups and academics share the underlying concern for animal welfare. French welfare groups also have such campaigns. The UK is probably the country where animal welfare groups – the British Humanist Association, the Farm Animal Welfare Council, the British Veterinary Association – and the public have the greatest voice for the prohibition of slaughter without stunning. As a consequence, there is little ritual slaughter without stunning in the UK and some welfare groups still fight for a legal ban (www.bbc.co.uk/news/uk-17966327). These welfare groups mainly ask three questions regarding ritual slaughter:

- is there pre-slaughter stress? (Grandin and Regenstein, 1994),
- is the neck incision painful? (Gibson et al., 2009) and
- are sensibility and consciousness lost quickly enough following exsanguination by neck cutting (Grandin and Regenstein, ibid.)?

Only the second and third questions are specific to ritual slaughter. There are two major camps about the pain issue. Some think the cut is quick and painless and agree with ritual slaughter without stunning. Others claim that severe pain is inevitable. Both camps rely on scientific methods to measure pain. Proponents of ritual slaughter assert that nothing proves that stunning reduces pain, while opponents argue that there is no proof that cutting the neck is not painful. The time delay to loss of consciousness after the neck is cut is another concern. Researchers study time to loss of brain function and report evidence that neck cutting may delay time to loss of consciousness (Anil et al., 1995).

How do European Muslims engage in this debate? Since the early 1990s, more Muslims have become opposed to stunning (Bergeaud-Blackler, 2012). According to them, an animal slaughtered without stunning is *mayta*: any animal that doesn't die from exsanguination is, according to the Islamic ritual, unsuitable for consumption. Furthermore, Muslims suppose that stunning prevents blood from flowing correctly and then prevents bacteria contained in this blood to be expelled. The meat is then impure and not fit for consumption. During the 1990s, Muslims declared stunning as non-ritual. In the early 2000s, the absence of stunning started to add value to halal meat, thus testifying to the halal quality of products and distinguishing them from impure products.

Rather than interviewing Muslims opposed to stunning and Muslims involved in the industrial production of halal meat, I interviewed Muslim members of the association Green Halal who were concerned about ethical issues related to animal welfare. All of them were opposed to stunning for several reasons. There is first a religious justification, as God and the Prophet Mohammed recommend a sacrifice without stunning. Moreover, according to several members, stunning is a technique to kill animals that does reduce their suffering. For instance, nothing guarantees that chickens survive electro-narcosis. After talking about these issues, Gerlando and Meriem added free-range chicken in the meat consignment in December 2014 because they were certain that such chickens do not experience electro-narcosis and are fed with 100 per cent organic food. More radically, Gerlando and Meriem define stunning as an additional suffering for animals, be it prior to or post-stunning. According to them, industrial slaughter rather than ritual slaughter is a source of suffering. As Gerlando declared, 'we have to show non-Muslims that ritual slaughtering is a benediction for animals if it is done correctly', that is to say by a good slaughterer who knows where to cut, cuts only once, and doesn't follow an industrial method.

Green Halal members also refer to scientific justifications. They mentioned various individuals who they referred to as experts: Bernadette Bresard, a French veterinarian; Temple Grandin, an American ethologist; Joe Regenstein, referred to as an academic – but in fact an academic from Cornell highly involved in halal certification; and Yves-Marie Le Bourdonnec, defined as an expert, but, in fact, a French butcher. All of these individuals agree with ritual slaughter without stunning. Some even propose practices to reduce animal suffering at slaughter, be it ritual or not. Others assert that ritual slaughter in a non-industrial context induces less suffering than conventional slaughter with stunning. Green Halal members collect information on the positions and arguments of these 'experts' from Internet websites – such as Al Kanz.[8] None of them read any of the online writings except Meriem. It is this information on which they base their argument and call for Green Halal members to assert their opposition to the practice of stunning.

I questioned Green Halal members about the GAIA audio message. Some of them had heard it and many commented on the campaigns carried out by societies for the protection of animals (30 millions d'amis, Fondation Brigitte Bardot, GAIA). They criticized these societies for presenting ritual slaughter as the sole source of suffering for animals. They considered themselves victims of this stigmatization and asserted that Muslims, more than Jews, were the targets of these campaigns. They were also convinced that stunning before slaughter does not prevent animals from suffering, or prevent stress during transportation, or when they wait to be slaughtered at the slaughterhouse. To them, stunning is at best partially effective in reducing animal suffering at slaughter. According to Gerlando, stunning is not an ethical practice, as it doesn't take account of animal welfare before slaughter. One member also evoked the allusion to the deportation of Jews during World War II in the GAIA audio message. This allusion had been, by the way, abundantly discussed in the media. However, no one mentioned the risk of integrating the debate about stunning and the stigmatization of ritual slaughter into extreme right-wing discourses, as evidently happened in France during the 2012 electoral campaign.

As this specific event shows, the general debate about stunning is an ethical debate, related to animal suffering and to the behaviours and norms implemented to reduce this suffering as much as possible. In the view of Green Halal members, opposition to industrial halal indicates respect for animals. This opposition is part of a more general ethic.

Sacrificing animals with Green Halal

Meriem and Gerlando not only spread principles and advice for a new ethic of consumption. They also try to apply them. Much like other Green Halal members, they consume organic food; they also buy organic cosmetics. They are however discreet about their religious practices. In the following description, I focus on the realization of ethical principles related to respect for animals at slaughter. I take as an example a day spent in a temporary slaughter site on 17 October 2013 for Aïd el-Kebir.

Gerlando had bought 26 Texel and Limousin sheep and most members came to choose their own. Once chosen, the sheep crossed the seven meter distance between the run and the slaughter room surrounded by two men – Gerlando and a family member. In the room, the sheep were laid down on their backs on a table and slaughtered; they were then moved to another room to be skinned and butchered. All of this happened in a festive atmosphere: Green Halal members met each other, greeted each other, talked to each other. They also took a picture of their sheep. In order to respect sheep and their welfare, and to realize their ethical principles, Meriem and Gerlando are committed to sacrificing on the third day of the Aïd. They underline, with the help of religious texts, that this temporality is licit. Hadîths tell that the sacrifice must occur between the Aïd prayer and the sunset of the third day of *tachriq* (eleventh, twelfth and thirteenth days of the twelfth month of the Muslim calendar, *dhou al hijjia*, the three days following the day of the Aïd). More interestingly, for Meriem and Gerlando, this temporality allows sheep to avoid the stress resulting from the first day fever. The slaughterer, who was also in charge on the first two days, described the massacre during these days: sheep were slaughtered four by four and blood was flowing everywhere.

Moreover, Meriem and Gerlando gave a homeopathic treatment to the sheep the day before the sacrifice in order to reduce their stress. This treatment, TIVAPA, is a capsule produced by Boiron that mixes lime tree, valerian and passionflower. The capsules are diluted in water with honey and given to the sheep. Bernadette Bresard, a French veterinarian professional specializing in biotherapies (homeopathy, aromatherapy), had the idea of this mix to reduce the pain and harm of any animal species before slaughtering. With the aim of further reducing their stress, Gerlando rubbed the sheep's head and legs with lavender essential oil before they left the run. When he took one sheep, Gerlando declared that he 'pampered' the sheep. He was of course aware that it was impossible to totally prevent sheep from being stressed, because sheep are 'instinctive' and stressed when they see their group vanish. Finally, Gerlando underlined the importance of sheep being slaughtered one by one, separately, and through a slow slaughter process. A closed partition separated the slaughter room from the run so that sheep did not see the other sheep being slaughtered. After each slaughter, Gerlando cleaned the blood from the slaughter room with water. The slaughterer also waited at least three minutes before giving the sheep to the butcher. Gerlando insisted on the respect for these principles. When the slaughterer or the members of the slaughterhouse wanted to accelerate the pace, or when the slaughter room was not properly cleaned, Gerlando waited outside with the sheep. Due to the observance of these principles, Gerlando and the slaughterer often paid attention to the atmosphere and the smell in the slaughterhouse. For instance, the lavender oil and the integral cleaning of the slaughtering room between each slaughter softened the smell.

Conclusion: ethics and halal

In this chapter, I took as my starting point the debate about animals suffering during ritual slaughter. I chose the specific example of a Belgian association, Green Halal, which promotes a new Muslim ethic, a new 'ethic of consumption'. After the presentation of their ethics, I described the campaign led by GAIA in October 2013 against ritual slaughter without stunning. I looked at how Muslims from Green Halal, promoting an ethical halal, reacted to this campaign. It appeared that the debate about animal suffering and stunning was highly ethical.[9] As I wrote in the introduction, ethical issues are linked to responsibility. GAIA militants ask the Belgian government to act on its responsibilities and ban slaughter without stunning, and they believe that they act responsibly when they speak out in the name of animals. Green Halal members engage in ethical halal in order to be responsible for their food and their commitment to their religion. These responsible engagements shed light on the affective and cognitive attachment of human actors to values, and on their competences, expertise and knowledge. Green Halal and GAIA members prove their attachment to principles – the absence of animal suffering. This attachment is both cognitive – they refer to religion to explain their commitment – and affective – they feel better being committed to the reduction of animal suffering. The members of the two associations moreover have competences, capacities and knowledge allowing them to evaluate situations and to act responsibly. Both of them also refer to experts and scientific results to assert their position for or against stunning.

Green Halal and GAIA meet in their ethical defence of animals, in their fight against animal suffering. Their involvement with ethical issues is similar to a certain extent. Nonetheless, GAIA and Green Halal are opposed to and accuse each other – with regard to stunning and ritual slaughter – of not being ethical and making animals suffer. While GAIA considers the debate about animal suffering to be mainly ethical and asks for legal treatment of this problem – a legal ban of ritual slaughter without stunning – Green Halal act in the domestic world according to religious traditions and conventions, and promotes its own actions. In this context, it can be said that GAIA proposes more formalized ethical issues, actions and solutions whereas Green Halal is less formalized. While the former appeal for a responsibility of duty – to help animals that have no voice – the latter promotes a responsibility of freedom – to be in good health and to act according to one's religion. Finally, GAIA addresses the three main questions linked to ritual slaughter (pre-slaughter stress, pain during the cutting of the neck and time to loss of consciousness) while Green Halal is concerned only with stress.

As well as illustrating the matter of responsibility in ethical debates, I have throughout this chapter shown various forms that ethics can take: principles and actions against animal suffering; principles and actions promoting the respect for animals, the environment and human beings; principles and actions for better food. The theory of conventions (Boltanski and Thévenot, 1991) helps us to deal with these multiple forms. Ethic is not a world or a justification, but a worth, a quality, present in several worlds: civic, religious, economic, ecological, domestic. For instance, on the basis of food worlds defined by Murdoch and Miele (2003), it is possible to categorize Green Halal and its ethical claims in three worlds. First, Green Halal belongs to the domestic world, based on confidence and tradition; there is no label for the halal or ethical quality of meat. The second world is the civic one, with the defence of religious and ethical collective principles. The last world, the ecological world, is featured with respect for the environment and its balance. Green Halal and its ethic of consumption are then opposed to the commercial world in which competition prevails, the industrial world characterized by standardization, and the public world in which brands reign.

Due to this presence in multiple worlds, ethic cannot be a taken-for-granted quality and does not essentially link with things, but results from a process of qualification. The ethical quality involves a device of qualification composed by all the mediations[10] that participate in the qualification (Legrain, 2012). Among the mediations in this case are Gerlando's awareness after he witnessed a documentary about industrial food production, the rental of a slaughterhouse in order to be alone and to not mix with other animals, the blog that offers information about a new Islamic ethic, concerns about an animal's health and respect, and the homeopathic treatment given to sheep. Senses and emotions also influence the qualification of food as ethical. According to Green Halal members, ethical meat is supposed to have a good colour and a good taste. Green Halal members are also nostalgic for the mythical practice of sacrifice performed by the Prophet. They are committed to respecting their religious prescription as much as possible; they also fear for their health.

The global assemblage of ethical halal in Belgium did not appear out of the blue. Several variables were involved in its development and in the form it took. These variables are economic (the presence of a halal market), religious (the recognition of Islam as an official religion), technological (Internet websites), political (promotion of good food) and ethical (a citizen movement for good food and respect for the environment and animals). The focus on ethical variables is partly due to its importance in the global assemblage. Belgian governments have already enacted laws about ritual slaughter, the presence of Islam and a taken-for-granted halal market. Many citizens, be they Muslims or not, are looking for good food and are involved – or at least concerned – with environmental and animal welfare issues. Citizens may give voice to and act around ethical concerns, as they are still subject to debate.

Notes

1 www.rtbf.be/info/economie/detail_le-marche-belge-des-produits-halal-estime-a-1-7-milliard-d-euros?id=8086187

2 www.levif.be/actualite/belgique/le-halal-a-plus-de-succes-que-le-bio/article-normal-147253.html
3 http://oumma.com/198945/viande-bio-halal-vente-directe-reportage; http://www.theguardian.com/lifeandstyle/2014/may/18/halal-food-uk-ethical-organic-safe
4 Author's translation.
5 www.gaia.be/fr/campagnes/abattages-sans-tourdissement-souffrances-pour-une-tradition
6 www.gaia.be/fr/actualite/une-lueur-d-espoir-
7 Author's translation.
8 www.al-kanz.org/. An article published by Halal AVS, a French Halal certifier, also presents various arguments against stunning before slaughter: http://www.halal-avs.com/PrintArticle.aspx?id=204.
9 I do not focus on the legal aspect of the debate. For more information, see Bergeaud-Blackler (2007).
10 According to Latour (2005), a translator delivers a message without deforming it, while a mediator associates, stops, diverts, objects and acts as an agent. Mediators, or their performance named mediation, are not at the origins of relations (they do not create relations) but they are a means for agents to be in relation with each other. Mediations are not face-to-face relations between objects and subjects, but mutual definitions of agents on the basis of the holds they offer to each other. As such, mediations do not act separately but constitute heterogeneous devices.

Bibliography

Anil, M. H., McKinstry, J. L., Wotton, S. B. and Gregory, N. G., 'Welfare of calves. Investigation into some aspects of calf slaughter', *Meat Science*, n°41, 1995, pp. 101–12.
Armstrong, S. and Botzler, R., *The animal ethics reader*, Oxford and New York, Routledge, 2008.
Barnett, C., Cloke, P., Clarke, N. and Malpass, A., 'Consuming ethics: articulating the subjects and spaces of ethical consumption', *Antipode*, vol. 37, n°1, 2005, pp. 23–45.
Bergeaud-Blackler, F., 'New challenges for Islamic ritual slaughter: a European perspective', *Journal of Ethnic and Migration Studies*, vol. 33, n°6, 2007, pp. 965–80.
——, 'Islamiser l'alimentation. Marchés halal et dynamiques normatives', *Genèses*, vol. 89, n° 4, 2012, pp. 61–87.
Boltanski, L. and Thévenot, L., *De la justification: les économies de la grandeur*, Paris, Gallimard, 1991.
Bonne, K. and Verbeke, W., 'Muslim consumer's motivations towards meat consumption in Belgium: qualitative exploratory insights from means-end chain analysis', *Anthropology of food* [Online], 5, 2006, on http://aof.revues.org/90, 05/09/2012.
Brahami, M. and Otmani, F., *Le marché du Halal. Entre références religieuses et contraintes industrielles*, Lyon, Tawhid, 2010.
Eisnitz, G., *Slaughterhouses: The shocking story of greed, neglect, and Inhumane treatment inside the U.S. meat industry*, New York, Prometheus Books, 1997.
Garcia Sanchez, E., 'La diététique alimentaire arabe, reflet d'une réalité quotidienne ou d'une tradition fossilisée?', in Frédérique Audoin-Touzeau and Françoise Sabban, *Un aliment sain dans un corps sain. Perspectives historiques*, Tours, Presses Universitaires François Rabelais, 2007, pp. 65–92.
Genard, J.-L., *Sociologie de l'éthique*, Paris, L'Harmattan, 1992.
Gibson, T. J., Johnson, C. B., Murrell, J. C., Hulls, C. M., Mitchinson, S. L., Stafford, K. J., Johnstone, A. C. and Mellor, D. J., 'Electroencephalographic responses of halothane anaesthetized calves to slaughter by ventral-neck incision without prior stunning', *New Zealand Veterinary Journal*, vol. 57, n°2, 2009, pp. 77–83.
Goodman, D., 'The quality "turn" and alternative food practices: reflections and agenda', *Journal of Rural Studies*, vol. 19, n°1, 2003, pp. 1–7.
Grandin, T. and Regenstein, J. M., 'Religious slaughter and animal welfare: A discussion for meat scientists', *Meat Focus International*, 1994, on http://www.grandin.com/ritual/kosher.slaugh.html, 10/08/2012.

Al-Hafiz, B. and Masri, A., *Animal welfare in Islam*, the Islamic Foundation, CIWF, 2007.

Holloway, L., Cox, R., Venn, L., Kneafsey, M., Dowler, E. and Tuomainen, H., 'Managing sustainable farmed landscape through "alternative" food networks: a case study from Italy', *The Geographical Journal*, vol. 172, n°3, 2006, pp. 219–29.

Latour, B., *Reassembling the social. An introduction to the actor-network theory*, Oxford, Oxford University Press, 2005.

Legrain, L., *S'attacher à transmettre, transmettre un attachement. Les Darhad, leur répertoire et le continuum sonore en Mongolie contemporaine*, Paris, EPHE, 2012.

Levkoe, C., 'Learning democracy through food justice movements', in Carole Counihan & Penny Van Esterik, *Food and culture – a reader*, New York and London, Routledge, 2013, pp. 587–601.

Marsden, T., 'Food matters and the matter of food: towards a new food governance?', *Sociologia Ruralis*, vol. 40, n°1, 2000, pp. 20–29.

Murdoch, J. and Miele, M., 'Culinary networks and cultural connections: a conventions perspective', in Alex Hughes and Suzanne Reimer, *Geographies of Commodity Chains*, London, Pearson Education, 2003.

Ong, A. and Collier, S., *Global assemblages. Technology, politics and ethics as anthropological problems*, Malden and Oxford, Blackwell Publishing, 2006.

Prigent-Simonin, A.-H. and Hérault-Fournier, C., 'The role of trust in the perception of quality food products: with particular reference to direct relationships between producer and consumer', *Anthropology of Food*, n°4, 2005, on http://aof.revues.org/204, 05/09/2012.

Shaharudin, M., Pani, J. J., Mansor, S. W., Elias, S. J. and Sadek, D. M., 'Puchase intention of organic food in Malaysia, a religious overview', *International Journal of Marketing Studies*, vol. 1, n° 2, 2010, pp. 447–66.

Turner, S. B. and Nasir, M. K., *The sociology of Islam*, Farnham and London, Ashgate, 2013.

Van Waarden, F. and van Dalen, R., 'Halal and the moral construction of quality: how religious norms turn a mass production into a singularity', in Jens Beckert and Christine Musselin, *Constructing quality. The classification of goods in markets*, Oxford, Oxford University Press, 2013.

9

HALAL, DIASPORA AND THE SECULAR IN LONDON

Johan Fischer

In November 2005, the Halal Exhibition at the major World Food Market (WFM) in London was held for the first time. The WFM also included an Ethnic Specialty Food Exhibition, as well as a Kosher Exhibition. In 2006, a delegation from the Malaysia External Trade Development Corporation (MATRADE) had a booth at the Halal Exhibition. As discussed in this chapter, Malaysia holds a special position in the global halal market. In 2004 Malaysia launched its first Malaysia International Halal Showcase (MIHAS) in the capital of Malaysia, Kuala Lumpur. The Malaysian Prime Minister, Abdullah Haji Ahmad Badawi, argued in his opening speech that establishing Malaysia as a "global halal hub" was a major priority of the government, and that MIHAS was the largest halal "trade expo" to be held anywhere in the world.

I attended both exhibitions. In addition to the large number of booths displaying halal products, the WFM also offered seminars on the business potential of halal in the rapidly expanding "ethnic food" or "world food" market. In a way, the Halal Exhibition and the various groups and organizations participating in it bring out the complexity of the problems this chapter addresses: how the proliferation of halal sits uneasily between Islamic revivalism, commercialization and secularism as political doctrine and "the secular" as an epistemic category in everyday life.

The controversial question of halal certification surfaced on the first day of the WFM seminars. A former director of environmental health and consumer affairs services who was also an advisor to the London Central Mosque on halal questions accused many of the companies present of promoting halal products that were not properly certified as halal by an Islamic authority. From this advisor's perspective, the lack of a state body in Britain that was and is capable of inspecting the "totally unregulated halal market" has left this market open to fraud and corruption and without any kind of standards, uniform certification or legislation. This, in turn, is distorting the commercially promoted image of halal as a healthy, pure and modern food in an era of food scares.

Present at the WFM were numerous Islamic organizations, groups and individuals who understand and practise halal in divergent ways. One example of such an organization is the Halal Food Authority (HFA), an organization set up in 1994 to certify halal meat, which I return to later in the chapter. A number of government institutions, such as schools and hospitals, were also represented; they are experiencing an increase in halal sensibilities among Muslim groups. Several market-research firms specializing in "ethnic markets" participated to provide an in-depth understanding of the transformation of halal. Finally, a large number of confused Muslim consumers were there to learn how contemporary understanding and practices of halal are being transformed.

For the MATRADE delegation at the Halal Exhibition mentioned above, the United Kingdom, and London in particular, is potentially an extremely lucrative market. At this exhibition I discussed the halal potential of this market with a young Malay Muslim woman I knew from attending MIHAS in Malaysia in 2006. She holds degrees in accounting and business studies from Britain and is currently involved in promoting halal in Britain for the Malaysian state through her private company. She is an example of a Malaysian entrepreneur with a global orientation, that is, she represents a modern type of Malay diaspora group privileged by the Malaysian state. The Malaysian state has financially supported her education and her promotion of halal in Britain. In return, the state expects these highly educated Malay Muslim entrepreneurs to embody a modern type of Islamic diaspora on the global stage.

Over the last three decades, a powerful state nationalism represented by the United Malays National Organisation (UMNO), the dominant political party in Malaysia since independence from Britain in 1957, has emerged. In contrast to the fragmented and complex halal market in the United Kingdom, which is characterized by a whole range of competing Muslim diaspora groups, the state in Malaysia has effectively certified, standardized and bureaucratized Malaysian halal production, trade and consumption since the early 1980s.

The Malaysian state's vision is to export this model; for that purpose, being represented at the WFM is essential. While the secular state is largely absent in halal in the United Kingdom, the Malaysian state is very much present in the everyday lives of Malay Muslims in Malaysia, not as a secular force, but in the form of an Islamic bureaucracy. Focusing on Malays in London, I show how understanding and practices of halal are incomprehensible without comparing Malaysia and Britain as two countries in which secularism and "the secular" are signs of quite different trajectories and meanings. This endeavour can be said to be a comparative anthropology of the state that explores how Malay halal consumption is practised in the interfaces between two powerful "languages of stateness" (Hansen and Stepputat, 2001, 37) in Malaysia and Britain that help shape state governance, its effects and its subjectivities. In other words, my focus is on how Malay diasporic groups consume and negotiate halal in the interfaces between powerful Malaysian state discourses, the secular state and Islamic organizations in Britain, and the commercialization of halal.

Following Talal Asad, I argue that we should unpack the various assumptions that constitute secularism as a political doctrine. Moreover, current meanings associated with secularism have come to embody much more than the progression from religion to secularism. From its origin in modern Euro-America, secularism in its most simple form represented an idealization of separating religious from secular institutions in government (Asad, 2003, 1). Studying halal among Malays in London is a way of exploring "what people do with and to ideas and practices before we can understand what is involved in the secularization of theological concepts in different times and places" (Asad, 2003, 194). The proliferation and transformation of modern forms of halal in Malaysia and Britain shed light on the way in which halal as a theological concept is being re-signified. Insightfully, Asad asks what the connection is between "the secular" as an epistemic category and "secularism" as a political doctrine (Asad, 2003, 1). A preliminary answer is that "the secular" comprises concepts, practices and sensibilities that conceptually are prior to secularism (Asad, 2003, 16). Unpacking secularism involves a focus on how people live the secular in everyday life, as I show in the case of halal. The secular is ubiquitous in modern life and not easily grasped, so it may most fruitfully be "pursued through its shadows" (Asad, 2003, 16).

My exploration of halal in everyday life among Malays in London gives ethnographic specificity to meanings and practices associated with secularism. In the majority of debates about secularism, "there is an unfortunate tendency to understand the secular state in rather undifferentiated terms: modern, homogenizing and driven by objectifying scientific modes of governance" (Hansen, 2000, 255). Ironically, Islamic revivalist critiques of "secularism" and the "secular state" in Malaysia have helped shape and reinforce not only a unique type of powerful state nationalism in Malaysia but also a highly commercialized version of Islam, in which halal plays a significant role. While this type of state nationalism can be said to be secular in nature, it feeds into and is itself fed by a whole range of divergent Islamic discourses.

Based on the ethnography of halal understanding and practice among Malay Muslim middle-class migrants in London, this chapter also speaks to points raised in the introduction of this book, that is, halal as integral to globalized Islam (Roy, 2002) and halal as a global assemblage with particular emphasis on how the proliferation of the halal market signifies broader global shifts in domains such as circuits of licit and illicit exchange; systems of administration of governance; and regimes of ethics or values (Collier and Ong, 2005, 4).

This chapter is divided into seven sections. Following this introduction, I reflect on the methodology of the study. Then I discuss the relationship between Islam and the secular in Malaysia before moving on to the way in which these issues can be explored in Britain. The next section examines how halal certifiers in Britain claim authority in the market for halal products and services. The subsequent section investigates Malay middle-class Muslims' understandings and practices of halal in their everyday lives in London. The conclusion ties the findings of the chapter together and reflects on how diaspora is given a new expression in the interfaces between Islam, secularism, state and market.

A note on methodology

The fieldwork for this study was a multi-sited ethnography involving Kuala Lumpur and London. My methodology rests, first, on an intention to "follow the people" (Marcus, 1995, 106), which led me to focus on descriptions of Malays who migrated from Kuala Lumpur to London and on their migration narratives, with special emphasis on understandings and practices of halal in these two locations. Of Malaysia's 2008 population of more than 25 million, about 61% were indigenous Malays (virtually all Muslim) and tribal groups, also labelled *bumiputera* (literally, "sons of the soil"); 24% are Chinese, and 7% are Indian (IndexMundi). According to information supplied by the Malaysian High Commission in London on 21 August 2006, there are about 55,000 Malaysian citizens in the United Kingdom. How many are Malay, Chinese or Indian is unknown. In 2006, the Office of National Statistics estimated that there were 1,558,890 Muslims in Britain; the two largest groups are Pakistani (43.2%) and Bangladeshi (16.5%), while "Other Asians", including Malays, account for 5.8%.

The main reasons for focusing on Malays in multiethnic London are, first, that the Malaysian state's vision of and commitment to promoting halal specifically identifies London as a centre for halal production, trade and consumption; and, second, that London is home to a substantial number of Malays and Malaysian organizations such as UMNO and MATRADE. The focus on Malay halal consumption in London also allows me to offer comparisons to previous research on halal and consumption among middle-class Malay families in Malaysia (Fischer, 2008).

Second, I endeavoured to "follow the thing", that is, I traced the circulation of halal commodities as manifestly material objects of study (Marcus, 1995, 106). During fieldwork in London, I spent a great deal of time in Malaysian halal restaurants and butcher shops, grocery stores and supermarkets selling halal products. As discussed in the next section, ritually slaughtered meat is the primary halal commodity, but a whole range of new commodities is now being subjected to halal requirements by Muslim groups and consumers. During my fieldwork I also went shopping for halal with Malay consumers. More specifically, I explored the availability of halal products, including those certified by the Malaysian state's Jabatan Kemajuan Islam Malaysia (Islamic Development Department of Malaysia), or JAKIM. Moreover, a number of background interviews and participant observations were carried out with halal producers and traders, Islamic organizations and food authorities. Lastly, magazines, pamphlets, newspapers, websites and e-mail messages provided valuable insights into modern forms of halal production, trade and consumption.

Malaysia: Islamic and secular

Constitutionally, since Malaysia gained independence from Britain in 1957, Malays have been Malays only if they are Muslims. Malaysia is not an Islamic state, but

Islam is Malaysia's official religion, professed by over 50% of the population. In principle, Islam's "official" role was designated for ceremonial purposes and public occasions while the nation would remain a secular state (Nagata, 1994, 67). At the time of independence, UMNO played a major role in determining the constitutional position of Islam as "the religion of the country, a wording believed sufficient to convey the intended notion of a secular state" (Funston, 2006, 54). With Malaysia's rapid economic development over the past three decades, the meaning of Islam has become ever more contested.

The rise of divergent *dakwah* (literally "salvation") groups as part of the wider resurgence of Islam in Malaysia challenged the secular foundations of the Malaysian state. *Dakwah* is an ethnic as well as political phenomenon that has transformed Malaysia for both Muslims and non-Muslims. From the 1970s onwards Parti Islam SeMalaysia (PAS), the Islamic opposition party that still enjoys widespread popularity, together with *dakwah* groups, criticized the policies of the UMNO-led government for "un-Islamic colonial traditions and secular practices which separated religion from political, social and economic issues" (Jomo and Cheek, 1992, 85).

In order to preempt *dakwah* groups and PAS, the state began to "nationalize" Islam in Malaysia (Fischer, 2008). This nationalization has meant the increased centrality of Islam as a national and ethnic signifier in Malaysia; its logic is to see Islam equated with Malayness, viewing the latter as the naturalized core of the Malaysian nation. The nationalization of Islam has incited a broader fascination with the proper and correct "Islamic way of life", which, for example, entails consuming specific halal goods that are seen to have a beneficial impact on domains such as family, community and nation. The increasing importance of halal discourses and practices is both a result of the increase in revivalism and an instrument of that resurgence; together, they lead to ever greater involvement with Islam, which, in turn, helps to promote the movement that produced them. Thus, the nationalization of Islam subordinated the secular in Malaysia. The growing centrality of Islam in Malaysian society is also reflected in the bureaucratization of Malay ethnicity (Ackerman and Lee, 1997, 33). An example of an Islamic bureaucratic body set up by the state is the Institut Kefahaman Islam Malaysia (IKIM), or Institute for Islamic Understanding, established in 1992.

The priority of state organizations such as IKIM is to guide Malays to correct and rightful Islamic practice in everyday life, even as religious views are challenged by persistent secularists. In effect, this priority allies the bureaucratic state with Islam even while avoiding the ultimate step of calling Malaysia an "Islamic state". Simultaneously, through actual interference in the life of the country, guided by Muslims, the allegedly secular state is serving Islamic values, not those of the Chinese or Indian minorities. After coming to power in 1981, Malaysia's charismatic and outspoken Prime Minister, Mahathir Mohamad, set off a wave of institutionalizing and regulating halal in 1982. In this way Mahathir actively nationalized the proliferation of halal and concentrated its bureaucratization and certification in the realm of the state, where it has since remained.

In the 1970s, the state launched its New Economic Policy (NEP) to improve the economic and social situation of Malays *vis-à-vis* the Chinese minority in particular. The NEP entailed a number of benefits for Malays and other indigenous groups, such as increased ownership of production and preferential quotas in the educational system. The number and proportion of Malays engaged in the modern sector of the economy rose significantly as a result of these policies. Ideologically, the overall objective was to produce an educated, entrepreneurial and shareholding Malay middle class, which the state elite considered a necessary prerequisite for economic, national and social cohesion. At the same time, the NEP forged a new class of Malay entrepreneurs – New Malays. According to Mahathir, the New Malay embodies an aggressive, entrepreneurial and global "We can" mentality. In effect, the novel Islamic ethos in Malaysia is tied to allegiance to the state, evoked as a form of cultural kinship through religion (Ong, 1999, 226). Most of my Malay informants in London can be seen to belong to this group of New Malays. Moreover, among the political elite in Malaysia, there exists a fascination with discovering, or even inventing, a "Malay diaspora". The particularity of this "diaspora-envy" is a sign of modern Malay aspirations towards cosmopolitanism and "global reach" (Kessler, 1999, 23).

Since independence, notions of the sacred in Malaysia have taken on more political meanings. The bureaucratization and standardization of Islam and halal in Malaysia's modern history sit uneasily between Islamic and secular interests, ideas and practices. Interestingly, the state in Malaysia strategically employs halal as a material sign to overcome critiques of excessive secularism. In fact, halal is promoted as bridging the religious and the secular as an example of the compatibility of the ethnicized state, modern Islam, business and proper Islamic consumption. In a way, the Malaysian state's promotion of halal among Malays in Malaysia and on the global stage can be seen as a form of "buycott" (Fischer, 2007) that encourages Muslim consumers to buy locally manufactured and state-certified halal products.

Secular bodies in Britain?

As might be expected, the standardization, bureaucratization and certification of halal in Malaysia contrast with the far more fragmented and complex halal market in Britain, in which numerous groups, organizations and individuals have divergent ideas about halal. So far, scholarly attention to halal in Britain has for the most part focused on conflicts over the provision of halal in schools (Abbas, 2005) and on the politics of religious slaughter (Charlton and Kaye, 1985; Kaye 1993). In many parts of London, such as Finsbury Park and Whitechapel Road, halal is a distinctive presence on signs and in butcher shops and restaurants. Lately, halal certified products have begun appearing in supermarkets such as Tesco and ASDA. In effect, the new ubiquity of halal in some parts of London can be seen as a form of urban space making (Metcalf, 1996) and Islamic visibility (Esposito, 2003, 195). Simultaneously, Britain is experiencing the renewed political importance of religion.

Tariq Modood writes that "political secularism can no longer be taken for granted but is having to answer its critics, as there is growing understanding that the incorporation of Muslims has become the most important challenge of egalitarian multiculturalism" (2006, 37). Egalitarian multiculturalism builds on the idea that identities are partly given shape or denied by the recognition or non-recognition of others: "Due recognition is not just a courtesy we owe people. It is a vital human need" (Taylor, 1994, 26). More specifically, there is a demand, as in the case of halal, for public institutions to acknowledge "ways of doing things" (Modood, 2005, 134) privately as well as publicly. In Britain, secularism predominates at a cultural level in the context of institutionally complex ties between church and state (Fetzer and Soper, 2005, 38). The arrival of Muslims disclosed these intimate ties so that, over time, Islamic practices have been recognized (Fetzer and Soper, 2005, 61). Even as secularism grows in power and scope in western Europe, this type of moderate and pragmatic secularism tries to compromise with religion (Modood, 2005, 142) although this does not seem to be the case in contemporary France.

At the time of my 2006 fieldwork in London, several Labour Party ministers criticized and questioned Muslim women's right to wear the *niqab*, a veil that covers the face. Under the headline "This Veil Fixation Is Doing Muslim Women No Favours", *The Guardian* argued that "we need an honest debate about women and Islam. But the current politically driven campaign is making that more difficult" (Malik, 2006, 32). Another headline was "Tribunal Dismisses Case of Muslim Woman Ordered Not to Teach in Veil" (Wainwright, 2006, 4). Finally, an article titled "The Veil Controversy" made the point that "arguments about the Muslim veil in Britain are part of a wider debate taking place across Europe. Amid competing claims of religious freedom and official secularism, some argue that the debate is motivated by growing intolerance of Muslims" (Dodd and Whitaker, 2006, 13). *The Sunday Times* asked, "Is It Time to Take God Out of the State?"

> Faith groups are increasingly demanding new rights or complaining of being wronged. Some say the time has come for Britain to create a clear divide between state and religion. Are they right? Religion, long dormant as a force in British politics and society, is back. After 9/11 and 7/7, rows over niqabs, hijabs, Christian crosses, faith schools and dress codes have exposed deep rifts in our attitudes to the spiritual.
>
> *(Appleyard, 2006)*

Conversely, many British Muslims and organizations call on the state to help recognize and standardize halal. There is no state discourse on halal in Britain corresponding to the intense debate over veiling. Apparently, secularism as a political doctrine defines the secular in everyday life in terms of overt dressing on or of Muslim bodies, whereas more covert halal consumption by these bodies is seen as uncontroversial.

Slaughter in accordance with Islamic law has been permitted in the United Kingdom under the Slaughter of Animals Act of 1933 (Charlton and Kaye, 1985,

490) and Slaughterhouses Act 1974 (Charlton and Kaye, 1985, 495), both of which expressly permit the slaughter of animals without prior stunning. Animal-rights groups see these laws as inhumane, and controversies over the Jewish and Muslim slaughter of animals for food have surfaced periodically during the twenty-first century. Hostility to religious slaughter has "heightened awareness of Islamic practice and a sense of self-identity among a growing number of British Muslims" (Ansari, 2004, 355).

In this respect, the state has recognized religious needs and adapted policies to accommodate Muslim groups. However, as the understanding and practice of halal production, trade and consumption are being transformed to involve more and more types of products, as has already happened with kosher products, the state is increasingly called on to help regulate these commodities. While the British state recognizes traditional halal requirements such as religious slaughter without stunning, it has virtually no authority to inspect, certify or standardize halal. In the eyes of some British Muslims, this leaves consumers unprotected against the growing commercial interest in halal.

Claiming authority through halal

I have discussed above how Nizar Boga, a former director of environmental health and consumer affairs services who was also an advisor to the London Central Mosque, used an address at the WFM to criticize products promoted in Britain for not being properly certified. In front of a sizeable audience at the WFM seminar in 2006, he made clear that there is a large market for fraud and corruption within the halal trade, as well as in the local certifying bodies such as the HFA and the Halal Monitoring Committee (HMC) – both represented in the audience at the seminar. He called for members of the Muslim community to "wake up" and to "clean up their act". Finally, he declared that while state authorities might be willing to "take somebody to court" and "take enforcement action", these bodies "feel that the Muslim community has not decided yet what the definition of halal is in the first place". So-called expert certifiers (e.g. imams without any real knowledge of halal) are issuing certificates "as long as the money is sent first". In order to standardize this "totally unregulated" market, therefore, he requested that the government and the Food Standards Agency (The Food Standards Agency is an independent government department established in 2000 to protect public health and consumer interests in relation to food) "give us a hand so that we can come up with something like standards against which halal food can be inspected". These views are supported by Dr Yunes Teinaz, health advisor to the director general at the Islamic Cultural Centre in London. For ten years, he has worked on illegal halal food and brought cases to court. As he explained to me, "You can easily buy certification if you pay for it. And they get away with it because there is no control, regulation or inspection from the state."

As halal and the aspect of religious slaughter more and more infused Muslim identity in Britain, the need to establish a body of halal butcher shops was recognized. The HFA was consequently set up, in 1994, with encouragement from the Muslim Parliament (a Muslim interest group), and it then established a network of approved abattoirs and shops to provide the community with independently certified halal meat (Ansari, 2004, 355). Contrary to the certification and institutionalization of *kashrut* within the Jewish community, the approach to halal among Muslims in Britain has been more fragmented and disunited, and "the broad range of emerging political demands may have served to dilute organisational effectiveness" (Kaye, 1993, 251). Moreover, Muslim organizations in Britain claiming to represent the Muslim community are of relatively recent origin and often lack both resources and political experience (Kaye, 1993, 247). As we have seen, this call for halal standards is, to a large extent, modelled on Jewish *kashrut* certification. Jewish groups in the United Kingdom have been more concerted in their efforts to impose these requirements, which have therefore been recognized by the state to a greater extent.

Interestingly, the current situation in Britain is somewhat similar to that in Malaysia before state recognition and regulation of "national" halal began in the early 1980s. What some Muslim groups call for is such a national standard for halal, one that would mark a kind of British Muslim unity and identity. The central difference, of course, is that the secular state in Britain is reluctant to extend recognition of a relatively fragmented halal market beyond already existing regulation on food in general.

The HFA is a "voluntary, not-for-profit organization" set up in 1994 to license

> slaughterhouses, distribution centres, retailers and providers of meat and poultry for human consumption. These licenses are granted on an annual and contractual basis. The HFA inspectors are there to audit and monitor compliance of both Islamic laws and MAFF [Ministry of Agriculture, Fisheries and Food] and EU regulations of slaughter. The HFA is also assiduously engaged in regulating, endorsing and authenticating foodstuffs, pharmaceuticals, confectionary, toiletries, flavourings, emulsifiers, colourings [...] for Muslim usage.
>
> *(Halal Food Authority [HFA] 2009)*

In an increasingly complex food market, these activities seem bold for a voluntary organization. Interestingly, the intentions and activities of the HFA take place in the interfaces not only between the secular and the religious but, apparently, also between local, national and international organizations and forms of legislation on food. From my conversation with HFA president Masood Khawaja, information on the HFA's website and Khawaja's attendance at the WFA, it is clear that halal is formative of more and more "network events", indicating the emergence of a global halal "network" or "community". As an example, we learn that the HFA president attends a large number of national as well as international halal seminars, and the speeches delivered are there for us to see on the HFA Web site. In fact, the president attended the International Muslim Trade Exhibition (IMTEC) held in 1998 in Kuala Lumpur. As the Malaysian state claims authority through halal, the HFA is "regulating, endorsing and authenticating" halal.

With reference to halal in Malaysia, Khawaja made clear to me that, unlike the HFA, Malaysia's Jabatan Kemajuan Islam Malaysia (JAKIM) is "supervised and works under government instruction". Only "reluctantly" is JAKIM recognizing the work of the HFA as a non-governmental organization. Whereas in Malaysia halal is a major prestige project supported financially by the state, the HFA is independently "generating" its funds through audit fees paid by slaughterhouses and cutting plants.

When I visited the HFA, there seemed to be a discrepancy between its vision, the scale of its ambitions and policies, and the modest offices the organization occupies in London. Such status markers can be important; because halal is a significant and contested discursive space for claiming recognition in a fragmented religious market, competition can be intense. At the WFM gatherings in 2005 and 2006, the HFA president was also present, as was the vice-chairman of the HMC. The HMC was established in 2003 in Leicester; unlike the HFA, it opposes the stunning of animals before slaughter. These two organizations can be seen as competitors with overlapping interests and claims for authority in the halal market.

A young Malay man who had studied in London since 2001 and was a student councillor with an Islamic student organization told me plainly that most of all halal in the United Kingdom is about politics and business. In fact, many of my informants saw the proliferation of halal as an overwhelmingly commercial endeavour for which Islam was a vehicle that was pragmatically employed by Islamic organizations, Islamic nations and the halal food industry. However, the HFA president objected to this form of commercialization of halal and maintained that there is a distinctive religious or ethical aspect to halal as well. This is a significant point because in the current halal market, a large part of production and trade is carried out by non-Muslims; maintaining that there is a definite religious aspect to halal is also a way of linking halal to Muslim groups, their interests and, perhaps, their further domination of the practice.

A large part of the research into halal in the United Kingdom is carried out by "secular" market-research companies such as Mintel and Ethnic Focus, which are starting to recognize the commercial aspects of halal. The HFA president critiqued Mintel's overly commercial approach to halal but failed to mention the fact that major supermarkets in London, such as Tesco and ASDA, require the halal products they sell to be certified by locally recognized bodies such as the HFA and the HMC. In this way, halal is being lifted out of its traditional base in halal butcher shops to become part of a range of "world foods" sold by major supermarkets.

The huge Tesco Extra store in Slough, outside London, boasts of having the widest range of "world food", including halal, in Britain. In November 2006 in this store, I found Maggi chilli sauce produced in Malaysia and certified by JAKIM, a halal "Curry Special" butter chicken with no certification or logo, and, downstairs in the same store, a more traditional halal butcher operating as a concession selling fresh meat. Anecdotal evidence from fieldwork in this area suggests that

Tesco, by using this store in Slough as an entry into the halal market, has reduced sales among halal butchers in the surrounding area. In the ASDA supermarket in north London, around the same time, I found HFA-certified chilled chicken and mutton.

Supermarkets such as Tesco and ASDA have introduced halal chocolate bars (see Ummah Foods). Among the slogans used to advertise this product is this one: "Community & chocolate close to your heart? Isn't it time your chocolate bar did something more than just taste good?" The fine print on the chocolate-bar wrapper announces that "10% of net Profit goes to Charity". Interestingly, I could not identify any certifier of this product. While halal in Malaysia expands to cover more and more products that are certified by either the state or by an Islamic organization recognized by the state, many new halal products in Britain are not properly labelled or certified, from the perspective of many Muslim consumers.

Islamic organizations in Britain claim authority through and compete over halal in the interfaces between expanding markets, the secular order and the rights and demands of Muslim consumers. At the same time, these organizations push for a form of national halal standard that could be seen as a sign of Muslim unity and identity. So far, these organizations have not been able to unite Muslim groups around a shared vision of standards. As more and more products appear in this expanding market, both Islamic organizations and commercial interests compete over standards and certification in the margins of the secular state. The emergence of this type of Islamic consumption draws attention to the state's incapacity to regulate halal and thus recognize a Muslim "community". The question is how Malays in London navigate this market in terms of halal understanding and practice.

"You just have to shut one eye": halal in Malay migration narratives

The halal narratives of Malays in London emerge as plotted storylines, narrations or sequences of events that involve mobility, contact and the embrace of halal as important to the lives of those who have migrated from Malaysia to London; hence, these narratives can be seen as embodying truly "spatial trajectories" (de Certeau, 1984, 115). From previous fieldwork in Malaysia, I learned that many middle-class Malays, shaped by the ways in which halal has been institutionalized by the Malaysian state since the early 1980s, see themselves as being quite fastidious about halal. This investment in halal manifests itself in several forms.

Three narratives dominated Malay halal sentiments. First, Malays attribute their concern about halal (and the lack of it in others) to the relatively strict Shafi'i school of jurisprudence within the Sunni division of Islam dominant in Malaysia. A young woman in her twenties who moved to London with her husband in 2005 to study international marketing explained to me that

> I would always say that Malaysian Muslims are stricter. It is just the way that we were taught, I think. We are Sunni, Shafi'i school of thought, we are the

strictest. Even if you go to Mecca there is a lot of people who pray differently, or eat differently [and] they say that this is considered halal, but for us it is not halal. I have Pakistani friends here in London and they still go to KFC and eat the chicken, they don't care. I guess to them if you have been in a country for a long time you can eat whatever in that country whether it's halal or not.

(Interview, 2006)

Second, on several occasions when I had the opportunity to discuss halal with a Malay imam who has lived in London with his family since 2002, the role of homeland experience in halal practice and discourse was emphasized in another way. The imam works at Malaysia Hall, which I frequently visited as part of this research. This facility provides accommodation for Malaysian students who have just arrived in London; the on-site canteen serves Malaysian halal dishes. The imam's work of introducing students to living in Britain includes guidance on proper halal food practice. In this capacity, he can be seen as a kind of Islamic bureaucrat in a diasporic context. He sees that in the homeland, living with non-Muslim Chinese may well sharpen Malays' alertness to contamination from non-halal sources. This alertness about and apprehension of the food habits of the Other can also be significant in a British context, where general indifference about food is in clear contrast with Malay particularity.

Third, there was a forceful evocation of the impact of halal discourses and practices transmitted through schooling and the school system in Malaysia, an impact that ultimately involves the state. Most immigrant informants narrated the details of their acquisition of both basic and extended knowledge of halal as part of their school experience. As expected, halal knowledge and practice was generated in families, yet the role of halal in the school system was far more pronounced in informants' accounts. A young student in his early twenties who has lived in London since 2005 described how a basic knowledge of halal was taught in "normal" school as well as in Islamic school in Malaysia. Other, younger informants repeatedly referred to this type of knowledge as a natural part of "a national curriculum", as "a common understanding", "general knowledge" or "a syllabus". A young Malay woman studying at the London School of Economics outlined her memory of halal in the school system in the following way: "At seven you are being taught that basic stuff about how to pray and not about halal until you are older and it's more concentrated, in-depth. I remember I learned about halal when I was fifteen or sixteen years old." It is these homeland experiences, in the private space of the home and in the semi-public spaces of school, that give shape to Malay immigrants' understanding and practice of halal when in London; both kinds of remembered experience are "crucial to the formation of subjects who will eventually inhabit a particular public culture" (Asad, 2003, 185).

Younger informants told a story about leaving the haven of Malaysia to study or work in London, where a good dose of pragmatism was necessary in Muslim food consumption. One young Malay man provided the heading of this section of the chapter when he reasoned that when you live outside Malaysia, where halal availability is unsatisfactory, "you just have to shut one eye". For most informants, everyday pragmatism was the order of the day when living abroad, without the imagined security of being able to rely on JAKIM-certified products. This form of pragmatism was obvious in my fieldwork when I accompanied Malays going halal shopping in London – thrift, convenience and trust in local butchers and shops were key in shaping everyday halal consumption. Thrift is important because many of these Malays are students who have to be economical about their spending. Local halal butchers were favourites with many Malay consumers in London because the meat there was affordable compared with halal meat in supermarkets. However, the meat in these halal butcher shops was still often seen to lack proper certification. Conversely, halal in supermarkets was more routinely certified by the HFA, the HMC or another Islamic organization – whose standards may vary and, at any rate, are not transparent. Consequently, for consumers, insisting on the proper "branding" of halal commodities can become a luxury that is not always affordable.

Malay migrants in Britain work hard to navigate the complex halal market, in which no single standard that inspires trust prevails. For the observant Malay Muslim, real and imagined perils abound. For instance, the Malay imam discussed above told me that if you fall ill in London, the medication you receive may contain pork gelatine without this being stated on the label. Less anecdotally, too, my empirical data suggest that the majority of respondents and informants are dissatisfied with the labelling of products. Hence the increasing advocacy by Malays and other Muslim groups for more specific information on labels about potentially haram or mashbooh substances, such as gelatine or alcohol; the latter is often present in medications in small amounts. Although its presence is spelled out in the fine print, no easily visible notification that this renders the medication haram is provided.

Strikingly, for this particular imam as for many others, the practice of halal labelling in Britain is unconvincing because the secular state has no authority to carry out inspections, unlike JAKIM in Malaysia. The imam advocated such authority even as he admitted that even in Malaysia, maintaining standards through JAKIM inspections is very difficult because this body is responsible for "monitoring" the entire country. Given the insufficiency of staff, it is actually impossible for the agency to verify that correct practice is followed in every instance that produces a halal product. In other words, the imam I spoke to and many others in Malaysia are well aware that JAKIM inspections are symbolic practices of an ethnicized state involved in legitimizing halal. Conversely, in Britain, because of the lack of state involvement in halal, trusting halal producers, traders and butchers becomes essential, even as this lack of state involvement in establishing standards is considered deplorable. In the end, the imam told me he prefers to go to a restaurant where he knows the owner personally. Lacking such personal knowledge of reliable suppliers, Malays who are alert about halal in London often become sceptical about eating meat. However, none of my informants were strict vegetarians. Instead, Malays often consume vegetarian food as an alternative strategy when halal is unavailable or when the certification standard is considered unreliable.

There are several Malaysian halal restaurants in London, and many other restaurants are advertised as halal. Advising Muslim consumers about halal in London has become a small industry in its own right – as demonstrated by the handbook *Halal Food: A Guide to Good Eating – London* (Azmi, 2003), published by a Malaysian company. Yet despite the availability of such guides, most of my Malay informants cited a number of reasons for preferring to eat at home. Again, as many of them are students on tight budgets, there is an economic aspect to this preference, but it also matters that eating in ensures a higher degree of control over halal consumption. Only a few of my London informants would admit to frequenting fast-food outlets otherwise popular with the young, such as McDonald's or KFC, because these are not halal.

The great majority of my informants preferred JAKIM-certified products if these were readily available; immigrant informants recognize the JAKIM-issued halal logo on these products because of their everyday experience and the habits instilled in their lives in Malaysia. State-certified halal in Malaysia was described as "familiar", "trustworthy", "reliable" and "convincing". Some informants argued that JAKIM certification is more reliable because producers pay only a small fee for certification, whereas certifying bodies in Britain actively seek to "profit" from certification. This economic consideration, combined with the knowledge that JAKIM appeared to all to be more dedicated to the Islamic ethos, reinforced their confidence in state certification and undercut their confidence in non-state, commercial certification. In London, my informants preferred local certification by organizations such as the HFA or HMC, because the bureaucratization of certification under the auspices of the state, on which they learned to rely in the homeland, suggested to them that a standard set of procedures would be followed more reliably than by either a "food expert" or even a local imam. The practice of halal certification in Malaysia has made a religious practice supervised by the state more reliable than the same practice without state involvement.

Older informants who had been living outside Malaysia for a longer period had not been equally exposed to Malaysian state halal. One of these Malays, a man in his late forties who left Malaysia in the 1970s and is now a British citizen, sees himself as "a flexible Muslim" who willingly escaped the politicized piety and excessive focus on proper Muslim consumption of modern Malaysia. He was quite unaffected by the bureaucratization of Malay Muslim identities that has taken place in Malaysia since the 1970s. In Malaysia at that time, he told me, halal was mainly about trusting the authority of the local halal butcher shop.

Interestingly, this story about shopping for halal in Malaysia in the 1970s parallels younger Malays' accounts of contemporary shopping for halal meat in local butcher shops in London. Pragmatically, most of my informants simply have to trust the authority of these butcher shops, which for the most part are not certified by any organization. In my experience of shopping with Malays for halal meat in these shops, in most cases there was no visible or recognizable certification. Malay consumers tend to feel embarrassed about inquiring about certification, because this means questioning the authority of the butcher. My informants were well aware that because there was no actual state authority involved in this type of halal consumption, the butcher shop was not really accountable for the halalness of the meat. The Muslim consumer who doubts whether a product is halal or not has two alternatives. One strategy is to eat only vegetarian food; the other is, as the informant discussed above put it, "There are times when you don't know whether it's halal or not so you just say a Muslim prayer before you eat." This reflects another aspect of the transformation of halal. Several informants explained to me that it is legitimate for Muslims to consume mashbooh or even haram food and drink if halal is not available. As the current halal market expands and is transformed, however, it becomes increasingly difficult to disregard or bend halal requirements.

Conclusion

The young Malay man mentioned earlier, who is a student councillor with an Islamic student organization in London, argued that the practice of halal is, crucially, not just a public and communal, but also intensely personal and private, matter: as "Malays, [as] Muslims we believe that what becomes part of your body stays on. So it is very important that you make sure it is the right things [sic]." In London, Malays live at the margins of the Malaysian state, in a space between bodies, laws and discipline (Das and Poole, 2004, 10). The state that has helped to create these New Malays and has encouraged and supported their stay in London – to mend the "diaspora-envy" of the state – cannot maintain for them in Britain the certification practices to which they are habituated and which facilitate halal practice. In the homeland, the state disciplines Muslim bodies and minds even as these modern forms of Islamic bureaucratization reformulate a new Malay ethnicity and offer it recognition. Moreover, this disciplining is reinforced by the global commercialization of halal that is taking place. This article has explored the ways in which the halal practices of the Malaysian state, which cannot be fully enforced in Britain, combined with the lack of practices of halal certification and regulation on the part of the British state, have created a space in which memories of state regulation and state-certified identity must coexist with commercial practice and with inadequate, not fully trustworthy religious participation in certification; this coexistence creates an interstitial space in which Malaysian immigrants work in a typically mixed diasporic space to combine pragmatism and commitment to halal ideals, producing novel forms of management of life in terms of proper conduct. This study of halal among Malays in London exposes a whole range of ambiguities involved in the tension between religion and the secular, as well as between private and state involvement, in determining the patterns and identity-affirming practices of everyday life.

Bibliography

Abbas, Tahir (2005). *Muslim Britain: Communities under Pressure*, London: Zed Books.
Ackerman, Susan E. and Lee, Raymond L.M. (1997). *Sacred Tensions: Modernity and Religious Transformation in Malaysia*, Columbia: University of South Carolina Press.

Ansari, Humayun (2004). *The Infidel Within: Muslims in Britain Since 1900*, London: Hurst.
Appleyard, Bryan. "Focus: Is It Time to Take God Out of the State?" *Sunday Times* 22 October 2006. 19 May 2009 <www.timesonline.co.uk/toynews/uk/article608998.ece>.
Asad, Talal (2003). *Formations of the Secular: Christianity, Islam, Modernity*, Stanford, CA: Stanford University Press.
Azmi, Jumatuun (2003). *Halal Food: A Guide to Good Eating – London*, Kuala Lumpur: KasehDia.
Badawi, Abdullah Ahmad. "Window to the Global Halal Network". Malaysia International Halal Showcase. Malaysia Int'l Exhibition and Resort Ctrt, Kuala Lumpur. 16 August 2004. 31 March 2009 <http://mymall.netbuilder.com.my/index.php?doit=showclass&cid=36&domain=ehalal>.
Certeau, Michel de (1984). *The Practice of Everyday Life*, Berkeley: University of California Press.
Charlton, Roger and Kaye, Ronald (1985). "The Politics of Religious Slaughter: An Ethno-religious Case Study". *New Community* 12(3): 490–502.
Collier, Stephen. J. and Ong, Aihwa (2005). "Global Assemblages, Anthropological Problems". In *Global Assemblages: Technology, Politics, and Ethics as Anthropological Problems*, eds. Stephen J. Collier and Aihwa Ong, 3–21, Oxford: Wiley-Blackwell.
Das, Veena and Poole, Deborah (2004). "State and its Margins: Comparative Ethnographies". In *Anthropology in the Margins of the State*, eds. Veena Das and Deborah Poole, 3–33, Oxford: James Currey.
Dodd, Vikram and Whitaker, Brian (2006). "The Veil Controversy". *The Guardian* 21 October: 13.
Elliot, Rose (2009). "Something Fishy in Your Pasta?" *The Guardian* 26 October <www.guardian.co.uk/lifeandstyle/2006/oct/26/foodanddrink.uk>.
Esposito, John L. (2003). *Modernizing Islam: Religion in the Public Sphere in the Middle East and Europe*, New Brunswick, NJ: Rutgers UP.
Ethnic Focus. Home page. 30 March 2009 <www.ethnicfocus.com>.
Fetzer, Joel S. and Soper, Christopher J. (2005). *Muslims and the State in Britain, France and Germany*, Cambridge: Cambridge University Press.
Fischer, Johan (2007). "Boycott or Buycott? Malay Middle-Class Consumption Post-9/11". *Ethnos* 72(1): 129–50.
——(2008). *Proper Islamic Consumption: Shopping among the Malays in Modern Malaysia*, Copenhagen: NIAS P.
Food Standards Agency [FSA]. Home page. 30 March 2009 <www.food.gov.uk>.
Funston, John (2006). "Malaysia". In *Voices of Islam in Southeast Asia: A Contemporary Sourcebook*, eds. Greg Fealy and Virginia Hooker, 51–61, Singapore: Inst. of Southeast Asian Studies.
Halal Food Authority [HFA]. Home page. 27 March 2009 <www.halalfoodauthority.co.uk>. Halal Monitoring Committee [HMC]. Home page. 30 March 2009 <www.halalmc.co.uk>.
Hansen, Thomas B. (2000). "Predicaments of Secularism: Muslim Identities and Politics in Mumbai". *Journal of the Royal Anthropological Institute* 6(2): 255–72.
Hansen, Thomas B. and Stepputat, Finn (2001). "Introduction: States of Imagination". In *States of Imagination: Ethnographic Explorations of the Postcolonial State*, eds. Thomas B. Hansen and Finn Stepputat, 1–38, Durham, NC: Duke University Press.
IndexMundi. *Malaysia Demographics Profile 2008*. 18 December 2008. 31 March 2009 <www.index-mundi.com/malaysia/demographics_profile.html>.
Jomo, Sundaram K. and Cheek, Ahmad Shabery (1992). "Malaysia's Islamic Movements". In *Fragmented Vision: Culture and Politics in Contemporary Malaysia*, eds. Joel S. Kahn and Francis Loh Kok Wah, 162–93, North Sydney: Asian Studies Assoc. of Australia/Allen & Unwin.
Kaye, Ronald (1993). "The Politics of Religious Slaughter of Animals: Strategies for Ethno-religious Political Action". *New Community* 19(2): 251–61.

Kessler, Clive S. (1999). "A Malay Diaspora? Another Side of Dr Mahathir's Jewish Problem". *Patterns of Prejudice*: 23–42.
Khawega, Masood. Interview with the author. 1 November 2006.
Malik, Mohamad, (2006). "This Veil Fixation Is Doing Muslim Women No Favours". *The Guardian* 19 October: 32.
Marcus, George E. (1995). "Ethnography in/of the World System: The Emergence of Multi-sited Ethnography". *Annual Review of Anthropology* 24: 95–117.
Metcalf, Barbara D. (1996). *Making Muslim Space in North America and Europe*, Berkeley: University of California Press.
Mintel. Home page. 30 March 2009 <www.mintel.com>.
Modood, Tariq (2006). "British Muslims and the Politics of Multiculturalism". In *Multiculturalism, Muslims and Citizenship*, eds. Tariq Modood, Richard Zapata-Barrero and Anna Triandafyllidou, 37–56, New York: Routledge.
——(2005). *Multicultural Politics: Racism, Ethnicity and Muslims in Britain*, Edinburgh: Edinburgh University Press.
Mohamad, Mahathir (1995). "Views and Thoughts of Dr Mahathir Mohamad, the Prime Minister of Malaysia". In *Malaysia's Vision 2020*, ed. A. Sarji Abdul Hamid, 1–51, Kelana Jaya, Malaysia: Pelanduk.
Nagata, Judith (1994). "How to Be Islamic without Being an Islamic State". In *Islam, Globalization and Postmodernity*, eds. Akbar S. Ahmed and Donna Hastings, 63–90, London: Routledge.
Office of National Statistics (2004). "Population of Great Britain by Religion: April, 2001". 11 October. 1 April 2009 <www.statistics.gov.uk/cci/nugget.asp?id=954>.
Ong, Aihwa (1999). *Flexible Citizenship: The Cultural Logics of Transnationality*, Durham, NC: Duke University Press.
Riaz, Mian N. and Chaudry, Muhammad M. (2004). *Halal Food Production*, Boca Raton, FL: CRC Press.
Roy, Olivier (2002). *Globalised Islam: The Search for a New Ummah*, London: Hurst & Company.
Taylor, Charles (1994). "The Politics of Recognition". In *Multiculturalism: Examining the Politics of Recognition*, ed. Amy Gutmann, 25–73, Princeton, NJ: Princeton University Press.
Teinaz, Y. Interview with the author. 6 September 2006.
Ummah Foods. "Products". 30 March 2009 <www.ummahfoods.com/products.html>.
Wainwright, Martin (2006). "Tribunal Dismisses Case of Muslim Woman Ordered Not to Teach in Veil". *The Guardian* 20 October.

10

MUSLIM FOOD CONSUMPTION IN CHINA: BETWEEN QINGZHEN AND HALAL[1]

Yukari Sai and Johan Fischer

Introduction

In China today, halal is generally referred to as *qingzhen* (清真), meaning "Islam", "Islamic" or "Muslim". Alternate terms include *haliale* (哈俩勒), *haliali* (哈俩里) and *hala* (哈拉), all of which are phonetic equivalents of the original Arabic term. Hui people rarely use the word "halal" or phonetic equivalents; rather, they prefer qingzhen and consider the mark to denote cleanliness, goodness and as an indication that the provider of the food or services is Muslim (Gillette, 2000; Sai, 2013b, 2014a, 2014b, 2014c). However, as a Hui *Ahong* (Imam) in his thirties explained to the researcher in the southeastern province of Fujian in September 2010, religious specialists argue that qingzhen only means "adhering to Islamic law". He told the researcher that the exact meaning of qingzhen is "lawful to Islamic belief and what is required from Islamic teaching". He also emphasized that we cannot interpret qingzhen by simply dividing it into "qing" and "zhen", as non-Chinese scholars tend to do when they argue that qingzhen signifies the pure, true or authentic. As we shall see, the definition of qingzhen is subject to a range of divergent degrees of understanding and practices in contemporary China.

Pigs and pork perform significant roles in daily life and ritual in Chinese culture (Ahern, 1973; Anderson, 1988; Simoons, 1991). Pork products occupy large parts of meat counters in shops and fresh markets in contemporary China and alcohol consumption is widespread. It is in this context we explore how qingzhen is being resignified in China among Muslims with a long and distinct history. The People's Republic of China (PRC) identifies ten Muslim ethnic minorities including the Hui, the Uyghyr, the Kazakh, the Kyrgyz, the Tajik, the Uzbek, the Tatar, the Dongxiang, the Salar and the Baoan – about 23 million in total. Most of the Muslim minorities reside in densely populated areas in north-west China while the Hui can be found nationwide. Generally speaking, the Hui create mosque-centred communities in which qingzhen food shops and restaurants are common and they apply qingzhen marks to stores and restaurants to indicate that they are proper spaces for Muslim consumption.

Simultaneously, several Chinese terms employ the word qingzhen as related to Islam: *masjid* (mosque) is referred to as *qingzhensi*; *Shahadah* (literally, "testimony") as *qingzhenyan*, the Islamic calendar as *qingzhenli* or *huili*. Before halal certification and standardization were introduced to China, two characters or symbols were traditionally used to denote qingzhen: a water pot and a hat. For example, in the early twentieth century, an American missionary in China described these "traditional" (before halal/qingzhen standards were officially regulated in China) signs as follows: "The water-pot signifies ceremonial cleanliness, and is a guarantee that no pork is used, while the hat indicates respect to customers … the two characters on the tea-pot are 'pure and true'". (Broomhall, 1987[1910], 224). After implementing regulation of qingzhen food these traditional signs gradually disappeared and they were no longer evident in Muslim shops near masjids in urban areas (Figure 10.1).

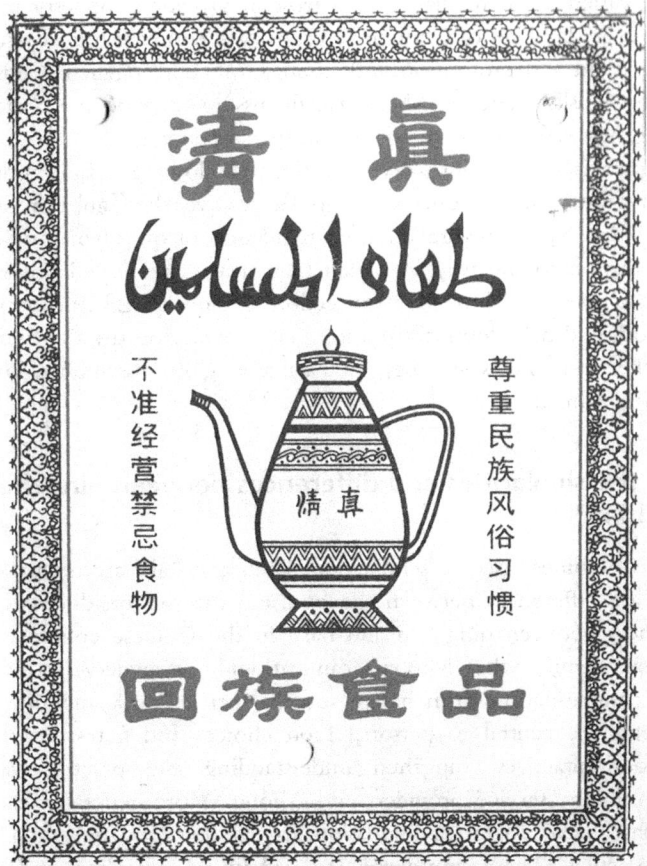

FIGURE 10.1 A qingzhen sign with "traditional" motifs at a Muslim shop in Beijing in the 1990s. Photograph by Yukari Sai

As global awareness of the halal market has increased, local governments in China have introduced standards for qingzhen food management. The drive to take economic advantage of this market, as well as to address food safety concerns, has raised the need for agreement between domestic qingzhen and internationally accepted halal standards (Li, 2009). Additionally, there is considerable variation between official Chinese qingzhen definitions and the perceptions of qingzhen among Muslims and non-Muslims in everyday life (Sai, 2013a). Arguably, in the case of the Hui, human agency and social capital are formative of the gap between official definitions and micro-social understandings and practices (Gillette, 2000). The central research question here is *how do Muslims and non-Muslims understand and consume qingzhen foods in contemporary China?*

Based on ethnographic fieldwork carried out by Yukari Sai, the chapter argues that the availability and consumption of qingzhen food in China are premised on the government's qingzhen/halal food policies and the sentiments of the surrounding Han majority. Even if personal attitudes to qingzhen understanding and practice are varied, both regulation and trust in providers' honesty play essential roles in the everyday lives of Chinese Muslims. We compare top-down qingzhen/halal management and promotion with the bottom-up qingzhen needs and practices of both Muslims and non-Muslims, discussing how people understand and practise qingzhen eating in its temporal and spatial context.

This chapter is divided into seven sections. Following this introduction, we highlight how it contributes conceptually to debates over the regulation of qingzhen/halal food. Then we discuss government regulation of qingzhen food production before moving on to the way in which these issues are played out in the local context of the research. Thus, the next sections explore qingzhen food in everyday life: eating out and halal food distribution. The conclusion ties the findings of the article together and reflects on qingzhen/halal as a "global assemblage" (Collier and Ong, 2005) in China.

What are the similarities and differences between qingzhen and halal in China?

In the eyes of Chinese Islamic scholars qingzhen and halal are inseparable. However, there are differences between the two and this section discusses similarities and differences between qingzhen and halal in the Chinese context. Obviously, both concepts signify what Muslims can eat without anxiety, most notably in relation to contamination from haram sources such as pork and pig derivatives. Both concepts are central to personal food choices and tastes. At the level of everyday food practices, qingzhen understanding and practice vary among Muslim consumers, service providers and Ahong. More generally, the tendency is to see that "halal" logics of regulation are standardizing qingzhen understanding and practice. These approaches to redefining qingzhen and halal align with the dynamics of modern and global halal markets and their regulation around the world.

The relationship between qingzhen and halal is deeply contextualized and contested in the interfaces between "Islamic"/"Chinese" culture and government policies. Conventionally, qingzhen is an ethnic term of Chinese-speaking people and its practical usage is linked to ethnic, religious and cultural understandings of Muslims. Qingzhen is inseparable from Hui identity and tradition and the Hui mostly use the term qingzhen rather than the relatively new term halal that is considered "transnational" and denotes globalizing markets, authority and power. Qingzhen is a term that signifies faith and practice embedded in everyday lives: being Muslim as well as the way of life of the Hui (Su, 2012, 106).

Moreover, qingzhen cuisine is considered and consumed as a variation of Chinese cuisine while halal cuisine is seen to be a variation of "western" cuisine or cuisine from abroad. Qingzhen food is consumed by non-Muslims as an ethnic, local and "clean" cuisine. Images of qingzhen as representing cleanliness in China are inspired by ambiguous understandings that qingzhen is Muslim food that requires careful preparation. These characteristics are now being reinforced by state regulations and international transactions of modern halal knowledge.

In sum, the relationship between qingzhen and halal has developed historically through negotiations between Islamic, Chinese and transnational cultural values. Qingzhen has been shaped through everyday food practices as well as sophisticated by Muslim intellectuals. Premised on the existence of others, practising proper foodways is a core part of constructing and maintaining ethnic identities among Muslim minorities in China. Market interests and the regulation of qingzhen/halal production and service by local governments rediscovered and redefined qingzhen as a form of cultural capital for constructing ethnic, religious and national identities.

Regulating qingzhen/halal food: central concepts

Conceptually, this chapter engages with a number of themes raised in the introduction to this book. Islam and politics in the Chinese context involve various actors and organizations, everyday politics and micropolitics. We explore halal at the intersection of these different levels where the field of politics is constituted in practice (Soares and Osella, 2010, 1). The Chinese government's certification, standardization and bureaucratization of halal production, trade and consumption is a relatively recent endeavour that must be seen in the context of Hui ethnicity, that is, qingzhen food and eating is an essential ethnic identity marker in contradistinction to the surrounding Han majority. This type of ethnicity is based on kinship, body, language, a common cult/religion and a shared history of origins together with symbolic and political accoutrements (Nash, 1989, 5–6).

Claude Lévi-Strauss (1968, 87) argued that exploring food could generate "a significant knowledge of the unconscious attitudes of the society or societies under consideration". The underlying logic in this type of analysis is that religion and dietary understandings and practices are linked forces shaping cosmological understandings, as is the case with qingzhen/halal among the Hui. In seminal studies of food and religion/cosmology by Lévi-Strauss (1968) and Mary Douglas (1972, 2004), binaries such as edible/inedible, sacred/profane and raw/cooked are vital. Informed by such seminal studies, this chapter explores the emergence of a global and regulated market for halal food in China and how the Hui respond to and are affected by these transformations.

Arguably, halal in China evolved from being a sensitive Hui minority question to become a major national focus of the government and market. An important question is how government politics and policies of regulation help brand halal in China. This is where standardization and certification play important roles. Standards refer to the design and qualities of products as well as proper conduct of companies, for example with regard to the production, preparation, handling and storage of halal products, states, organizations and individuals. Simultaneously, standards work as instruments of control and forms of regulation attempting to generate elements of order (Brunsson and Jacobsson, 2000).

Certification together with standardization work is a "logo logic" that attaches political and moral messages to lifestyle brands and communicates these branded messages (Bennett and Lagos, 2007, 194). Thus, halal certification in complex ways links the different levels of the social scale such as individual consumption, the marketplace, Islamic associations and government. In a way, halal certification, standards and logos can be seen as a form of moral economy in which the ideal is to apply regulatory logics to the certification of virtue in increasingly formal ways (Busch, 2000; Brown, 2010).

Modern halal in China lends itself well as an example of "global assemblages" – halal is not only a product of multiple and emergent determinations, but subject to tensions at different levels of the social scale. As we shall see, the proliferation of the halal market in China signifies broader shifts in domains such as circuits exchange; systems of administration of governance; and regimes of ethics or values. These phenomena are distinguished by a particular "global" quality moving across and reconstitute "society", "culture" and "economy" (Collier and Ong, 2005). In China halal matters have created new fields of potential economic value within government and industries on the one hand and raised legal and ethical questions that shape and challenge social worlds of meaning in the everyday lives of Islamic organizations and consumers on the other. In this respect, regulation of qingzhen/halal is a site where multi-layered values are contested, negotiated and transformed as a form of "global assemblage".

Government regulation of qingzhen food production in China

The process of government regulation of qingzhen food in China was conducted under the aegis of ethnic policy. Moreover, the increased economic motivation to sell qingzhen food by both Muslims and non-Muslims, as well as increased calls for food safety, has highlighted the need to align localized and domestic qingzhen standards with the internationally accepted definition of halal. Since the founding of the PRC in 1949, special meat and food service measures for Muslims were enshrined in written policy (Suzuki, 1997; Guojia Minzu Shiwu Weiyuanhui

Zhengce Faguisi bian, 2006). Here, qingzhen was defined as an "ethnic minority custom" and the "food of the Hui people" with a particular focus on meat and pork. Hence, Muslims in this era were sometimes referred to as a "pig-prohibiting minority".

Early cases of qingzhen regulation were seen in Changchun in Jilin Province and Beijing in 1988, but started to flourish from the mid-1990s onwards – local governments began establishing official rules and regulations for qingzhen production and management, for example in the city of Xian in Shaanxi Province (Gillette, 2000). These policies also defined qingzhen as an ethnic minority custom, emphasizing the ethnicity of those engaging in qingzhen production, services and consumption. In the mid-2000s, government-run publishers began producing qingzhen- and halal-related books that treated "qingzhen food" and "halal food" as almost equivalent terms. For example, in definitions of the terms "qingzhen food industry" and "qingzhen food management", qingzhen was defined as "adhering to the laws of Islam", similar to the meaning of the term halal in Arabic (Ge, 2005; Wu, 2006; Zhou, 2005). Some of these texts excerpted regulations for domestic qingzhen and halal food management. These regulations state that Ethnic Affairs Commissions of local governments consigning to Islamic associations in the district can issue a qingzhen food operating licence in addition to general operating licences issued by health departments and industry organizations. Moreover, these qingzhen food regulations of local governments supervise qingzhen marks and penalties for any violators. Under these regulations relevant departments of local governments conduct official inspections of qingzhen food operating licences and marks at restaurants, food shops and manufacturers for the assurance of "food safety and health of ethnic minorities" – especially on the occasion of national holidays and ethnic festivals of Muslim minorities. In this way, official involvement with qingzhen management emphasizes ethnic definitions of qingzhen and attempts to control qingzhen food production and services. However, as we discuss later in the chapter, these forms of regulation create new challenges.

Around 2010, guidelines for halal food certification were introduced in the Ningxia Hui Autonomous Region. This document also equated qingzhen with halal, citing the Codex Alimentarius Commission's *General Guidelines for Use of the Term "Halal"*. In 2013, five provinces in western China agreed to adhere to these guidelines. The new halal logos and certificates, which were issued by Islamic associations, not only incorporate qingzhen in Chinese characters, but also halal in English or Arabic in some instances.

In addition to qingzhen standardization, China's economic policy has facilitated "international cooperation and collaboration" (Fischer, 2011) between qingzhen industries in China and other countries in the context of the emergence of halal as a global assemblage. For example, China has participated in international halal expos, held international trade fairs and launched a joint industry park with Malaysia in the Malaysian city of Kuantan. This globally motivated standardization and internationalization has facilitated openness and engagement with various actors in qingzhen food industries. Moreover, such efforts seem to reinforce the government's commitment to ensuring the reliability and authority of the qingzhen/halal mark in China. In sum, Chinese halal has been transformed from an esoteric and sensitive ethnic-minority market to become a major national and international focus of government and market in which standardization and certification play important roles.

Setting the scene

We now explore how Hui informants understand and practise their everyday consumption of qingzhen food products. Building on a practice theory perspective that sees practices as routinized ways in which bodies are moved, objects handled, subjects are treated and things are described (Reckwitz, 2002, 250), we examine how qingzhen is embedded in social practices (Bourdieu, 1990). As mentioned above, the Hui create masjid-centred communities and qingzhen food is available at qingzhen food shops and restaurants in such areas. Moreover, in these urban areas where the Hui or other Muslim ethnic minorities reside, the tendency is to see more and more specialized fresh markets, food stores and restaurants catering for Muslim use appear. These are labelled with the word qingzhen or sometimes Arabic words.

In the city of Yinchuan (population of about 1,990,000, including about 400,000 Hui), which is the capital of the north-western autonomous region of Ningxia, there is a special section for qingzhen food in supermarkets and fresh markets. This separation of the qingzhen food section from other sections where pork is sold is characteristic of the situation of the Muslim minorities in this particular spatial/temporal context. Of course this is different from super/hypermarkets in Malaysia, for example, in which halal and non-halal products are clearly separated in a national Muslim majority context (Fischer, 2011). Restaurants and small vendors serve local qingzhen dishes across the city, especially near the Hui communities. Recently, processed food and ready-made food are tagged with qingzhen marks on packagings and this reflects a move away from only displaying the word qingzhen in Chinese: now, the names of the authorities that certify products are added in English or Arabic to the processes of certification and standardization.

The central location for the research on which this chapter is based was a Hui community of about 20,000, located in a suburb of Quanzhou, a city of about 8,120,000 people in south-east China. Quanzhou is famous for its historical sites relating to the Maritime Silk Road trade. It is also a significant place for Islam in China because it was a great port and thus one of the main routes for the introduction of Islam in China. The Hui local community have different religious and food customs compared with other Hui communities around China. They have been described as "*Hanhuade*" or "sinicized", that is, in ethnic terms, that most of the Hui live and eat in the same way as the surrounding Han (Gladney, 1996). The Hui use the word "Hanhuade" themselves and informants told the researcher that Islam is the religion of ancestors, but not the religion of today. Their community is a lineage-based community and actually the majority of the ethnic Hui are not

Muslim, but "Buddhists" practising local folk religion and to a lesser extent Christian (Xiamen Daxue Minzu Diaochazu, 1984).

After implementation of an economic open-door policy in 1978 the Hui were granted ethnic status in 1979. A masjid was built in 1989 and in 1991 a plaque with the word Masjid in Chinese characters was used for the first time. As a local woman pointed out, "I did not know the building was the *gingzhensi* (masjid) until my daughter went there to study Arabic." Similar discourses by non-Muslim residents appeared in an earlier study (Fan, 2001). Some of the local youth began to venture outside their communities to study Arabic and converted to Islam – from 1991 to 1996 about 50 local youths including some Han youths joined this programme. Some of them kept practising Islam while others did not. Some youths, wishing to study continuously, studied abroad in countries such as Jordan, Saudi Arabia, Syria and Malaysia and became core members of the masjid later on.

Economic development in the region attracts businesspeople and workers from around China and the Islamic world as well. Many Muslims visit and reside in this region including Hui, Uyghyr and Kirghiz, as well as Muslims from inland China and from countries in North Africa, the Middle East and South Asia. Many of these Muslims are working in neighbouring towns, but visit the masjid in this community and join prayers and Islamic celebrations. Generally, the masjid community has become more and more diverse over the years. In this way, this Hui community is not a strictly Muslim community, but rather an emerging community of practice (Lave and Wenger, 1991) that includes Muslims who have diverse ethnic and cultural backgrounds and play an active role at the masjid.

Qingzhen food in everyday life

This section and the following ones explore access to and availability of qingzhen food in everyday life. Access to and availability of qingzhen food depends on marriage and resident statuses more generally. Local Hui Muslim youth told the researcher that they do not experience major difficulties finding qingzhen food because of the availability of live chickens, seafood and vegetables, for example. Non-Muslim family members respect the qingzhen foodways, and Muslims from inland China or abroad who cook their own meals or live with their family also narrate a positive picture about food availability. As a male Ahong in his forties from Xinjiang Province pointed out in 2001, "I do not have any difficulties with eating here because I visit a fresh market in front of the masjid and cook by myself, it is convenience for me." A wife of another Ahong from inner Mongolia explained that she can make everything herself if she has wheat flour or various vegetables. "We have enough food indeed", as she put it. A businessman, born in Iraq, his wife and children living in UAE, who cooked largely by himself, but also had meals prepared by Chinese colleagues, also painted a positive picture. He argued that while "Chinese cuisine is good we Muslims have some foods we cannot eat ... however, here is so much seafood and other types of food". In this way, the food availability for Muslims from outside the area, who cook their own meals, is good.

Conversely, Muslims who are single or work further away from their homes feel that it is often difficult to find qingzhen food.

Guoping, a male Hui Muslim from Shanxi Province, visited Fujian as an Arabic translator on referral from a local Hui Muslim in 2005. We had lunch several times at two qingzhen restaurants in a town near the masjid. He often complained about how difficult it was to find qingzhen meals in Fujian. His friend, a local Hui Muslim, advised him that he could choose Chinese vegetable cuisine or seafood restaurants. Attitudes towards seafood among Muslims vary from region to region across China and what is available depends on religious practice, the differences in local food habits and familiarity with the place of residence. Guoping was born in Shaanxi Province where he did not grow accustomed to eating seafood in everyday life. It seems he was not familiar with tastes in Fujian, and finds it difficult to work out whether dishes in such restaurants are qingzhen or not. In sum, therefore, the availability and properness of qingzhen foods often depends on marriage and resident status, as well as on experiences and familiarity with local food culture.

Eating out

There are several options for eating out divided between Chinese and foreign cuisines. Chinese food comprises local as well as a whole range of regional dishes, including vegetarian food. Qingzhen noodle stalls are the most common type of food outlet and they are mostly run by Muslim migrants from north-west China such as Qinghai and Ningxia. During fieldwork, local Muslims noted that they could choose between various dishes at qingzhen restaurants. However, the price of food in Arab restaurants was considered high and the food "lacking in variation" while other informants explained that they were tired of noodles.

Labelled qingzhen/halal food is not easily found in the suburb where the fieldwork took place and in most cases it is restaurants and personal distributors that sell this kind of food. There was a qingzhen Thai restaurant run by Hui from Thailand along the highway from Quanzhou to Shishi in the late 1990s, but it closed down after a short while. In 2003, two small qingzhen Ningxia restaurants were opened, but only one survived. In 2005, there were five qingzhen restaurants including two serving foreign cuisines in Shishi, three qingzhen restaurants in Qingyang next to the area where the masjid is located, and seven qingzhen restaurants and noodle shops by 2009. Shishi is a suburb famous for the garment trade and industry. It has several restaurants serving foreign cuisines in Arab, Turkish and Indo-Pakistani restaurants. These restaurants and noodle shops are small-scale, that is, the number of employees is under ten. Owners and employees are mobile individuals and in most cases these establishments are family-owned. In addition, as a local Hui man in his thirties explained during fieldwork in 2010–11, the number of qingzhen noodle shops increased rapidly like "bamboo shoots after rain". An informant, who distributes qingzhen food in this area, told the researcher that because noodle shops are family-operated, there is no need to pay employees, which means that business costs are low. Hence, running noodle shops has become a major ethnic business of Hui and Salar Muslims from the north-western coastal areas (Wang, 2009).

In this diverse setting, Muslims share information about where to eat through the masjid and personal communication. Ahongs play important roles in gathering information and communicating about qingzhen/halal restaurants and noodle shops through the owners and employees who frequently visit masjids to join activities or in connection with religious slaughter. The role of personal and social media networks such as BBS (Bulletin Board System), Weipo (the Chinese version of Twitter) and Weixin (a mobile text and voice messaging communication service) was also important.

Muslims have different choice criteria for ordering qingzhen meals. First, these Muslims address the risk of meals that may contain pork. In Minnan (historical name of South Fujian), restaurants and local food stalls specialize in serving dishes from stewed whole parts of cattle such as *niurougeng* (beef soup), *niurouwan* (meat balls), *niupai* (spare ribs) and *niudu/baiye* (tripe). During the research, there were numerous visits to these kinds of local food stalls with local Hui Muslim youth, who chose to eat at these stalls not only because local food was served but also because these stalls were guaranteed to sell non-pork dishes. When dining at non-qingzhen restaurants Hui customers request that no pork or ham should be in the ordered dishes.

Second, the qingzhen/non-qingzhen binary is complex. While qingzhen or halal marks on the one hand and Muslim owners/employees on the other are visible criteria for qingzhen, these are not always considered reliable. According to the local Ahong, sometimes an improper display of qingzhen takes place. For example, one case concerned a Muslim owner of a noodle shop who sold his business and all its furnishings to a non-Muslim. The Ahong visited the shop with a colleague and explained the rules and significance of qingzhen to the new owner, ultimately convincing him to remove the marks with qingzhen written on it. The Ahong later recounted the incident on a local BBS and provided photos. Besides, practical use of the word qingzhen in everyday conversation requires close attention. Baoguo, a local Hui male in his thirties, bought his wife, child and the researcher *yangrouchuan* (mutton kebabs). As we ate the food he explained that he himself did not eat the kebabs arguing that they were not qingzhen. This was because he was unsure about the slaughtering method and the vendor's reliability. To sum up, qingzhen can express a whole range of personal and social sentiments. In this way, availability and choice criteria of where and what to eat depend on price, variation, familiarity and taste. This suggests that although the need for qingzhen eating is essential for Muslims, simultaneously eating as recreation and pleasure is also an important motivation in food consumption (Warde and Martens, 2000). Thus, Muslims have different choice criteria for ordering qingzhen meals – pork avoidance as well as reliability and responsibility in qingzhen dealings.

Halal food distribution

According to the researcher's informants qingzhen foods can be obtained by asking the local Ahong to participate in animal slaughter, or from a personal contact.

Asking the local Ahong to slaughter living poultry is a common way to get fresh meat in Muslim communities in China. Moreover, ritual slaughter becomes a source of income for Ahongs. An example of a "personal contact" is Yiwen. He is a local Hui Muslim, who works as a translator of Arabic. He also distributes both fresh and frozen qingzhen meat and ingredients to local Muslims. He stores these goods in two large refrigerators at his house and distributes them to order. He told the researcher that the price of meat makes a major difference to consumers. Initially, he was the only person who distributed qingzhen food in this area, but now competition has increased. Previously, he went to wholesale markets around the country meaning that transportation costs were high and he would need several days for delivery. Now availability has improved and one of his customers, a woman Muslim restaurant owner specializing in local cuisine in Xinjiang, western China, told the researcher that she appreciated his effort as "he is so honest. He is not doing this for his own personal gain, he is doing it for us." This indicates that the honesty of the provider is an important element for consumers of qingzhen food. In this way, Muslim residents observe their daily foodways to the best extent possible within given circumstances and methods of access to qingzhen food suggest that Chinese Muslims prioritize service providers' honesty and responsibility.

The complex culinary image of qingzhen is influenced by religious, ethnic and local factors. Qingzhen cuisine is considered a culinary category in China, and is perceived as having specific qualities that overlap with local cuisine. For example, the covers of qingzhen cookbooks tend to emphasize Islamic motifs, such as the crescent and the dome of the Grand Mosque. Similar to its treatment in government policy, qingzhen cuisine is usually regarded as the food of ethnic minorities. Qingzhen cuisine is defined as the cuisine of Muslims in a wide sense and as a cuisine of Hui minority in a more narrow sense. For example, *youxiang* (deep fried bread), which is exchanged at ceremonial occasions, *niurou lamian* (Lanzhou beef noodle) and *yangrou paomo* (Xian mutton soup with flat bread) are all traditional ethnic foods of the Hui in north-western China.

Yang (1991) described qingzhen cuisine in the foreword to his cook book. Chinese qingzhen cuisine is a significant part of national food culture and it has been created by Muslims and chefs over hundreds of years. Qingzhen cuisine reflects a specific taste mixing selected food materials, sophisticated culinary arts and Islamic flavour with Chinese style (Yang, 1991, 1). This discourse illustrates a positive image of the syncretism of Islam and Chinese culture, which locates their food culture within national discourses as a part of Chinese cuisine (Appadurai, 1988; Swislocki, 2009). Even if qingzhen in China is recognized as a north-western regional cuisine it has its local variations. Non-Muslim Chinese tend to know little about the relationship between qingzhen and halal – most are only aware that Muslims require complex food preparation and that this has something to do with "cleanliness". Qingzhen cuisine is also perceived as characterizing the local fare of north-western China. This also shows the overlapping culinary image and non-qingzhen cuisine of north-western China sometimes incorporates religious images and Islamic motifs to attract customers. For example, a non-Muslim restaurant owner in his forties living in Fujian migrated from Xinjiang, western China, specialized in local cuisine. On his business card was an image of a masjid. When asked why he associates his restaurant with Islamic imagery, he explained that: "It will attract more consumers. I used to provide pork dishes, but have stopped because they were rarely ordered." This strategy is irrelevant for non-Muslims who enjoy the dishes as regional cuisine; however, it is obviously a critical issue for Muslim consumers. Muslim consumers advise each other not to eat in these restaurants and provide tips for obtaining qingzhen or halal cuisine via chat or other online communication.

Besides, the following narrative of a non-Muslim Han Chinese businessman in his fifties suggests the image of qingzhen is changing in response to economic demand:

> Originally I didn't like qingzhen, because when I visited areas such as Yunnan, where the Hui Muslim population is concentrated, there was bad hygiene there ... subsequently, now that I know qingzhen is clean and good, I am more and more interested in it. I have participated in MIHAS [MIHAS: Malaysian International Halal Showcase, an international halal industry exhibition held annually in Kuala Lumpur] several times. At first, I didn't expect a lot of the economic opportunities, but gradually I have become convinced of qingzhen and its potential. I have been to Tokyo, Aichi, Okinawa, Kyoto, Nikko, Sizuoka and other cities in Japan. Japan should move aggressively into the halal market. Japanese products have high standards and quality. Japan should fit naturally into qingzhen. Even though Muslim population is not so large there, the qingzhen industry might hold the promise of future growth in Japan.
>
> *(Interview, 2011)*

As exemplified by this narrative, the image of qingzhen is moving beyond the culinary to become associated with cleanliness, good quality, economics and future growth. These positive values are also inspired by Koranic influences and strict halal interpretations in South-east Asia. Thus, in China, halal matters have created a new field of potential economic value within industries as well as government (Ke, 2013; Ho, 2013; Wang and Ma, 2011; Yang, 2010). While Muslim informants agree with the inherent cleanliness and goodness of qingzhen, they are uncertain about the economic implications of modern halal as Fischer indicated in the case of Malays in London in the previous chapter. This transformation of social meanings of qingzhen reflects the everyday effects of commercialized halal.

Conclusion

This chapter has explored discourses and practices of qingzhen consumption among Muslims and non-Muslims in China. The relationship between qingzhen and halal is deeply contextualized and contested in the interfaces between Islamic/Chinese culture and government policies. Conventionally, qingzhen is an ethnic term and its practical usage is linked to ethnic, religious and cultural understandings of Muslims in China. Qingzhen is inseparable from Hui identity and daily lives. Qingzhen food production, trade and regulation take place in the context of ethnic policy, market drive and the need for food safety in China. The introduction of modern halal in China has resignified local qingzhen understanding and practice with regard to government, industry and economic interests.

Qingzhen food consumption varies with respect to individual experiences and knowledge in Muslim minority contexts. Access to and availability of qingzhen food depends on marriage and resident statuses more generally, but also personal experiences and familiarity with local food culture. Qingzhen can express a whole range of personal and social sentiments and the complex culinary image of qingzhen is influenced by religious, ethnic and local factors. Halal matters have created new fields of potential economic value within government and industries in China, within which the certification, standardization and regulation of qingzhen food production is essential. The ethnographic examples show how the relationship between qingzhen and halal can therefore be extended to describe social meanings of halal as a "global assemblage".

Note

1 This article draws on a number of Yukari Sai's (2014a; 2014b; 2014c) publications and she is thankful for permission to use these materials. This work was supported by the Islamic Area Studies Program of the National Institutes for the Humanities (NIHU), JSPS AA Science Platform Program, JSPS Core-to-Core Program, B. Asia-Africa Science Platforms and JSPS KAKENHI (Grant Numbers 20320113, 2330170 and 25870825).

Bibliography

Ahern, Emily M. (1973). *The Cult of the Dead in a Chinese Village*. Stanford: Stanford University Press.
Anderson, Eugene N. (1988). *The Food of China*. New Heaven and London: Yale University Press.
Appadurai, Arjun (1988). "How to Make a National Cuisine: Cookbooks in Contemporary India". *Comparative Studies of Society and History* 30(1): 3–24.
Bennett, Lance W. and Lagos, Taso (2007). "Logo Logic: The Ups and Downs of Branded Political Communication". *The ANNALS of the American Academy of Political and Social Science* 611: 193–206.
Bourdieu, Pierre (1990). *The Logic of Practice*. Cambridge: Polity.
Broomhall, Marshall (1987 [1910]). *Islam in China*. London: Darf Publishers.
Brown, Michael F. (2010). "A Tale of Three Buildings: Certifying Virtue in the New Moral Economy". *American Ethnologist* 37(4): 741–52.
Brunsson, Nils and Jacobsson, Bengt (2000). "The Contemporary Expansion of Standardization". In *A World of Standards*, eds. Nils Brunsson and Bengt Jacobsson, 1–20, Oxford and New York: Oxford University Press.
Busch, Lawrence (2000). "The Moral Economy of Grades and Standards". *Journal of Rural Studies* 16: 273–83.
Collier, Stephen J. and Ong, Aihwa (2005). "Global Assemblages, Anthropological Problems". In *Global Assemblages: Technology, Politics, and Ethics as Anthropological Problems*, eds. Aihwa Ong and Stephen J. Collier, 3–21, Oxford: Wiley-Blackwell.

Douglas, Mary (1972). "Deciphering a Meal". *Daedalus* 101(1): 61–81.
——(2004). *Purity and Danger*. London: Routledge.
Fan, Ke (2001). "Identity Politics in South Fujian Hui Communities". Ph.D diss., University of Washington.
Fischer, Johan (2011). *The Halal Frontier: Muslim Consumers in a Globalized Market*. New York: Palgrave Macmillan.
Ge, Zhongxing ed. 葛忠兴主编 (2005). *Qingzhen Shipin Chanye Fazhan: Lirun he Duice* 清真食品产业发展: 理论与对策. [*Development of Qingzhen Food Industry: Theory and Measures*]. Beijing: Minzu Chubanshe.
Gillette, Maris Boyd (2000). *Between Mecca and Beijing: Modernization and Consumption among Urban Chinese Muslims*. California: Stanford University Press.
Gladney, Dru C. (1996). *Muslim Chinese: Ethnic Nationalism in the People's Republic*. Cambridge: Harvard University Press.
Guojia Minzu Shiwu Weiyuanhui Zhengce Faguisi bian国家民族事务委员会政策法规司编 (2006). 国内外清真食品管理法律法规和政策汇编 [*Domestic and International Regulations for Halal Food Management*]. Beijing: Falü Chubanshe.
Ho, Wai-Yip (2013). *Islam and China's Hong Kong: Ethnic Identity, Muslim Networks and the New Silk Road*. London and New York: Routledge.
Ke, Zhixian 柯至嫻 (2013). Zhongguo Dalu Qingzhen Chanpin Ji Zhongxibu Shichang Shangji Dance 中国大陆清真產品及中西部市場商機探索 [*Halal Products in Mainland China and Searching Business Chance in the Midwest Market*]. Taipei: Taiwan External Trade Development Council.
Lave, Jean and Etienne Wenger (1991). *Situated Learning: Legitimate Peripheral Participation*. Cambridge: Cambridge University Press.
Lévi-Strauss, Claude (1968). *Structural Anthropology*, vol. I. Harmondsworth: Allen Lane, Penguin Press.
Li, Dekuang 李德宽 (2009). "Cong 'Qingzhen' dao 'HALAL': Tan Zhongguo Huizu 'Qingzhen Shipin' de Bentuhua yu Chanye Guojihua" 从清真"到HALAL": 谈中国回族"清真食品"的本土化与产业国际化 [From "Qingzhen" to "halal": Localization and Globalization of "Qingzhen Food" of the Hui in China]. In *Zhongguo Huishang Wenhua* 中国回商文化), [*Chinese Muslim Business Culture*], vol. 1, ed. Yang, Huaizhong 扬怀中主编, 205–13, Yinchuan: Ninxia Renmin Chubanshe.
Nash, Manning (1989). *The Cauldron of Ethnicity in the Modern World*. Chicago and London: University of Chicago Press.
Reckwitz, Andreas (2002). "Toward a Theory of Social Practices: A Development in Culturalist Theorizing". *European Journal of Social Theory* 5: 243–63.
Sai, Yukari (2013a). *Shokutaku kara Nozoku Chuka Sekai to Islam: Fukkien no fieldnote kara* [*Chinese and Islamic Food Culture on the Table: Food and Eating Field Notes in Fujian, China*]. Tokyo: Mekong.
Sai, Yukari (2013b). "Shoku no Halal wo Meguru Tayou na Koe to Jissen" [Multiple Voices and Practices in Halal Food and Eating]. *Waseda Asia Review* 14: 82–85.
Sai, Yukari (2014a). "Halal Policy, Practice, and Perceptions in China". In *Islam and Multiculturalism: Coexistence and Symbiosis*, eds. Asia-Europe Institute and Organization for Islamic Area Studies, 187–93, Tokyo: Organization for Islamic Area Studies, Waseda University.
Sai, Yukari (2014b). "Chugoku ni okeru Qingzhen to Halal" [Qingzhen and Halal in China]. In *Shoku no Halal* [*Halal Food in Various Cultural Contexts*], ed. Yukari Sai, 57–69, Tokyo: Institute for Asian Muslim Studies, Waseda University.
Sai, Yukari (2014c). "Policy, Practice, and Perceptions of Qingzhen [Halal] in China." *Online Journal of Research in Islamic Studies* 1(2): 1–12.
Simoons, Frederick (1991). *Food in China: A Cultural and Historical Inquiry*. Boston: CRC Press.
Soares, Benjamin and Osella, Filippo (2010). "Islam, politics, anthropology". In *Islam, Politics, Anthropology*, eds. Benjamin Soares and Filippo Osella, 1–22, Oxford: Wiley-Blackwell.

Su, Min 苏敏 (2012). "Hanwei 'Qingzhen': Shijie Zongjiao, Mixin yu Luxinan Huimin de Yisilan Xiangxiang" 捍卫 "清真": 世界宗教、迷信与鲁西南回民的伊斯兰想象 [Defending "Qingzhen": World Religion, Superstition, and Islam Phenomena of Luxinan Huimin]. *Zhongjiao Renleixue* [*Religious Anthropology*] 3: 105–32.

Suzuki, Ken 鈴木賢 (1997). "Chuugoku no Islam Hou" [Islamic Law in China]. In *Ajia ni okeru Islam Hou no Yishoku* [*Transplanting Islamic Law in Asia*], ed. Seiji Chiba, 39–103, Tokyo: Seibundo.

Swislocki, Mark (2009). *Culinary Nostalgia: Regional Food Culture and the Urban Experience in Shanghai*. Stanford: Stanford University Press.

Wang, Guoqiang and Li, Mazong 王国强，马宗礼 (2011). *Qingzhen Chanye yu Renzheng* 清真産業与認証 [*Halal Industry and Certification*]. Yinchuan: Huanghe Chuban Chuanmei Jituan and Yangguang Chubanshe.

Wang, Ping 王平 (2009). "Dongnan Yanhai Chengshi Qingzhen Shipin Hangye Xianzhuang yu Fazhan de Diaocha yu Fenxi" 东南沿海城市清真食品行业现状及发展的调查与分析—以福建厦门市清真食品行业为列 [Research on Development of Qingzhen Food Industry in a City of South-eastern Part of China]. *Huizu Yanjiu* 回族研究 [*Journal of Hui Muslim Minority Study*], 2010(4): 137–44.

Warde, Alan and Martens, Lydia (2000). *Eating Out: Social Differentiation, Consumption and Pleasure*. Cambridge: Cambridge University Press.

Wu, Junzhu ed. 吴俊主编 (2006). *Qingzhen Shipin Jingji* 清真食品经济 [*Economies of Islamic Food*]. Yinchuan: Ninxia Renmin Chubanshe.

Xiamen Daxue Minzu Diaochazu 厦门大学民族调查组 (1984). *Jingjiangxian Chendai Gongshe Huizu Diaocha Baogao* 晋江陈埭公社回族调查报告 [*Field Report on Jinjiangxian Chendai Community of Hui*]. Xiamen: Xiamen Daxue Renleixuexi, Xiamen Daxue Renleixue Yanjiusuo and Xiamen Daxue Renleixue Bowuguan.

Yang, Guotong ed. 扬国桐主编）(1991). *Qingzhen Caipu* 清真菜谱 [*Qingzhen Recipe*]. Beijing: Jindun Chubanshe.

Yang, Huaizhong ed. 扬怀中主编 (2010). *Zhongguo Huishang Wenhua* 中国回商文化 [*Chinese Muslim Business Culture*], vol. 2. Yinchuan: Ninxia Renmin Chubanshe.

Zhou, Ruihai ed. 周瑞海主编 (2005). *Qingzhen Shipin Guanli Gaishu* 清真食品管理概述 [*Outline of Halal/Qingzhen Food Management*]. Beijing: Minzu Chubanshe.

11

HALAL TRAINING IN SINGAPORE

Johan Fischer

This chapter discusses halal training in Singapore arranged by the Majlis Ugama Islam Singapura (MUIS) or in English the Islamic Religious Council of Singapore. Based on participation in MUIS halal training that is mandatory for relevant companies and institutions in Singapore, I explore how this particular form of training tries to standardize halal understanding and practice. I also discuss how halal regulation plays an essential role in these processes, and training to a large extent focuses on developing proper halal skills among employees.

In the global market for halal products, Singapore holds a special position in that it is state bodies that certify halal products and spaces (shops, factories and restaurants) as well as work processes. In shops around the world, consumers can find state halal-certified products from Singapore that carry distinctive halal logos. Globally, companies are affected by the proliferation of halal that to a large extent is evoked by Southeast Asian nations such as Singapore, Malaysia, Indonesia and Thailand. I situate my analysis of halal in a framework of new governing practices by different Southeast Asian countries such as Singapore (Ong, 2006). Sovereign rule creates new economic possibilities, spaces and techniques – for instance, an increased legal focus on halal in Singapore (Ong, 2006, 7).

The everyday political economy of halal commodities and services such as training raises some broader questions about how the state and Islamic authorities in Singapore attempt to create and regulate new markets around halal products in a local context. I explore the rise of a halal commodity regime and how and why processes are changing and their implications in Singapore (Nevins and Peluso, 2008, 1). More specifically, in analysing how this emerging commodity regime relates to the production of "trained" people and places in Singapore, this chapter traces how cultural, economic and political processes shape, consolidate and expand the market for halal products. The central research question here concerns how MUIS subjects the everyday workings of participants in halal training to expanding

"Islamic" requirements and forms of regulation and how these respond to, and are affected by, these processes.

Singapore is small in size and there are not many manufacturing industries in the country. Moreover, the number of Muslims in Singapore is limited and most of these are relatively relaxed about everyday halal consumption. Consequently, the Singaporean market for halal products and services is not so much driven by local demand; the main impetus for the widening and deepening of halal markets in Singapore is the country's vision to become the world leader in global halal markets. Thus, the marketing and regulation of halal in Singapore is to a large extent framed and formatted by a number of transformations in the global market for halal that took place from the 1990s onwards. The connection between Singapore and Muslim Southeast Asia more generally and the global proliferation of halal is no accident. As this chapter shows, halal has a particular and unique historical, political and cultural trajectory in Singapore.

During fieldwork in Singapore, I found a large number of food as well as non-food products certified by the state in convenience stores, grocery stores, supermarkets and hypermarkets. What is more, in Singapore virtually all of the multinational fast food chains such as McDonald's and Burger King are fully halal certified by MUIS and this is also the case with many smaller restaurants, even those owned and run by ethnic Chinese. In Singapore and the modern world at large, halal commodities and services are no longer expressions of esoteric forms of production, trade and consumption but part of a huge and expanding globalized market. The fieldwork for this study took place in 2009–10. This chapter forms part of a larger research project with the title *Global Halal Zones: Islam, Regulation, and Technoscience*. In terms of methodology, this chapter is based on participant observation and interviews carried out among halal producers, traders, Islamic organizations, companies, Islamic authorities, restaurant owners and supermarkets.

This chapter is divided into seven sections. Following this introduction, I reflect on the relationship between everyday political economy, standards and skills and halal in Singapore. Then I discuss the trajectory of halal in Singapore with a particular emphasis on its history and institutionalization. The next section explores how MUIS regulates halal markets. The two subsequent sections comprise the ethnography on halal training. The conclusion ties the findings of the chapter together and links the ethnography and the broader conceptual issues of the chapter.

Everyday political economy, standards and skills

Over the past three decades, the state in Singapore has effectively certified, standardized and bureaucratized halal production, trade and consumption and this has had a profound effect on the everyday experiences of consumers, companies and regulatory institutions in the country. I am inspired by a take on political economy that explores how anthropological subjects in everyday life are situated at the "intersections of local and global histories" (Roseberry, 1988, 173), that is, ways in which the lives of informants, in this case teachers and participants in halal training, can be studied in particular conjunctions or tensions between capitalism and the cultural freedom of subjects that define anthropological political economy (Roseberry, 1988, 174). Studies in this tradition typically examine their subjects in the context of the world economy, the development of capitalism and structures of power that shape and constrain activity (Roseberry, 1988, 179) – for example, how markets and MUIS as a regulatory institution interact and diverge in Singapore.

This chapter speaks to points raised in the introduction of this book, that is, how halal as a global assemblage also involves training or education with particular emphasis on systems of administration of governance and regimes of ethics or values (Collier and Ong, 2005, 4). I also explore how halal training is formative of new types of knowledge in terms of politics of scientific authority and representation, expertise and skills (Boyer, 2005). Building on the Singaporean case I explore the production of knowledge about halal in a particular national setting in which conceptualizations of power/knowledge work as operations/procedures that Foucault calls disciplinary technologies (Rabinow, 1984, 17).

As halal proliferated in the 1980s in Singapore, it contributed to new forms of space making, thus lifting halal out of its base in halal butcher shops and wet markets into standardized space such as abattoirs and super/hypermarkets. Economic growth, the emergence of large middle-class groups and globalization of the food market have pluralized shopping choices, that is, in urban Singaporean shops and restaurants there is availability of a very wide range of local and imported foods. My research shows that before super/hypermarkets became dominant, halal was mainly about trusting the authority of the local halal butcher shop. Consumers now rely on the authority involved in proper Islamic branding through marking commodities with logos or accompanying certificates (Fischer, 2008; 2011).

Standards and standardization can be seen to be instruments of control and forms of regulation attempting to generate elements of global order (Brunsson and Jacobsson, 2000, 1). The Singaporean state can impose sanctions on companies that do not live up to halal standards. What is more, standards can also refer to persons with certain qualifications, knowledge or skills (Brunsson and Jacobsson, 2000, 5). An example of this is the mandatory requirement to set up a Muslim Halal Team and participate in training to ensure not only the halalness of products but also as a means of mitigating the risk of non-halal contamination, that is, a form of standardized Muslim risk management.

With the declining importance of personal loyalty (in halal butcher shops and wet markets, for example) in the labour market, the importance of previous experience, training, skill and formal qualifications among staff increases (Fanselow, 1990, 258). In the neoliberal imaginary of contemporary capitalism, workers' employment value depends on their skills. Skills terms, especially "communication", "team" and "leadership", formulate aspects of personhood and modes of sociality as productive labour. All skills are assumed to be commensurable and readily available for inculcation into workers (Urciuoli, 2008). Discourses of communication, team and leadership skills all come together in halal training, as we shall see. Ideally, team members complement each other's capacities; they should be productive, high-functioning, make great decisions, resolve conflict, gain consensus and communicate/collaborate fluidly. Team training is about the ideal flexible worker who is seen as self-monitoring, self-assessing, continuously self-improving and internalizing the organization's key interests (Urciuoli, 2008, 216). Thus, the team as a paradigm of productivity and organizational control is internalized through the reconstitution of expertise and redistribution of worker responsibility in small, impermanent teams (Urciuoli, 2008, 219). Team training is seen to promise optimal labour coordination resulting in higher productivity and personal transformation (Urciuoli, 2008, 222).

Current studies on the entanglements of capitalism, Islam and the state in Southeast Asia explore, for example, how moderate Islamic "spiritual reform" movements in Indonesia combine business management principles and techniques from popular life-coaching seminars with Muslim practice. This form of "market Islam" and "spiritual economies" merges entrepreneurship as a way to produce new Muslim subjects, Islamic practice, capitalist ethics and effective self-management (Rudnyckyj, 2009; 2010). Rudnyckyj's research conducted in Krakatau Steel, a state-owned steel enterprise in Java, Indonesia, explores training sessions and the methods known as "Emotional and Spiritual Quotient" (ESQ) developed by spiritual reformers. These motivational speakers fuse economic progress with spiritual reform. In this case training is a powerful tool in shaping and guiding individual ethical comportment in line with national interests and strategies. In the Indonesian case, Microsoft PowerPoint was the preferred technology through which a rapidly growing movement for spiritual reform was mediated. Narrating PowerPoint presentations indicates the ability to participate in circuits of transnational business that combine corporate matters and Islam. This technology or technique is powerful in producing representations of the world and truth about the world (Rudnyckyj, 2009) and the same can be said about halal training in Singapore.

Standards and standardization can refer to the design and qualities of products as well as people with certain qualifications, knowledge or skills – for example, with regard to the production, preparation, handling and storage of halal. Halal standardization represents a particular take on political economy that explores how everyday life in Singapore is situated at the intersections of a range of opposite: between local economies of consumption and a globalizing halal industry; between religious principles and administrative practices; between the country's economic ambitions and the everyday experiences of participants in halal training.

Halal in Singapore

The Singaporean vision is to become a world leader in halal. To achieve this, halal commodities and handling are subjected to increased forms of everyday regulation. Singapore is a Chinese majority country while Muslims – of whom most are ethnic Malays – constitute the largest minority and this has a significant bearing on halal production, trade, consumption and regulation. Out of 3.77 million Singapore residents in 2010, the Chinese formed about 74 per cent, Malays 13 per cent and Indians 9 per cent, while "Others" accounted for the remaining part (www.singstat. gov.sg/pubn/popn/c2010acr/key_demographic_trends.pdf). Singapore exists in a "double minority" setting: the Chinese are a majority in Singapore but a minority in the region whereas the Malays are a minority in Singapore but a strong majority in the immediate region (Mauzy and Milne, 2002, 99–100). This complex relationship is essential to understand halal in Singapore.

Singapore's colonial history dates back to 1819 when the British East India Company chose it as a settlement because it was centrally located for trade. In 1959, the People's Action Party (PAP) formed a government led by Lee Kuan Yew, who was the first Prime Minister of the Republic of Singapore. Lee Kuan Yew governed for three decades until 1990 and he can be said to have been the architect behind Singapore's impressive performance and continuous economic growth. The reasons for this growth are many, but his strategies to make use of technology with multinational corporations have helped the country achieve first-world status. To this day, PAP governs Singapore driven by the pursuit of economic growth, which it delivers – and this is PAP's "performance" principle and single legitimacy to rule. The party will go to all lengths including curtailing conventional democratic rights and practices to "deliver the goods" to the people (Chua Beng Huat, 2003, 3). Certain laws and controls on political participation and civil rights such as freedom of the press can be said to determine that Singapore is not a liberal democracy, but rather some form of authoritarian state. More broadly, authoritarianism is intimately linked to the political history of Singapore and PAP's quest for political dominance (Chua Beng Huat, 1995, 204). What is more, the "moral performance" of the PAP state defines the political rule and shapes the quality of social and political life (Yao, 2007, 180). Singapore's judicial system has received high international acclaim and this is also relevant to the way in which religion – and in connection with halal in particular, Islam – is regulated and managed legally.

From the early 1980s the Singapore nation-building project moved towards a more "ethnic-cum-racial form", with conceptions of "Chinese" ethnicity and a peculiar Singaporean notion of "Chinese values" playing increasingly important roles (Barr and Skrbis, 2008, 5). What is more, this ethnicization includes the upholding of Singapore's two main national myths, that is, multiracialism and meritocracy that facilitate and legitimize rule by a self-appointed Chinese elite (Barr and Skrbis, 2008, 5). Interestingly, halal aspirations that emerged in the 1980s occurred in parallel to the stress on Confucian ethics and, more broadly, a form of Chinese ethnicization of society. Confucian ethics includes obedience to benevolent and paternalistic hierarchical authority, and emphasizes societal duties and obligations. Ironically, it is this transformation that plays a key role in the proliferation of halal in Singapore and beyond.

The state promotion of halal in Singapore presents a paradox: halal as an ancient Muslim food taboo is promoted as a national and neutral brand that benefits the economy, while the moral implications are downplayed – especially in a Chinese majority cultural context where Chinese social, religious and economic rituals are unavoidably intertwined. Gambling, eating pork and drinking alcohol are important ways of establishing identity and group membership and rituals involving these things permeate all aspects of Singapore life (Stimpfl, 2006, 74). It is in this context that Malay Muslims are called upon to handle halal properly. In other words, no matter how forcefully halal is promoted as a highly lucrative global market in which countries such as Singapore want to find their rightful place, halal is essentially an Islamic moral injunction and not socially neutral in nature. Before halal became part of a global and growing market the state in Singapore considered it an expression of excessive religiosity and minority rights that separate Muslims and non-Muslims in a "multiracial context".

MUIS and halal regulation

Islam is heavily state regulated in Singapore. MUIS is the state Islamic institution and its main decision-making body is the council headed by a president. It also comprises the Mufti of Singapore and members nominated by Muslim organizations. The state in Singapore promotes religiosity even though Singapore is officially a secular state, that is, the "religious economy" is heavily regulated and governed by a very pragmatic state (Pereira, 2005, 172). When the Administration of Muslim Law Act (AMLA) was enacted in 1965 it allowed for the establishment of MUIS in 1968 and the consequent culmination of the fusion of Malay and Muslim identities in Singapore (Kadir, 2004, 360). The management of Islam in Singapore is acheived through the institutionalization of AMLA and the formation of MUIS. Issues addressed in AMLA are the Shariah Court; Muslim financial provisions; mosques and religious schools; halal and haj (pilgrimage); marriage and divorce; property; conversions; religious offences and miscellaneous others. MUIS' functions, duties, responsibilities and powers are clearly defined in AMLA. It states that MUIS was established and functions to administer matters relating to the Muslim religion and Muslims in Singapore including any matter relating to halal certification (http://statutes.agc.gov.sg/). MUIS started to provide halal services in 1972 and the first halal certificate was issued in 1978. MUIS is solely responsible and performs a regulatory function in halal under the state. MUIS also facilitates halal food trade through certifying local exporters to export their products to a global halal market; certifying local establishments and participating in forums on standardization of halal certification (Riaz and Chaudry, 2004, 53).

An amendment of AMLA was passed in 1999 giving MUIS new powers in allowing it to regulate, promote and enhance the halal business. This bill endows MUIS with the sole authority to regulate the halal certification of any product, service or activity in Singapore. On 1 December 2009 a further amendment of AMLA with specific reference to halal certificates took effect so that it was now a serious offence to display false halal logos, that is, false MUIS logos.

MUIS is vested with the powers to act as the sole authority to administer and regulate halal certification in Singapore and this is clearly stipulated in AMLA's

Section 88A(1). Persons who without the approval of MUIS issue or misuse a halal certificate in relation to any product, service or activity are guilty of an offence and shall be liable on conviction to a fine not exceeding S$10,000 (on 10 January 2013, one Singapore Dollar or S$ was worth US$0.81) or to imprisonment for a term not exceeding 12 months or both. In 2009, MUIS certified more than 2,600 premises (www.muis.gov.sg/cms/services/hal.aspx?id=1714).

In a MUIS (2007, 11) publication the definition of the mandatory Muslim staff or Halal Team is outlined as follows: a group of appointed personnel responsible for implementing, monitoring and maintaining the halal system, as well as ensuring that all requirements have been met in accordance with this document. The team shall be led by an appointed management representative and shall comprise at least one Muslim staff and members from a multidisciplinary background who possess relevant knowledge and expertise. The company shall ensure that the Muslim staff and at least one other member of the Halal Team are sent for halal training recognized by MUIS. Obviously, this can be a controversial aspect of halal production, trade and regulation.

Halal in the Singaporean context evolved from being a sensitive Malay minority question to becoming a major national focus of state and market. Singapore's "double minority" setting has been a driving force in the promotion of halal – Malay Muslims are simultaneously seen as a "problem" as well as instrumental to the production, promotion, regulation and consumption of halal. The stress on Chinese ethnicity, ethics and values also embodies a powerful narrative about the hard-working and economically successful Chinese that must "tap" the global and expanding market for halal. All this takes place in the framework of Singapore's unique form of government that can be characterized as some kind of authoritarianism that allows for close networking between key organizations and institutions, but also a standardized culture around the commoditization of halal. MUIS as a statutory body plays a pivotal role in regulating the halal market in Singapore.

Halal training at MUIS Academy

In 2009 I participated in MUIS' halal training held at MUIS Academy, Singapore that develops and conducts courses on Islam. MUIS Academy "serves as a conduit for MUIS to share Singapore's model of religious administration and service, expertise and technology" (MUIS Academy folder, n.d.). This training consisted of two courses: *Level 1: Halal Foundation Programme with an Introduction to the Singapore MUIS Halal Quality Management System (HalalMQ)* and *Level 2: Halal Training Programme. Developing & Implementing Halal Quality Management System (HalMQ)*. The objective of Level 1 is to be able to understand the definition and basic concepts of halal certification; be better prepared to comply with MUIS halal requirements and gain an overview of the principles of HalMQ (The Singapore MUIS Halal Quality Management System). The course is mandatory for one Muslim member of staff and one other staff member in the Halal Team (www.muis.gov.sg/cms/services/hal.aspx?id=7156).

MUIS Academy is a modern type of conference facility equipped with all the latest teaching equipment. It is part of Singapore Islamic Hub (SIH) that comprises the Muhajirin Mosque, Madrasah Al-Irsyad Al-Islamiah (Islamic school) and MUIS headquarters. About 30 participants are in the Level 1 class and it is important to sign in before the course starts. The basic structure of the training is a series of Microsoft PowerPoint slides narrated by the Malay teacher. He explains about the day's programme that runs from 9 am to 5 pm and consists of lectures, team exercises, problem solving and case studies, as well as questions and answers. The course is aimed at Halal Team members, Halal Liaison Officers, managers and supervisors from companies and state institutions who are responsible for halal certification, as well as Muslim employees.

The atmosphere is relaxed among the mainly Malay and Chinese participants. The teacher writes his name on the whiteboard and explains about his relationship with MUIS. He recognizes several of the participants from his earlier role as MUIS inspector in companies and institutions. Hence, these participants know that the teacher also represents the audit/inspection authority. He has worked in the civil service for some years and has also been involved in business so his knowledge of halal is extensive. He now works for Warees Halal Division, a subsidiary of MUIS, which helps firms attain MUIS halal certification through the process of consultation. Once companies are certified, Warees Halal undertakes the task of ensuring that firms comply with requirements of the halal certification, that is, conducting site audits, engaging local Muslim organizations abroad to conduct regular periodic audits and sending halal-certified products for laboratory tests on an annual basis.

The course starts with a round of introductions focused on participants' type of organization and business and the role halal plays in their working life, as well as course expectations. For example, one participant is from Singapore General Hospital. In Singapore there is an increasing focus on public institutions such as hospitals and halal because Muslims from the Middle East in particular have become medical tourists, she explains. Between introductions the teacher jokingly asks why participants attend this mandatory course. A man works as a lawyer representing a local company. He is interested in some "basic knowledge" on halal. Yet another participant is employed by an enterprise that is to implement the HalMQ system and she hopes to be better equipped to do this after the course. A man who works as a manager wants to improve halal management in his canteen. When all participants have introduced themselves, the teacher explains that all questions and critique relating to MUIS halal regulation are welcome – the system cannot be improved without critique, he says. The training is not about "right and wrong", but "interaction and discussion" so participants should come forward with all enquiries and not be shy.

Quiz 1 is on *What is halal?* This question is discussed in groups for a while. A woman is the first to give her opinion and she thinks that pork and lard avoidance and proper ritual slaughter essentially define halal. A man adds that alcohol should be avoided and another man argues that carnivores are haram. The teacher nods approvingly and asks if any other participants have additional ideas. As there are not, he poses a question about the halal status of amphibians such as frogs that are a delicacy among some Chinese in Singapore. The teacher repeats that participants should be "brave in your answers" and that "no one is punished for wrong answers". When participants offer no further explanations five slides with definitions of halal from the Koran are shown. The teacher adds that in principle everything is halal except for what is mentioned as haram in the Koran and ruled as haram by *ulama* (Islamic functionaries). He describes the Koran as a "manual" of "religious aspects" Muslims live by.

Quiz 2 is on *What is Halal Certification?* Groups again discuss and the accompanying slides to a large extent focus on MUIS' role in halal certification and its accompanying legislation. Thus, in Singapore only MUIS can certify halal and other types of halal certification must be approved by MUIS. Halal certification by JAKIM in Malaysia and MUI in Indonesia are examples of bodies, which are also approved elsewhere in the region. The teacher poses the question of what certification is. This seems to be a challenging question among participants who speculate whether halal certification can be compared with non-religious certification, which is familiar in everyday consumption. The teacher clarifies that in order to understand halal certification it is imperative to understand halal. One thing is clear, a proper halal mark "sells".

This is certainly not the case if you go to China or Holland, for example. In these countries there is no centralized state authority that can define and certify halal and certification is carried out by competing Muslim organizations. This means that where there is no clear halal certification in the form of logos, consumers and companies must be on their guard and critically ask about the halalness of products, raw materials and services. Is it enough to build trust in food on race, the teacher asks? In multiethnic Singapore, trust in food cannot be based on race, he reasons, and to ensure halalness state-regulated certification provided by MUIS has to be efficient. Halal certification is by far the most reliable indicator of halal assurance, the teacher concludes.

The course then moves to discuss the origin of MUIS in 1968, the fact that in Singapore it is only MUIS that can certify halal, and that MUIS as a statutory board "exists because of law" and that there is "a law behind it", that is, the Administration of Muslim Law Act (AMLA). Warees Halal, the company that employs the teacher, is an expression of the way in which MUIS and halal in Singapore have global aspirations: Warees is now handling halal globally as this is not within the jurisdiction of MUIS. As halal is lifted out of its local context to become a global assemblage, MUIS and Warees Halal are differentiated, systematized, specialized and bureaucratized in order to promote and regulate it. The Halal Certification Strategic Unit of MUIS is ISO 9001 certified (deals with the requirements that organizations wishing to meet the standard have to fulfil) and provides a range of "personalized" services for companies and there is also an E-Halal Kiosk in MUIS Halal Consultation Room within the Singapore Islamic Hub. Even if Singapore's halal vision to a large extent focuses on global Muslim markets due to the fact that the local market is limited, halal promotion and regulation in

Singapore itself are extensive in order to demonstrate national dedication to tap this lucrative market.

Before moving to Team Exercise 1: *What are the benefits of halal certification?* the fees for the different number of MUIS halal certification schemes are outlined. The different schemes are as follows: Products Scheme, Food Preparation Area Scheme, Storage Facility Scheme, Poultry Abattoir Scheme and Endorsement Scheme. When asked about the benefits of halal certification to their organizations, participants mainly give economic reasons such as expanding markets. However, benefits of halal certification also generate questions among participants about challenges posed by such certification. Questions relate to halal and ethnicity, for example. A man asks why he has to take this mandatory course when he is a Muslim who is supposed to be knowledgeable about halal. A supermarket Director of Food Safety and Quality from the largest supermarket chain in Singapore, NTUC FairPrice Co-operative LTD, has logistic challenges marking the separation of halal and non-halal products in her store. FairPrice received complaints from Muslim consumers that frogs were placed next to halal crabs in the supermarket. Customers wanted to know what MUIS' position was on that issue. Yet other questions relate to announced/unannounced inspections, their frequency and nature. The teacher answers to the best of his ability and most of his answers tend to rely on the way in which halal is legally regulated in Singapore, that is, MUIS as a statutory body in Singapore regulates halal and it has employed a number of Contact Officers that deal with particular challenges participants may experience.

The teacher then asks about disadvantages of certification and participants argue that the cost, time, "restrictions", "hassle" and audits can be considered disadvantages. The teacher draws attention to a case of a primary school canteen he was involved with. In 2008, a Singaporean primary school insisted that only halal food could be taken into the canteen causing a stir among non-Muslim parents. In a letter to all parents, the school's principal said that because the whole school canteen had been certified halal, children would not be allowed to bring non-halal food onto the premises. The school security guard and discipline master were also checking lunch boxes to ensure that pupils complied. The Ministry of Education declared that this decision was a mistake and it was reversed. MUIS clarified that it certifies only the food stalls in a school canteen, not the premises as a whole and added that once a stallholder has obtained his halal certificate, non-halal foods cannot be brought in or out of that halal-certified stall. The teacher stresses that this story exemplifies the importance of knowing what kind of halal scheme to apply for.

During the coffee and lunch breaks I had the opportunity to discuss halal with some of the participants. The Director from the large Singaporean supermarket, NTUC Fairprice Co-operative LTD discussed above, explained to me that there is an increased focus on halal in Singapore and thus the need for halal training has risen. The other representative from FairPrice present at the training was the Malay Muslim man mentioned above who wondered why he as a Muslim had to take this course. The Director was handling Muslim complaints about frogs' legs placed next to crabs and found that translating halal into actual corporate practice in the supermarket had been demanding on resources, but that rules and regulations were becoming clearer. Separating halal and non-halal products in supermarket outlets, for example, that are not designed for this poses a challenge. For a period of time, a "green mark" on the floor signified this separation, before halal and non-halal were separated in different sections of the supermarket. These are some of the issues that a company such as this one consults MUIS on. Other aspects brought up during the break concern the role of law in halal in Singapore and more broadly the transformation halal is undergoing in the local setting and how this affects participants' organizations.

Even though the teacher emphasized that it is preferable to have questions asked during class, a number of queries relating to the individual situation of participants surface during breaks. These take many forms, also very mundane issues such as who one can contact in MUIS are addressed. The teacher recommends emailing MUIS for answers to questions. Another aspect he introduces is that while different auditors audit differently, there is no question about the legal background and enforcement of halal in Singapore, that is, MUIS is a statutory body inseparable from AMLA and ensures that any advice is firmly based on a legal foundation.

The training then moves to a discussion of the different halal schemes MUIS offers. Participants are advised to carefully consider the characteristics and relevance of these schemes. A man argues that selecting the most appropriate scheme can be complicated and this question leads to a discussion of more general points relating to submitting applications. The teacher offers an example of the importance of certification: at a dinner with guests from Malaysia and Brunei there was a discussion about where the duck on the plates was from. Uncertainty can easily arise when meat or other products do not carry a logo with a recognizable certifier such as MUIS. While Malaysia and Brunei are recognized as countries with stringent halal certification, China, for example, does not have the same kind of state halal system. The teacher stresses that more and more consumers are accustomed to identifiable and reliable halal logos, and certification helps create confidence in the expanding market for halal in which grey zones are common – "can artificial pork flavour be halal certified?" the teacher jokingly asks to the amusement of participants as well as the researcher.

A woman asks if other types of halal certification have to go through MUIS. The teacher replies that MUIS has a list of recognized halal certifying bodies worldwide including JAKIM and that this ensures the integrity of halal regulation. This point clarifies the relationship between MUIS and other certifying bodies among participants and more broadly speaking this is an example of the kind of clarity that this training can offer participants.

The discussion then centres on a case of alleged halal certified pork in the FairPrice supermarket. Of course, pork cannot be halal certified everybody agrees, but somehow a MUIS halal logo was supposed to have ended up on pork in the supermarket. Fair-Price and MUIS systematically explored the case and it was concluded that the incident referred to arose because of a rumour in an email that halal pork was on sale in

Singapore. MUIS inspectors did not find any halal pork when investigating the matter and it was referred to as a case of "sabotage", but a police investigation could not place the responsibility. This case increased the call for fixed halal standards and guidelines among companies such as FairPrice.

Next, Singapore's role in an international halal network is presented, that is, Singapore's formal international network within ASEAN and Unofficial Meetings of Religious Ministers in Brunei, Indonesia, Malaysia and Singapore on the one hand and "informal" overseas networks of bilateral meetings and exchange visits as well as international conferences and seminars on the other. All this testifies to the global scope of Singapore's halal recognition.

After a brief question and answer session, the basic concept of halal food is discussed. Special dietary requirements of different "belief systems" such as halal, kosher and "vegetarian"; general criteria of halal food and halal slaughtering inform discussions. A video on slaughter processes in Australia raises ethical questions about meat eating in general. The question of stunning is also discussed and the teacher explains that after stunning the animal must show signs of life. In Brunei, for example, stunning is not allowed.

Now the question of halal status verification is on the agenda. The main point is that halal status verification can take three forms: halal certificates; halal certification labels such as the MUIS logo on products and food labels and ingredient lists. The teacher provides examples of rumours about the questionable halalness of products and how halal status verification can address such issues. In Singapore, halal status verification is inseparable from AMLA, that is, halal status verification is solely handled by MUIS.

Types of halal offences include misuse of the MUIS mark and thus AMLA, false or misleading claims about halalness in violation of the Sales of Food Act and Sedition Act, and forgery related to the penal code. The Singaporean Parliament enacted a law giving MUIS sole certification rights and legislation was tightened. A number of specific halal offences are discussed and after a couple of questions from participants on the aspect of offences the course looks into the Singapore MUIS Halal Quality Management System (HalMQ). The teacher shows that the benefits of HalMQ increased competitive advantage of certified companies, enhanced halal compliance through a more structured and systematic approach, increased credibility of Singapore halal certification, meeting the rising expectations of Muslim consumers and widening international recognition of Singapore halal certification.

Now HalMQ implementation plans for new and existing halal certificate holders are discussed as well as ten detailed HalMQ principles, for example establishing the Halal Team. After a discussion of the application process, Team Exercise 2 deals with the issues touched upon in groups. After group work, groups present their discussions and findings and there is also room for queries: a woman asks how large the MUIS halal logo on products can be and the teacher replies that this depends on the size of products, that is, there has to be a fair relationship between the size of the logo and the product surface. Finally, the teacher issues certificates to participants.

Level 2: Developing and implementing Halal Quality Management System (HalMQ)

The objective of MUIS' Level 2 training is that participants understand the basic concepts and requirements of HalMQ, learn how to prepare and document HalMQ procedures and gain an overview of internal audit and assessment techniques. This training is strongly recommended for Halal Team leaders/members within halal certified premises (www.muis.gov.sg/cms/services/hal.aspx?id=7156). The teacher who taught Level 1 is also responsible for Level 2 and the basic structure of the course is the same. Compared with Level 1 fewer participants attend Level 2. The two-day course takes place in the same room as Level 1. The teacher starts out by explaining how this Level 2 course continues some of the points raised in Level 1 and can be seen to lead to a Level 3 course on *Conducting Halal Internal Audits*. After having introduced himself the teacher outlines the course objectives. Participants should be able to understand MUIS' general halal certification requirements, identify basic concepts of HalMQ, comprehend the benefits and rationale for HalMQ, learn how to prepare the documentation for HalMQ and gain an overview of internal audit and assessment techniques.

The teacher asks participants why they spend time and money on Level 2 and what their expectations are before a round of introductions starts. A Pizza Hut representative, who also attended Level 1, explains that she is there to deepen her halal knowledge. Another representative from a local company says she wants to "merge halal and management systems together". A woman from Singapore General Hospital, also present at Level 1, has the same aim. A man from Brunei explains that he is there because Brunei does not offer such a course even if the Brunei government encourages institutionalization of halal. A chef at the National University of Singapore (NUS) Cultural Centre (a venue for events that reflect the cultural heritage of Singapore and international arts and entertainment) wants to learn more about halal management in his canteen. The National Trades Union Congress (NTUC) FairPrice representative is also present and so are representatives from about 15 other state institutions and companies.

The basic structure of the course is General Halal Certification Requirements, Introduction to HalMQ, ten principles of HalMQ and a maintenance programme. In other words, keys to maintaining a good halal system. In terms of the General Halal Certification Requirements three areas are essential: halal basic requirements (documentation for raw materials); staffing (mandatory participation in halal courses for establishing the Halal Team) and systems with particular reference to tightened legislation and complying with HalMQ principles. In all this, the teacher explains, logos and certificates are essential. A man asks if it would be possible to have mandatory and recognized certificates for imported raw materials and the teacher replies that this would be desirable, but unlike Singapore most countries do not have a state certification body like MUIS that can issue reliable certificates. What is more, the teachers make clear that even if imported raw materials come with a logo, the certifier and thus the logo are not necessarily recognized by MUIS. A man asks about the role of the Muslim staff or Halal Team. The teacher reasons that the mandatory Muslim staff and Halal Team play an "advisory role" to give "public assurance".

In Exercise 1 participants are asked to list the benefits of implementing HalMQ. After discussing this question in groups the following arguments are presented: increased sales, standardization, confidence, "HalMQ is good for Singapore" and increased recognition, that is, "a good system that can be recognized abroad. Singapore is positioning itself globally and is recognized for technology", as a man puts it. A woman from a multinational fast-food chain tells the class that the company had to undergo *sertu* (ritual cleansing) by MUIS in 1998 when the restaurant was first halal certified. She likes this kind of standardization "because then it's the same for all companies". The teacher adds that actually demands to standardize and proliferate halal in Singapore also come from companies and not only from MUIS and the state. Each of the chain's outlets has a MUIS halal logo on the door and a certificate behind the counter, but she would prefer that all outlets could be certified together and not on an individual basis as it is the case.

The teacher now moves to Principle 1 of HalMQ – establishing the Halal Team. This Team should comprise a Team Leader, at least one Muslim staff and "relevant personnel from multidisciplinary backgrounds". What is more, the Terms of Reference (TOR) as well as roles and responsibilities of individual members should be established. Team members should be sent for halal training. The "team approach" the teacher explains is central when dealing with halal. A couple of participants ask about the ideal size of the Halal Team in their particular workplace; this varies according to the number of employees the teacher explains. Another question is as follows: how many employees must complete MUIS halal training? The teacher replies that Level 1 is compulsory and every employee on the Halal Team must go, whereas Level 2 is optional and "recommended" because then companies will be better equipped to work with auditors. In any case, if problems arise they will be settled by MUIS.

Principle 2 of HalMQ is concerned with the definition of the product or nature of business and the teacher makes clear that MUIS has a helpline that can always assist in case of questions. It is important that applicants carefully consider the particular scheme or product they apply for. In Exercise 2 participants are told to imagine that they are Halal Team members and document the profile of the Team and the nature of products and business. The teacher explains that it is important that the whole group supports the individual group member presenting findings in the form of posters on the wall. In their presentation, the first group goes over the different group members' experiences relating to the task at hand. The teacher praises the presentation and poster, but also asks about possible improvements. A man answers that the certification process could perhaps be spelled out and the teacher nods. Another participant adds that in his company the Halal Team is appointed by the company management. A central concern is to make sure that certified products have logos and non-certified products do not, he makes clear.

In general, the atmosphere is relaxed and many jokes blend in with the course contents. When presenting their poster a group explains that when applying for halal certification the Muslim staff on the Halal Team should endorse incoming raw materials. The Halal Team's TOR is to satisfy such halal requirements and all members should have completed MUIS training. The teacher says that the exercise is there for participants to know what to do, for example to appoint a Halal Team leader. The group should remember that each Team member should have different roles and at least one Muslim staff member should be on the Halal Team in order to comply with HalMQ requirements. What is more, the "halal file should be signed by Muslim staff", as a man from the group makes clear.

The teacher stresses that if one Halal Team member fails, the whole Team fails. A couple of questions concern the relationship between halal legislation and how companies should live up to this. Many questions relating to the particular situations of participants surface during the break – for example one question concerns the process of tightened legislation taking place in Singapore and how this relates to legislation and regulation of halal more globally. Another question focuses on sentencing in connection with different types of halal offences and how companies can ensure that they are not punished for using raw materials with fake halal logos.

Principle 3 concerns the construction of a flow chart and Principle 4 is to identify halal threats and control measures. In Exercise 3 groups should now develop the flow chart for business operation and identify possible threats and control measures. Both the teacher and participants think that the poster presented after group work should read more like a "real" flow chart and the group presenting takes this advice into consideration. The teacher stresses that it is important that group work flow charts on posters are depicted as realistically as possible in order for groups to receive the most accurate comments. Groups gather around the poster again to go over it and learn how the teacher would "monitor" this particular flow chart in real life. A man from a local company has a specific question: does a truck have to be halal for transport? The teacher explains that the driver has to know about transporting halal and that if the truck has been carrying any *najis* (filth) such as pork it must be ritually cleansed. In case of "heavy pork pollution several ritual washings" carried out by MUIS are necessary.

In connection with Principle 5 on Halal Assurance Points (HAP), Exercises 4 and 5 are to identify the HAPs including allowable limits and prescribed practices. During group work the teacher circulates among groups and discusses and answers questions before the first day of the course ends. The second day of the course starts with a discussion of Principles 6 and 7 on the establishment of a monitoring system and corrective action for each HAP followed by Exercise 6 on these topics. During the first group's presentation the question of controlling suppliers is brought up: how can companies and restaurants control raw materials from suppliers?

During the break the teacher explains about the confusion in Malaysia in the wake of the tension between JAKIM and HDC and that halal is more tightly regulated in Singapore. He brings up the issue that essentially halal is an Islamic injunction and that quite a number of questions about halal are for religious scholars to answer. For example, for fish to be halal they must have scales and Imams determined this in a *fatwa* (opinion concerning Islamic law issued by an Islamic scholar). Another issue is that these interpretations and rulings differ between the different schools of Islamic jurisprudence. The teacher contends that halal is not an exact science, but open to interpretation and that MUIS plays a central role in this type of interpretation and regulation. A couple of Chinese participants argue that halal is mainly important in Singapore for business reasons as the Chinese do not really observe any kind of religious food taboos. After discussing Principles 8 (establishing documentation and record keeping), 9 (verifying the halal system) and 10 (reviewing the halal system), the teacher issues certificates to all participants and this concludes the course.

Conclusion

To conclude, halal training plays an essential role in Malaysia and Singapore – especially in the context of changing landscapes of halal legality and regulation. Moreover, as halal is lifted out of its local context to become a global assemblage, MUIS and Warees Halal are differentiated, systematized, specialized and bureaucratized in order to promote and regulate it. The training structured around Microsoft PowerPoint slides pushes halal control and self-control into companies and state institutions such as universities and hospitals to satisfy the need to connect internal organizational arrangements to national visions and strategies. Most importantly perhaps, training instils a common managerial model that emphasizes the encouragement of internal compliance systems. In other words, training technologies and techniques encourage standardized halal understanding and practice in employees and institutions. Moreover, halal training also signifies standards and standardization, that is, the design and qualities of products as well as proper conduct of companies, for example with regard to the production, preparation, handling and storage of halal. Training is aimed at enhancing skills in terms of communication, team cohesion and leadership and is in itself a form of skills-related product that offers workers advice about acquiring, assessing and enhancing their own skills. In Singapore halal training is mandatory for companies and so is the setting up of the Halal Team; reflecting how standards can also refer to persons or teams as it were with certain qualifications, knowledge or skills.

The ethnography shows that in Singapore halal as a global assemblage also involves training in the context of national administration of governance and regimes of ethics or values. Training is also formative of new types of knowledge in terms of politics of scientific authority and representation, expertise and skills. Halal training plays an important role in the production of halal knowledge in Singapore. What is more, halal training works as a disciplinary technology that attempts to instil proper halal understanding and practice in participants.

Bibliography

Barr, Michael D. and Skrbis, Zlatko (2008). *Constructing Singapore: Elitism, Ethnicity and the Nation-Building Project*, Copenhagen: NIAS Press.

Boyer, Dominique (2005). "Visiting Knowledge in Anthropology: An Introduction", *Ethnos* 70(2): 141–48.
Brunsson, Nils and Jacobsson, Bengt (2000). "The Contemporary Expansion of Standardization". In *A World of Standards*, eds. Nils Brunsson and Bengt Jacobsson, 1–20, Oxford and New York: Oxford University Press.
Chua Beng Huat (1995). *Communitarian Ideology and Democracy in Singapore*, New York: Routledge.
——(2003). *Life is Not Complete without Shopping: Consumption Culture in Singapore*, Singapore: Singapore University Press.
Collier, Stephen J. and Ong, Aihwa (2005). "Global Assemblages, Anthropological Problems". In *Global Assemblages: Technology, Politics, and Ethics as Anthropological Problems*, eds. Stephen J. Collier and Aihwa Ong, 3–21, Oxford: Wiley-Blackwell.
Fanselow, Frank S. (1990). "The Bazaar Economy or How Bizarre is the Bazaar Really?", *MAN New Series* 25(2): 250–65.
Fischer, Johan (2008). *Proper Islamic Consumption: Shopping among the Malays in Modern Malaysia*, Copenhagen: NIAS Press.
——(2011). *The Halal Frontier: Muslim Consumers in a Globalized Market*, New York: Palgrave Macmillan.
Kadir, Suzaina (2004). "Islam, state and society in Singapore", *Inter-Asia Cultural Studies* 5(3): 357–71.
Majlis Ugama Islam Singapura (2007). MUIS-HC-S002: General Guidelines for the Development and Implementation of a Halal Quality Management System: Principle 1 – establish the Halal Team. Singapore: Majlis Ugama Islam Singapura.
Mauzy, Diana K. and Milne, Robert S. (2002). *Singapore Politics Under the People's Action Party*, London and New York: Routledge.
Nevins, Joseph and Peluso, Nancy L. (2008). "Introduction: Commoditization in Southeast Asia". In *Taking Southeast Asia to Market: Commodities, Nature, and People in the Neoliberal Age*, eds. Joseph Nevins and Nancy L. Peluso, 1–24, Ithaca: Cornell University Press.
Ong, Aihwa (2006). *Neoliberalism as Exception: Mutations in Citizenship and Sovereignty*, Durham and London: Duke University Press.
Pereira, Alexius (2005). "Religiosity and Economic Development in Singapore", *Journal of Contemporary Religion* 20(2): 161–77.
Rabinow, Paul (1984). "Introduction". In *The Foucault Reader*, ed. Paul Rabinow, 3–32. New York: Pantheon Books.
Riaz, Mian N. and Chaudry, Muhammad M. (2004). *Halal Food Production*, Boca Raton: CRC Press.
Roseberry, W. (1988). "Political Economy", *Annual Review of Anthropology* 17: 161–85.
Rudnyckyj, Daromir (2009). "Market Islam in Indonesia", *Journal of the Royal Anthropological Institute* (N.S.): S183–S201.
——(2010). *Spiritual Economies: Islam, Globalization, and the Afterlife of Development*, Ithaca: Cornell University Press.
SPRING (2011). Global Halal Food Industry. Guide to tapping the fast growing Halal food market, Singapore: SPRING Singapore, available at: www.spring.gov.sg/industry/fm/documents/global_halal_food_industry.pdf.
Stimpfl, Joseph (2006). "Growing up Malay in Singapore". In *Ethnicity, and the State in Malaysia and Singapore*, eds. Lian Kwen Fee, 61–93, Leiden and Boston.
Urciuoli, Bonnie (2008). "Skills and Selves in the New Workplace", *American Ethnologist* 35(21): 211–28.
Yao, Souchou (2007). *Singapore: The State and the Culture of Excess*. Oxon: Routledge.

12

WHO OWNS HALAL? FIVE INTERNATIONAL INITIATIVES OF HALAL FOOD REGULATIONS

Florence Bergeaud-Blackler

"One halal logo – one standard halal: united we succeed, divided we fail"
Motto of the Middle East OIC Halal Exhibition, UAE, 2012

Introduction

The chapter describes the current initiatives set up to create international halal standards. It concludes with some reflections on the low plausibility of the emergence of a long-awaited "single halal standard".[1]

The intensification of the halal trade has led many countries to advocate the creation of an international halal standard, ostensibly to fight fraud, unofficially to get ahead of the game. The pioneer of this approach is Malaysia. Committed since the 1980s, Malaysia inspired the drafting of the very first Codex Alimentarius global halal guidelines,[2] the impact of which was more symbolic than real. Far too vague and ambiguous, these guidelines did not allow for the harmonization of diverse halal standards within the global assemblage. There is also a problem of implementation. The guidelines refer to "Islamic law", which has no existence in international trade law, with undefined "religious authorities" replacing state responsibility. There is no power of sanction and therefore no power to control. However, the Codex initiative remains a reference point for the World Trade Organization (WTO), opening up new horizons for international standardization initiatives.

The international battle for the establishment of an international standard actually began in the mid-2000s. It reached a period of stabilization in the 2010s when the Organisation of Islamic Cooperation (OIC[3]) argued that the halal economy should primarily be a Muslim matter and that halal standards should be set by Muslim countries.

In December 2012, the first Middle East OIC Halal Exhibition took place in the United Arab Emirates (UAE), bringing together 37 Muslim and European countries.[4] For the first time, a single halal standard was explicitly designed as a priority by OIC

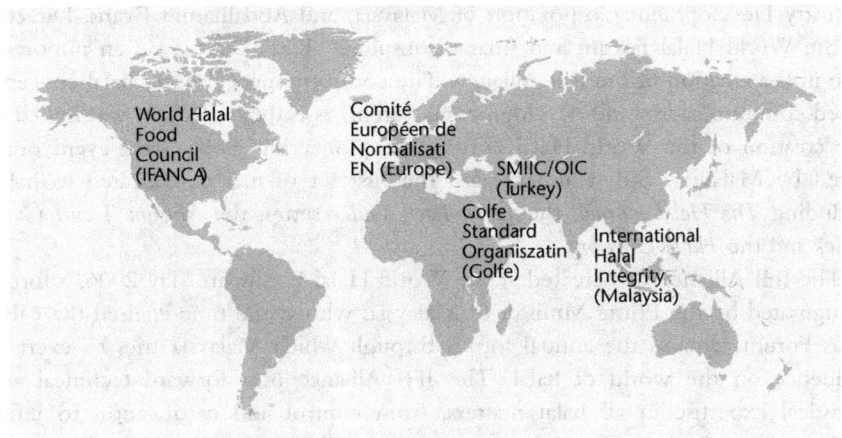

FIGURE 12.1 International standards: the quest for a unique halal standard

members; the motto of this meeting was: "one halal logo, one standard, united we succeed, divided we fail". This call did not appear in a vacuum; five main international regulatory initiatives from different parts of the world were already under way.

The World Halal Food Council (WHFC): "the liberal option"

The WHFC is one of the oldest international halal regulatory initiatives. Established in Jakarta in September 1999, it was officially backed by the Council of Indonesian Ulama. The project was initiated by the main American halal agency, Islamic Food and Nutrition Council of America (IFANCA),[5] along with agencies from the Netherlands and Australia. It then slowly spread to form an international network of national agencies of various sizes. After changing its name into the World Halal Council (WHC) the organization has since split into the WHC and WHFC. The latter has regional representations such as the Halal Food Council of Europe, focused on European members. In 2014, the WHFC had 35 members, including the main certification agencies in the US; Halal Instituto of Spain; Halal Quality Control of Netherlands; The Grand Mosque of Paris in France; FIANZ of New Zealand and the Halal Feed and Food Inspection Authority (HFFIA), which are mainly first-generation agencies.[6] The WHFC is more a network than an organization. It puts forward a liberal view of halal standards based on the principle of *mutual recognition*. Although different, a certificate from one WHFC member must be recognized by other members as halal.

The International Halal Integrity Alliance/World Halal Forum: "the experts"

The IHI Alliance is an agency based in Malaysia. It was founded by Jumaatun Azmi, Managing Director of KasehDia,[7] Darhim Hashim, Director of the Halal

Industry Development Corporation of Malaysia, and Abdalhamid Evans, Director of the World Halal Forum and Imarat consultant. KasehDia played an important role in the creation of the IHI Alliance. The company specialized in halal concept-based communication and developmental systems as early as 1999. It was linked to the creation of the World Halal Forum, the pioneering global halal event organized by Malaysia, and it also created the first set of media dedicated to halal, including *The Halal Journal*, the *Halal Food Guide* series, the *Muslim Travel Guide* series and the *Halal Directory*.

The IHI Alliance was created at the World Halal Forum in May 2006, a forum inaugurated by the Prime Minister of Malaysia, who at the time chaired the OIC. This Forum remains the annual forum through which Malaysia tries to exert its influence on the world of halal. The IHI Alliance puts forward technical and logistical expertise in all halal matters, from control and certification to infrastructure organization. Through the programme "Halal in a Box", it sells a comprehensive training programme that aims to ensure that all certification bodies adhere to common standards and procedures in order to harmonize halal certification globally.[8] The IHI Alliance's aim is not to promote a unique standard, but rather a single accreditation body of halal standards. Malaysia is perceived by market players to be a country with excellent expertise in halal matters. However, while it is a worldwide reference point in the global halal world it is seen to lack religious legitimacy. This type of legitimacy lies with Arab countries, in particular Saudi Arabia and the Gulf states, who have less technical expertise but more financial capacity.

The Gulf Organization for Standardization: "the Landlord"

The Gulf countries are rather new to the world of halal, at least compared to Malaysia and Southeast Asian countries. They have been playing catch up recently and do not have the food resources and the experience of Malaysia, Singapore and even Thailand. The Gulf Cooperation Council (GCC) is an international organization composed of Saudi Arabia, Bahrain, the UAE, Kuwait, Oman, Qatar and Yemen. Following the lead of Bahrain and Qatar, in 2008 the GCC launched the standard GSO 1931: Halal Food.

There are very few experts in the area. One of the influential figures is Hani Mansour Al-Mazeedi, a Kuwaiti and food safety researcher trained in the US.[9]

Every year since 2011, the Gulf Conference on the Halal Industry has drawn major scholars, thinkers and specialists from around the world, none of whom risk refusing an invitation from the major financiers of the world Islamic economy. At the inaugural conference he organized in Kuwait in 2011,[10] Al-Mazeedi called on Muslim countries to reconquer the halal market from the West and warned Muslim countries of "an international conspiracy against the requirements of Halal". "The West does not care for the requirements of Islamic law", he said in his presentation,[11] calling for a Muslim-based halal standard.

The GCC halal standardard stands in direct competition with another initiative overseen by Turkey, who is following a similar line: promoting the halal market through opposition to Western countries while, at the same time, trying to control the European halal standard.

The Standards and Metrology Institute for Islamic Countries (SMIIC): "the Community"

The SMIIC has also developed its own standards.[12] The main player in this initiative is Turkey. From his position of Secretary General of the OIC, and following the Malaysian line, Ekmeleddin İhsanoğlu decided to set up a halal standard that would be marketed as an OIC standard. The OIC commission drafted three guidelines: "OIC/SMIIC 1:2011, General Guidelines on Halal Food", "OIC/SMIIC 2: 2011, Guidelines for Halal Certification Bodies" and "OIC/SMIIC 3: 2011, Guidelines for Accreditation Bodies Accrediting Halal Certification". Despite the adoption of these guidelines by some of the OIC member countries, disagreement remains between Muslim countries over clauses relating to mechanical slaughter, aquatic animals and, most significantly, stunning. Turkey is generally in favour of stunning, but other countries are divided. In such circumstances, one way of overcoming the dispute within Islamic countries may be to find a common "enemy". Ekmeleddin İhsanoğlu said in an Arab newspaper that Turkey was *"ready to develop this standard as soon as possible before Europe claims its rights over halal, much as it has made London the main centre for Islamic banking"*. And indeed, the European Union (EU) is already working on a draft to issue a European certificate for halal food.

The halal standard of the European Committee for Standardization (CEN): "the legal option"

The CEN for the creation of a European halal standard was initiated by Austria, a country where Islamic institutions have legal recognition, and where trade ties with Turkey and Bosnia are very important. In October 2010, a first meeting of the CEN was held at the Austrian Standards Institute (ASI). A working group was set up with the task of analysing "the feasibility of a European norm standard for halal food requirements". Among the countries in the working group, only four, Austria, Bosnia and Herzegovina, Croatia and Germany, already have halal standards recognized by the state. In the others, there are dozens of halal standards with no legal recognition. A first step feasibility study was completed in 2012, which resulted in a report calling for the creation of a committee to develop a "European Standard of Halal Food"; 21 out of 29 countries voted for the standardization project. Germany proved reluctant, but ultimately did not vote against the proposal; only France opposed. It was therefore decided that Europe would develop halal standards. A committee was set up in April 2013 with the Turkish Standards Institute (TSE) appointed as chosen secretary. It is up to Turkey to initiate the proposals and the first draft of the standard. Since 2014, the member countries have been working on mirror commissions in each country to discuss and develop the European halal standard that, if successful, could be issued in 2017.

This chapter has attempted to provide an initial overview of the international halal regulation initiatives. The most important variations between standards are not due to different legal schools (*madhhab*) but are due to logical marketing differentiation on both economic and religious markets. I have reviewed the main five international regional initiatives that attempt to standardize halal and show that they would not compete with each other. Each initiative has adopted a pragmatic approach in line with their own requirements and each attempts to impose their views on their trade partners. Malaysia opts for the expertise, the US, to build a network of mutual recognition, the Gulf countries are competing to be the worldwide religious reference point, Turkey plays the community card and attempts to take OIC leadership to Malaysia, and the Europeans are trying to impose their standard by erecting legal barriers. It needs further research in the coming years to assess these initiatives, but at least we can observe that so far the target of a worldwide single standard seems unlikely.

Notes

1 The analyses produced here are based on surveys conducted over the past five years with expert and industry players in the global market for halal certification during professional events in Europe (Paris, Brussels), Africa (Meknes, Casablanca) and Asia (Tokyo). This approach is supplemented with Internet-based documentary research.
2 General guidelines for use of the term "Halal" were adopted by the Codex Alimentarius Commission at its 22nd session, 1997.
3 The Organisation of Islamic Cooperation (OIC) (formerly Organization of the Islamic Conference), established in 1969, presents itself as "a collective voice of the Muslim world [...] ensuring to safeguard and protect the interests of the Muslim world in the spirit of promoting international peace and harmony among various people of the world". It has membership of 57 states spread over four continents, www.oic-oci.org/.
4 With the participation of Mohammad Al Qassimi (Islamic board of Emirates), Ekmeleddin İhsanoğlu, the Secretary General of the OIC, the mufti of Bosnia etc. Representatives of different countries and minorities of Sunni and Shia Islam participated: Algeria, Austria, Egypt, Germany, India, Iran, Italy, Kyrgyzstan, Lebanon, Malaysia, the Netherlands, Pakistan, Spain, Thailand, Turkey, the UAE and the US.
5 In the "about us" page on the WHC website, one can read that "Halal Certification started in the West in the mid '60s in the United States by Muslim food and technical experts". This view of the halal certification market history is the one promoted by IFANCA who claim to be the first, and to have been influenced by the Kosher route: "It was observed that the Jewish people which are fewer in numbers than the Muslims are enforcing their religious requirements on products to be acceptable to them through their certification and accreditation called the 'kosher'. So Muslims in the United States started to follow the precedent established by the Jews in the U.S. so the establishment of the halal logo, although different from what we have now to those that are considered 'halal'". Source: www.worldhalalcouncil.com/about-us.
6 Cf. our classification (first/second generation) in our article "The halal certification market in Europe and in the world: a first panorama".
7 KasehDia is a company that specializes in halal concept-based communication and developmental systems which were at the origin of the World Halal Forum, the first and

pioneering halal global event organized by Malaysia. Her company was at the origin of the very first set of media dedicated to halal: *The Halal Journal*, the *Halal Food Guide* series, the *Muslim Travel Guide* series and the annual *Halal Directory*.

8 "The focus of this training program is to ensure that each country regardless whether it is a Muslim or non-Muslim majority country, shall have at least one accredited certifying body ensuring Halal certification. This training program will enable a country to set-up a Certifying Body for domestic certification by using the IHI Alliance Global Halal Standard as a reference during the certification process". Source: http://www.ihialliance.org/hiab.php.

9 "My first experience in relation to halal foods was in the summer of 1972 in Buffalo, NY, when a Pakistani student warned me about the existence of extracts of pork in some kind of cake. I was 18 at the time, and it was that which increased my interest in studies and research on the nature of the food ingredients". Source: Interview with ASIDCOM Dr Hani Mansour Al-Mazeedi, 6 October 2010, www.asidcom.org/Interview-with Dr Hani Mansour-M.html.

10 H. M. Al-Mazeedi, who was given the Halal Award 2009 for his personal achievements for the halal industry, was the organizer of the first halal Gulf conference in 2011 in Kuwait.

11 The document can be found online on Mazeedi's blog L20 – Halal Services: Obstacles Over the Past 30 Years, by Dr Hani Mansour Al-Mazeedi (pdf), http://azkahalal.wordpress.com/the-first-gulf-conference-on-halal-and-its-services/.

12 The 13 countries that initiated the SMIIC are: Algeria, Cameroon, Guinea, Jordan, Libya, Mali, Morocco, Pakistan, Somalia, Sudan, Tunisia, Turkey and the UAE.

Bibliography

Bergeaud-Blackler, F. (forthcoming) Le "Halal World" pour les marchands un conte néo-libéral du XXI siècle? in *Les Sens du Halal*. Paris: Editions CNRS.

Bergeaud-Blackler, F. and Bernard, B. (2010) *Comprendre le halal*. Belgium: Edipro.

INDEX

Note: Numbers in *italics* indicate figures

Abi Taleb, Ali ibn 13, 55, 56, 57, 59, 69
Administration of Muslim Law Act (AMLA) 180–1, 183, 185, 186
AHC-Europe 45
Äid el-Kebir 81, 84, 128, 129, 134–5, 138
AKP *see* Justice and Development Party
alcoholic drink prohibition 3, 127, 160, 180, 182
Al-Mazeedi, Hani Mansour 101, 194
al-Qaradawi, Yusuf 6, 93
animal welfare: Belgium and animal suffering considerations 127, 128, 129, 134–7, 139; European Union concerns 27, 38, 46, 47, 51, 52, 114; farm animal welfare 45; Green Halal and sacrifice of animals 128, 134, 135, 138–9, 140; head-only stunning, acceptability of 110; Islamic associations, objective alliance with 112; Ministry for Agriculture and Food, responsibility for animal welfare 46; Morocco, respect for animals in 84; public sensitivity and halal considerations 14, 30; Quran, emphasis on humane treatment of animals 59, 67, 133, 134; *see also* stunning of animals
ARGML *see* Ritual Association of the Grand Mosque of Lyon
Asad, Talal 145
ASDA supermarkets 148, 152, 153
Atatürk, Mustafa Kemal 40–1
audit culture 9–10

Australia 106, 111–12, 186
Austria 119, 195
A Votre Service (AVS) 100, 102n14, 116–17, 120

Badawi, Abdullah Ahmad 108, 143
baraka 83–4
beldi products 13, 72, 73, 77, *83*, 84–7, 88n4
Belgium: animal suffering considerations 127, 128, 129, 134–7, 139; halal market 130, 131, 132, 140–1; *see also* Green Halal
Bernama 21, 30
blood: drainage after slaughter 46, 48, 49, 99; as forbidden 2, 3, 96; stunning and proper blood flow 136
Bresard, Bernadette 137, 138
Britain *see* United Kingdom
Büyükzer, Hüseyin Kami 44

Carrefour stores 30, 48, 50
carrion prohibition 2, 3, 96, 99
CEN *see* European Committee for Standardization
Chaudry, Muhammad M. 4, 92, 113
China: halal certification and standardization 15, 162, 163–4, 165–6, 183, 185; Han ethnic majority 2, 14, 162, 163, 166; Malaysia, Chinese presence in 21–2, 24–5, 146, 148, 154;

pigs and 160, 165; poultry slaughter 170; religious food taboos 190; Singapore as Chinese-majority country 178–80, 181; *see also* Hui; qingzhen
Codex Alimentarius Commission (CAC) 26, 28, 34n1
Cola Turka 52
COMCEC *see* Standing Committee for Economic and Commercial Cooperation

dakwah groups 23, 147
Darul Arqam 23
Dialrel project: European Union funding 12, 19, 99; focus groups 49; as a research source 21, 28, 39
diaspora: of European Muslims 115; halal considerations 93, 94, 95, 96, 99, 100–01; Malay diaspora 25, 33–4, 144, 146, 148, 154–5, 157
Douglas, Mary 4, 94, 95
Dünya Helal Birliği 51

Egypt 7, 106
ethics: alternative food ethics 13, 32, 56, 60, 68; animal suffering and 127; ethical halal 14, 128, 129–31, 132, 139, 140–1; ethically proper food 77; ethic of consumption 83–4, 129, 130, 131–4, 138, 139, 140; halal and haram, ethical line between 122; home-processed foods, ethical considerations of 74, 84, 87; stunning, ethical debate on 3, 137
Europe: animal stunning and slaughter 27, 48, 129; animal welfare concerns 27, 38, 46, 47, 51, 52, 114; Dialrel project, EU funding of 12, 19, 99; European Halal Food Park 31; European Standard of Halal Food, developing 195–6; exports as problematic 49, 51; halal certification and standardization 34, 45, 114–19, 130, 195–6; halal market 30, 100–01, 114–15; Islamic Food Council of Europe (IFCE) 4, 9; Malaysian presence in European markets 32; Muslim population increases 20, 114–15; Turkey, European influence on 40, 45, 47
European Association of Halal Certifiers (AHC-Europe) 45
European Committee for Standardization (CEN) 195–6

FairPrice supermarket chain 184–5, 185–6
fatwas 5–6, 7, 93, 117, 118, 189

Federation of Islamic Associations of New Zealand (FIANZ) 110–11, 193
Food and Agriculture Organization (FAO) 45, 48
Food Auditing and Certification Research Association (GİMDES) 43–4, 45, 51
France: animal stunning and slaughter 30, 98, 99, 117, 137; AVS certification 100, 102n14, 116–17, 120; consumer control of halal recognition 79; government role in halal standardization 97–8, 100; halal petition as a unifying force 101; mosques and halal 30, 98, 99, 100, 102n13, 116, 193; opposition to European Standard of Halal Food 195; prohibition of private slaughter 96, 97; secularism and religion 149; sheep sacrifice as offensive 101n6
French Society for Control of Halal Meat (SFCVH) 116

GAIA *see* Group of Action for the Interest of Animals
gelatine in medicines as problematic 1, 6, 44, 155
Germany 30, 44, 102n9, 195
GİMDES *see* Food Auditing and Certification Research Association
global assemblage of halal: alternative food networks 32, 60; beldi example 77; defining 10, 39, 52; ethical halal as an assemblage 128, 129–31, 140–1; fatwas and discourses playing into 7; halal training as a part of 177; in Iran 55, 56, 60, 67–8; proliferation of halal market, signifiers of 145; qingzhen example 164, 165, 172; Singapore, moving from local context 183, 190; stem cell analogy 33; systematic disassembly, lacking 11; in Turkey 43–6; vertical alliances 51
Grandin, Temple 134, 136, 137
Green Halal: as eco-Muslim movement 14; ethical food, concern with 130; GAIA, debate with 134–8; Meriem and Gerlando, foundational work of 128, 131–4, 136–7, 138–9, 140; organic halal associations, inspired by 129
Group of Action for the Interest of Animals (GAIA) 128, 134–5, 137, 139–40
Gulf Cooperation Council (GCC) 29, 31, 194, 195

Hadiths 27, 57, 58, 133, 138
halal, general: defining 1, 182; ethical halal 14, 128, 129–31, 132, 139, 140–1; halal

exhibitions 143, 144, 192–3; halal experts as scholar Muslims 92–3; halal focus groups 49–51; halalization 107, 108, 109; halal restaurants 155–6, 160–1, 168–9, 176; Islamic identity through halal 23, 33, 34, 38, 76, 94, 95–6, 101; mosques and halal 30, 98, 99, 102n13, 116, 193; Quran, halal food rulings based on 2–3; Shia interpretation of halal 55, 56–7, 58–60, 65, 68; *tayyib*, connection with 76, 133; *see also* qingzhen

halal certification: competition 105, 107; distinction between certification agencies 14; legal signification 11; local butchers, lack of certification 155, 156–7; local muftis, certification through letters 12, 38, 45, 47, 48, 49; mashbooh items as difficult to certify 5; mosques as certifiers 30, 98, 99, 100, 102n13, 116, 193; MUIS certification 107, 114, 180–1, 181–6; in non-Muslim countries 109–10; poultry concerns and calls for certification 39, 45–6, 49; second generation certification agencies 110, 116, 117, 119–22; self-certification 73, 77, 134; third-party certification 27, 43–4, 106; *see also under* individual countries

Halal Correct 119

Halal Feed and Food Inspection Authority (HFFIA) 118

Halal Food Authority (HFA) 30, 115, 144, 150, 151–3, 155, 156

Halal Food Laws 113

Halal Food Production (Riaz/Chaudry) 4–5, 92

Halal Industry Development Corporation (HDC) 26, 108, 189

halal market: annual value 1; defining 92; fraud factor 99, 106, 107, 113, 121, 143, 150, 192; generational differences in approach 120; as a global assemblage 73; growth of 10, 14, 91, 100, 157; market size estimations unavailable 123n1; neoliberalism, in wake of 8; opacity of 134; origins 91, 93–4, 107

Halal Monitoring Committee (HMC) 115, 150, 152, 155, 156

Halal Quality Control (HQC) 118, 119

Halal Quality Management System (HalMQ) 181, 182, 186, 187–9

halal standardization: fatwas, role in 5–6; halal training leading to 15, 175–6, 181–6, 187–9, 194; in Muslim *vs.* non-Muslim countries 13–14; OIC standard 195; single standard hopes 15, 26–9, 32, 107, 122, 192–3, 196; *see also under* individual countries

Halal Voeding in Voedsel (HVV) 118, 119

haram: consumption of 157; defining 1, 94, 101, 183; ethical line between halal and haram 122; haram medications 155; land creatures and carnivores as haram 3, 182; pork and pig derivatives 162; Shia perspective 59; as a social taboo 95

Harris, Marvin 4

Hazard Analysis and Critical Control Points (HACCP) 75, 109

Helalder 51

Hui: ethnic identity through qingzhen 2, 163, 165, 172; minority group status 164; qingzhen as preferred term 160, 163; qingzhen cuisine 167–71; Quanzhou community 166–7

Id al-Kabir *see* Äid el-Kebir

Ihsanoglu, Ekmeleddin 195, 196n4

ijtihad 58–9

Indonesia: halal status of food labels as problematic 5; imports 111, 113; Majelis Ulama Indonesia 107, 114, 117, 183; Netherlands, ties to 118; spiritual reform movements and market Islam 8, 178

Information of Islamic und Dokumentationszentrum Österreich (IIDZ) 119

institutional trust 75, 87

Institut Kefahaman Islam Malaysia (IKIM) 147

Institut Marocain de Normalisation (IMANOR) 75, 109

Instituto Halal (IH) 117

International Halal Integrity Alliance (IHIA) 27, 29, 31, 32, 51, 193–4, 197n8

Iran: challenges in Iranian poultry sector 63–5; global assemblage 55, 56, 60, 67–8; Iranian revolution, effect on poultry industry 55, 57, 60–2; Iranian slaughter requirements 106; poultry farm case 13, 56, 57, 60, 65–7, 68, 69; Shia Islam and halal 55, 56–7, 58–60, 65, 68

Islamic Food and Nutrition Council of America (IFANCA) 4, 92, 113–14, 193, 196n5

Islamic jurisprudence: certification agencies, weak effect on 14; halal and 55, 58–60; schools of 5, 27, *28*, 113, 153–4, 190; Shia perspective 56, 59, 60

Islamic Religious Council of Singapore *see* Majlis Ugama Islam Singapura
Islamic Services of America (ISA) 113, 114
Islamic Society of North America (ISNA) 113, 114
Islamische Glaubensgemeinschaft in Osterreich (IIGIO) 119
Issues on Halal Products (Office of State Mufti, Darussalam) 5–6

Jabatan Kemajuan Islam Malaysia (JAKIM) *see* Malaysian state Department of Islamic Development
Justice and Development Party (AKP) 12, 38, 43, 52

KasehDia 108, 194, 196n7
kashrut 98, 102n8, 117, 120, 121, 151
Khomeini, Ayatollah 61, 106
Koran *see* Quran
kosher products: halal, economic model different from 121; Hebrew food laws 4; as inspiration for design of halal 92, 112, 196n5; Jewish identity and 95; Kosher Food Laws 113; kosher products in United States 124n31; temporary resurgence 97
Kurban Bayrami 46–7

The Lawful and the Prohibited in Islam (al-Qaradawi) 6, 93
Lee, Kuan Yew 179
Lévi-Strauss, Claude 163–4
London *see* United Kingdom

Majelis Ulama Indonesia (MUI) 107, 114, 117, 183
Majlis Ugama Islam Singapura (MUIS): certification and 107, 114, 180–1, 181–6; halal training, providing 15, 175–6, 181–6; HalMQ, sponsoring 181, 182, 186, 187–9
Malaysia: Britain, colonial ties to 20, 21, 25, 144, 147; Chinese presence in 21–2, 24–5, 146, 148, 154; as global halal hub 108, 109, 143; halal certification 8, 108, 113, 156; halal market 12, 19, 20–1, 26, 29, 32; halal standardization 8–9, 20, 28–9, 31, 45, 108, 148; joint industry park with China 165; Malay diaspora in the UK 25, 33–4, 144, 146, 148, 154–5, 157; Malaysian branded halal 21, 25, 26, 30, 31, 34, 51; Malaysian standard (MS 1500) 25, 26, 28; Malay teachers at MUIS Academy 182; New Malay entrepreneurs 144, 148, 157; OIC and 29, 44–5, 52, 194; Shafi'i school, dominance of 5, 153–4; Singapore, ties to 21, 180, 181; supermarkets, separating halal and non-halal products 166

Malaysian International Halal Showcase (MIHAS) 25, 60, 108, 143, 144, 171
Malaysian state Department of Islamic Development (JAKIM): accreditation, providing 45, 108; American certification agencies, claiming approval of 114; halal standard, developing 26; HDC, tension with 189; HQC, recognition of 118; IH, non-acceptance of 117; Singapore, brand recognition in 183, 185; UK, certified products found in 146, 155, 156
Marrakech *see* Morocco
mashbooh 5, 155, 157
Matrade 21, 26, 30, 143, 144, 146
Migros supermarkets 48
Ministry for Agriculture and Food 44, 45, 46
Modood, Tariq 149
Mohamad, Mahathir 23, 24, 107–8, 147, 148
Mohammad, the Prophet 3, 27, 57–8, 134, 136, 140
Morocco: beldi and rumi products 13, 72, 73, 77, 83, 84–7, 88n4; consumer role in determining good food 76, 81; food processing practices 82–3; halal certification and standardization 73, 75, 87, 109; shopkeepers, trust in 79–80; sourcing in Marrakech food spaces 78–9
mosques and halal 30, 98, 99, 100, 102n13, 116, 193
MUI *see* Majelis Ulama Indonesia MUI
MUIS *see* Majlis Ugama Islam Singapura
mujtahids 58–9, 68

Nasr, S. H. 58–9
National Halal Food Group (NHFG) 30
Navaro-Yashin, Yael 43
Nestlé 25, 91, 99, 108, 109, 118
Netherlands 31, 118, 135, 183
New Economic Policy (NEP) 22, 24, 25, 148
New Zealand 106, 110–11
New Zealand Islamic Meat Management (NZIMM) 110–11
niqab 149

organic food industry: global assemblage of alternative food ethics 60; Green Halal founders, inspired by 132, 133, 138; growth of industry and consumer concerns 67; halal connection 32; halal food industry, emulating 56; halal products, compatibility with 92; halal standardization, compared to 122; organic halal 129, 130

Organisation of Islamic Cooperation (OIC): global halal standard, developing 26–7, 34, 44, 75, 108–9, 192–3; Halal World Institute, link to 60; Malaysia and 29, 44–5, 52, 194; poultry stunning 28; Turkey and 38, 51, 108, 195, 196

Ottoman Empire 39–41

Parti Islam Se-Malaysia (PAS) 23, 24, 147
People's Action Party (PAP) 179
pork: in China 160, 165; exclusion of pork in slaughter process 122; halal-certified pork scam 185–6; as haram 162; identity establishment through pork 180; non-pork dishes in restaurants 169, 171; pork avoidance as halal 127, 182; pork meat availability in Iran 61; Quran, prohibiting pork consumption 3, 96, 183; ritual washings to clean pork pollution 189; as taboo 4, 95
postliberalism 19–20, 32, 34
poultry: beldi *vs.* rumi chicken 85–6; China, poultry slaughter in 170; Doux-produced chicken, legality questioned 99; electro-narcosis applied to 136–7; ethical halal chicken 128; Iranian poultry industry 55–7, 60–2, 63–5; Morocco, chicken buying in 78–9, 80; poultry concerns and calls for certification 39, 45–6, 49; poultry farm case study 13, 56, 57, 60, 65–7, 68, 69; stunning before slaughter 28, 32, 121; support for poultry producers 13; Turkish poultry sector 46, 48–9, 51, 52
Poultry Industry Liberation Act 62, 63

qingzhen: defining 160–1; distribution 169–71; government regulation 164–6; halal, compared to 162–3; Hui identity and 2, 163, 165, 172; qingzhen availability 167–8
Quran: halal food rulings 2–3; humane treatment of animals emphasized 59, 67, 133, 134; mufti of Jordan on absolute verses 98; pork consumption prohibited 3, 96, 183; pre-stun position in alignment with 27; qingzhen, Quran as inspiring influence 171; Shia interpretations 58

red meat *see* ritual slaughter
Regenstein, Joseph M. 92, 137
Riaz, Mian N. 4, 92
Ritual Association of the Grand Mosque of Lyon (ARGML) 116
ritual slaughter: animal suffering 135–7, 139; Australia, slaughter in compliance with Islamic laws 112; commonly-held slaughter practices 122; Eid al Adha, during 47, 97; France, prohibition of private slaughter 96, 97; Green Halal and 14, 132, 133–4, 137, 138–9, 140; halal association 1, 3, 6, 146; halal food standards, most notable aspect of 127–8; industrial slaughter 96–8, 131, 137, 138; Muslim identity and 25; 'people of the Book', animal slaughter by 27, 94, 98, 100; poultry slaughter 28, 30; slaughterhouses as protected spaces 121; *tasmiyah* recited during slaughter 46, 48, 76, 94; Turkey and illegal slaughter concerns 12, 39, 47–8, 50; unionisation of halal slaughtermen 111; *see also* stunning of animals
Rotterdam as gateway for halal products 31, 118
Rudnyckyj, Daromir 66, 178
rumi products 72, 84–7, 88n4
Rusznak Ahmed, Günther 119

Saudi Arabia 106, 111, 113, 194
secularism: in Britain 14, 148–50; halal certification in secular countries 109, 122; in Malaysia 20, 22, 23, 147, 148; in Turkey 38, 41, 42, 43, 52; unpacking of 145
SFCVH *see* French Society for Control of Halal Meat
Shafi'i school 5, 153–4
Sharia law 6, 40, 46, 58, 180
sheep 110, 111, 128, 135, 138–9
Shia Islam and halal 55, 56–7, 58–60, 65, 68
Singapore: double minority status, effect on halal 179, 181; halal certification and standardization 8–9, 15, 175, 176–8, 180–1, 181–6, 187–9, 190; Malaysia, ties to 21, 180, 181; Shafi'i school of

jurisprudence 5; *see also* Majlis Ugama Islam Singapura
Spain 117–18
Standards and Metrology Institute for Islamic Countries (SMIIC) 44, 108–9, 195, 197n12
Standing Committee for Economic and Commercial Cooperation of the Organization of the Islamic Cooperation (COMCEC) 26, 28, 44, 108–9
stunning of animals: GAIA campaign for stunning use 128, 134–5, 137, 139–40; Green Halal, against stunning 136–7; modern stunning techniques 123n2; non-stunning as halal 98–9, 100; poultry, stunning before slaughter 28, 32, 49; reversible stunning 110, 111, 112; ritual slaughter, stunning as a challenge to ideal of 127; second-generation agencies 121–2; signs of life showing after stunning 186; stunning as controversial 3, 6, 27–8, 105, 113–14; *see also under* individual countries
Sunni Islam: animal stunning, attitude towards 27; Jafari jurisprudence 60; Saudi exports 106; sea creatures and locusts as halal 3; Shia, reasons for split 57–8, 58–9; in Southeast Asia 5, 6

taboos 4, 95–6, 100, 179, 190
Tesco stores 30, 108, 148, 152–3
Tunisia 107, 109
Turkey: animal stunning 46, 47, 48, 195; halal certification and standardization 38, 43–5, 48, 51, 109, 195–6; illegal slaughter concerns 12, 39, 47–8, 50; OIC and 38, 51, 108, 195, 196; poultry sector 46, 48–9, 51, 52, 64; Turkish meat as *prima facie* halal 12, 38, 39, 42, 45, 48, 51; Turkish state, birth of 39–41
Turkish Standards Institute (TSE) 43, 44–5, 51, 195

ulama 3, 183
ummah 10, 93, 101, 106, 115, 120, 121
United Kingdom: animal stunning and slaughter 30, 98, 102n10, 115, 135–6, 149–50; British Muslims perceived as organized 131; European Halal Food Park of Norfolk 31; farm animal awareness 45; halal certification and standardization 145, 149–50, 151–2, 155, 156, 158; Malay diaspora in UK 25, 33–4, 144, 146, 148, 154–5, 157; Malaysia, colonial ties to 20, 21, 25, 144, 147; organic halal food in Britain 129; secularism and 14, 148–50; Tesco stores, halal meat sold in 30; World Food Market held in London 143–4
United Malays National Organisation (UMNO) 22–3, 24, 144, 146, 147
United States 92, 109, 112–14, 124n31, 134, 196n5

Vandenbosch, Michel 135
vegetarian and vegan options 133, 155, 157, 168, 186
Vision 2020 20, 24

Warees Halal Division 182, 183, 190
white meat *see* poultry
World Food Market (WFM) 143–4, 150, 152
World Halal Food Council (WHFC) 193
World Halal Forum 27, 29, 45, 108, 193–4, 196n7

eBooks
from Taylor & Francis
Helping you to choose the right eBooks for your Library

Add to your library's digital collection today with Taylor & Francis eBooks. We have over 50,000 eBooks in the Humanities, Social Sciences, Behavioural Sciences, Built Environment and Law, from leading imprints, including Routledge, Focal Press and Psychology Press.

Choose from a range of subject packages or create your own!

Benefits for you
- Free MARC records
- COUNTER-compliant usage statistics
- Flexible purchase and pricing options
- 70% approx of our eBooks are now DRM-free.

Benefits for your user
- Off-site, anytime access via Athens or referring URL
- Print or copy pages or chapters
- Full content search
- Bookmark, highlight and annotate text
- Access to thousands of pages of quality research at the click of a button.

Free Trials Available

We offer free trials to qualifying academic, corporate and government customers.

eCollections
Choose from 20 different subject eCollections, including:

- Asian Studies
- Economics
- Health Studies
- Law
- Middle East Studies

eFocus
We have 16 cutting-edge interdisciplinary collections, including:

- Development Studies
- The Environment
- Islam
- Korea
- Urban Studies

For more information, pricing enquiries or to order a free trial, please contact your local sales team:

UK/Rest of World: **online.sales@tandf.co.uk**
USA/Canada/Latin America: **e-reference@taylorandfrancis.com**
East/Southeast Asia: **martin.jack@tandf.com.sg**
India: **journalsales@tandfindia.com**

www.tandfebooks.com

9781138812765